THE M-FORM
SOCIETY
how American teamwork can recapture the competitive edge

WILLIAM G. OUCHI

ADDISON-WESLEY PUBLISHING COMPANY
Reading, Massachusetts • Menlo Park, California
London • Amsterdam • Don Mills, Ontario • Sydney

Library of Congress Cataloging in Publication Data

Ouchi, William G.
   The M-form society.

   Includes index.
   1. Industry and state--United States. 2. Industry and
state--Japan. I. Title.
HS3616.U47088 1984   338.973   83-25749
ISBN 0-201-05533-3

Cover design by Marshall Henrichs
Set in 11 point Trump by Techna Type, Inc. York, PA

ISBN 0-201-05533-3

ABCDEFGHIJ-DO-86543
First printing, February 1984

This book is dedicated to
Shizuko and Sugao Ouchi,
my mother and father,
who instilled in me
the spirit of lifelong learning.

contents

PART 1
THE M-FORM SOCIETY
what it is, how it works

APPENDIX
NOTES
INDEX

____acknowledgments

I am the front man for a research team of sixteen scholars at UCLA, most of whom have devoted the major part of their working hours to this project for the past three years. The names of the thirteen principal team members are:

Professor William G. Ouchi,
    Director
Professor Jay B. Barney,
    Associate Director
Nicholas E. Benes
Joseph Wayne Brockbank
William Hesterly

Guido Krickx
Osamu Masaki
James Robins
Sharon Stevens
Mary Kay Stout
Osamu Suruga
David Ulrich
Shin Watanabe

These thirteen received a great deal of assistance from three others who were not officially part of the project but who rendered major assistance to it: Sayoko Benes translated many Japanese documents into English and prepared memoranda on small business in Japan; Atsuo Shiboota (a member of the MITI staff on leave to study at UCLA) attempted to steer us away from dead-end searches and also assisted in arranging contacts at MITI in Tokyo, and he corrected the second draft. Yoko Watanabe assisted both in translating documents into English and in performing simultaneous translation in some of the interviews.

As for the research team, their efforts have been and continue to be both strenuous and intelligent. Professor Jay B. Barney ran the research team on a day-to-day basis and oversaw the collection and analysis of most of the empirical data. More importantly, he taught me how to bring together arguments in financial economics with those more familiar to me from the field of organizational sociology. Those theoretical arguments are not revealed in any detail in this book, but they are developed in Professor Barney's many working papers and articles and provide the basis for the chapter on the organization of banking.

Nick Benes is a gentleman, a scholar, and a heck of a hard worker. He painstakingly translated many of the documents from Japanese into English, especially those documents that deal with the structure of joint R & D in Japan, the laws underlying the arrangements, and the financing of those arrangements. On our trips to Tokyo, Nick (who has just received graduate degrees in law and in business at UCLA) would stay with me until our last interview ended each evening, usually at about ten P.M. Then he and either Osamu Suruga or Osamu Masaki would go off to borrow a duplicating machine with which to do the copying for the day. Then Nick would return to sleep at the home of his in-laws, a one-hour train ride from downtown Tokyo. The next morning he would be waiting for me in the lobby of the Okura Hotel at 7:30, with never even a hint that he was overworked or underpaid. I wish him well.

Wayne Brockbank and Bill Hesterly took down many of the interview notes and oversaw the accurate transcription. Wayne organized the interview schedule in Washington, D.C., and Bill the schedule in Minneapolis. Each of them also gathered a vast array of library materials from which I have drawn.

Guido Krickx is a careful and determined scholar. He produced a memorandum on the Japanese computer industry that serves as the foundation of chapter five, and he also produced one on the photovoltaic project that is described in chapter six. Beyond that, Guido performed much of the data analysis for the project. Osamu Masaki and Osamu Suruga were pure volunteers. Both were M.B.A. candidates at UCLA, Masaki sponsored by the Mitsui Bank and Suruga by his employer, Nippon Steel. These two were invaluable in arranging interviews, in teaching us about business practices in Japan, and in countless other ways. Suruga prepared some of the appendices, which required a good deal of sleuthing as well as a lot of translation of materials.

Jim Robins prepared a memorandum on small business in the United States and participated in many interviews. He also helped out with the data analysis, as did Sharon Stevens. Sharon carried out much of the research on trade associations, visiting associations both in the United States and in Japan, and helping us all to formulate our thoughts on this part of the work. Mary Kay Stout prepared memoranda on the U.S. computer industry and the VHSIC project that appear in chapter six. David Ulrich, who is now on the faculty of business at the University of Michigan, was the first research assistant. An energetic and effective researcher, he made most of the 3,000 long-distance telephone calls and did much of the early data analysis.

Shin Watanabe was an iron man. He went off to Japan for six months with his wife, Yoko, and gathered critical research materials for us. He made countless telephone calls and personal calls in order to arrange our interview trips. As a result of his work, I was able to conduct as many as twenty-eight interviews in one week in Tokyo, with each interview having required in advance perhaps two letters and five or six telephone calls to various aides and secretaries. How he and Yoko subsisted in Tokyo on the wages of a UCLA research assistant I will never understand, but he did it with grace.

In addition to these sixteen, we depended throughout on Elaine Wagner, my administrative assistant, who scheduled all of us and did much of the typing, and on Alice Hirata, who typed the remainder of the transcripts. Their work was fast and accurate, and all of us were grateful for their patience with our demands.

Beyond this core team, the research drew from literally hundreds of people who helped out in one way or another. Some of the key leaders who consented to interviews are named in later chapters. Many of the interviews required an introduction by a friend who put his reputation on the line in getting us access to busy people. Ed Harper, who was domestic policy advisor to President Reagan, arranged most of our interviews in the executive branch. Edwin J. Gray was very helpful in introducing us to the subtleties of Washington politics. Senator Daniel Inouye and Congresswoman Lindy Boggs opened doors on Capitol Hill for us, as did Andy Manatos, who knows his way around and is respected in Washington.

Several leaders of government generously consented to interviews, including Paul Volcker, Chairman of the Federal Reserve; A.W. Clausen, President of the World Bank; John Shad, Chairman of the Securities and Exchange Commission; William Draper, President of the Import-Export Bank; Lionel Olmer, Under Secretary for International Trade of the Department of Commerce; Dr. Bruce Merrifield, Assistant Secretary of Commerce for Productivity, Technology, and Innovation; William Baxter, Chief of the Anti-Trust Division of the Department of Justice; and Tim McNemar, Under Secretary of the Treasury. Dr. William Miskanen, a member of the Council of Economic Advisers, was a perceptive and helpful interview subject. In the Senate, we were informed through conversations with Senators Bill Bradley, Alan Cranston, John Danforth, Daniel Inouye, Charles Percy, William Roth, Paul Tsongas, and Pete Wilson. In the House of

Representatives, we interviewed several members including Lindy Boggs, Bob Edgar, Tom Foley, Albert Gore, James Jones, John Lafalce, Bob Matsui, James Scheuer, James Shannon, Ed Zschau, and Timothy Wirth. James Colvard, who is Deputy Chief of Naval Material, and Roger Porter, who is Deputy Assistant to the President, offered many helpful observations.

We spoke with Dr. Richard Lesher, President of the U.S. Chamber of Commerce; with Alexander Trowbridge, President of the National Association of Manufacturers; and with Jack Albertine, President of the American Business Conference. Robert Galvin and Richard Heimlich of the Motorola Corporation generously shared their time and their thoughts with me. My thoughts on the financing of U.S. business were sharpened through conversations with several venture capitalists, including Ben Rosen of New York, Frank Chambers of San Francisco, and Dick Riordan of Los Angeles. Eugene Fama, one of the creators of modern capital market theory, sat down with me and helped me to see the faults in my analysis. I am grateful to all of them for the time and the thought that they gave.

In the early going, we received help from the Washington law firm of Finnegan, Henderson, Farabow, Garrett, and Dunner. Pete McCloskey of the Electronics Industry Association provided many insights, as did Ed Ferrey of the American Electronics Association. Frank Cary and Ralph Pfeiffer of IBM listened patiently to my arguments and offered their views, as did John Young, David Packard, and John Doyle of Hewlett-Packard. Paul Kaestle and his partners at the firm of Booz · Allen & Hamilton worked with me in developing the concept of the M-Form structure as it applies to business. Tom Murrin of Westinghouse taught me about joint research in Japan. Chauncey Medberry of the Bank of America not only talked with us but also introduced us to Willard Butcher of the Chase Manhattan Bank. Our insights were also sharpened through conversations with G. Bruce Baker of the First Interstate Bank of California, Yoshiaki Shibusawa of the California First Bank, Shigekazu Yamamoto of the Sumitomo Bank of California, and many other bankers in the United States. Edward Nakata of Touche, Ross & Co. advised us on Japanese accounting practices and introduced us to the Tokyo firm of Tohmatsu, Awoki & Co., which instructed us further on these issues.

In Japan, our most important advisor was Akio Morita, co-founder and now chairman of Sony. It was his broad understanding of the important differences between the United States and Japan that first set the directions of our investigation. The staff of the U.S. Embassy in Tokyo opened many doors for us, and they were among the most articulate critics of our early thoughts. Yoshio Okawara, the Japanese ambassador to the United States, was a helpful counselor. Professors Moriaki Tsuchiya and Hideaki Okamoto of the University of Tokyo were not only good critics but also willing helpers, as was Mr. Jiro Tokuyama of Normura Research.

Yuji Masuda of the Japan Society for the Promotion of Machine Industries helped us in many ways, as did Hunter Hale, a U.S. Department of Justice alumnus who now works in Japan. We are grateful to all of them.

The staff of MITI and of the Ministry of Finance permitted us to return time and again to clarify our understanding of their role, and they were always forthright and candid with us. MITI Vice-Minister for International Affairs Shohei Kurihara was especially helpful in developing our understanding, as was former Vice-Minister Naohiro Amaya. The staff of the Economic Planning Agency, the Bank of Japan, and members of the Diet were accessible and informative. In particular, we are grateful to Dr. Eisuke Sakakibara of the Ministry of Finance and to Masataka Okura, president of the Export-Import Bank of Japan, for their insights.

Much of our inquiry in Japan focused on the important role of industry trade associations. Toshio Takai and the staff of the Electronics Industry Association of Japan were particularly helpful, as were Tadashi Yoshioka and the staff of the Japan Electronics Industry Development Association. Both of these associations permitted us to return time and again for more information. At the Keidanren, which is the common ground for all industry in Japan, Masaya Miyoshi proved to be an exceptionally insightful observer. He and his staff were invaluable to our effort. The staff of the Japan Electronic Computers Corporation was always responsive to our requests for information, as was the staff of the VLSI Research Association.

We visited several electronics companies in Japan, including Sony, NEC, Toshiba, Hitachi, Fujitsu, Oki, Mitsubishi Electric, Matsushita, IBM Japan, and Honeywell. Haruo Seki, advisor to the board of Toshiba, and Kensuke Koga, director of Nippon Steel, were very informative. In fact, my curiosity about the business-government relationship in Japan was first stimulated by a conversation with the executive vice-president of Yokogawa Electric, whom I met at a University of Hawaii executive program several years ago. All of these people were gracious in putting up with the difficulty of interviews conducted through interpreters or in speaking English in order to accommodate me.

We also visited several banks in Japan, including the Long-Term Credit Bank, the Industrial Bank of Japan, Sanwa Bank, the Mitsui Bank, the Mitsubishi Bank, and the Sumitomo Bank. We also talked with the Tokyo staff of the Bank of America, the Morgan Guaranty Trust Company, the Chase Manhattan Bank, and with Baker and McKenzie, Booze, Allen & Hamilton, and the Boston Consulting Group of Tokyo. All were both informative and helpful.

Several people have listened to my thoughts in raw form and reacted to them. In the beginning, Steve Lohr of the *New York Times* Tokyo bureau and Urban Lehner of the *Wall Street Journal* Tokyo bureau were among the most skeptical and thoughtful. I greatly appreciate the time they spent with me. Arjay Miller has on several occasions listened patiently to my embryonic thoughts and poked holes in my arguments. Charles Angevine of the U.S. Embassy in Tokyo has been a reliable critic, and he took the time to review my first draft. Joji Arai of the Japan Productivity Center in Washington, D.C., was helpful in many ways. Rick Wheeler of the Asia Society in New York brought together a group to evaluate my thoughts, as did Congressman Albert Gore, Congressman Robert Edgar, and Congressman John Lafalce.

The research that led to this book has consumed approximately $700,000 in funds. That money has gone to pay for data collection, travel, staff salaries, and computer time. The key funding came first from the Office of Naval Research, which has a direct interest in the competitive vitality of the U.S. electronics industry. The Office of Naval Research support has been overseen in a careful and disciplined manner by Dr. Bert King. It was that funding that led to the massive data collection and analysis, only a small part of which is reported in this book. The great body of that work continues under analysis and writing. So far, it has yielded some twenty-five working papers of a technical nature and will yield important research articles. Other funding has come from the Alcoa Foundation, which has been a steady and reliable supporter, and from the General Electric Foundation, the Westinghouse Foundation, AMP Incorporated, and from IBM Americas/Far East Corporation. Other support has come from Sperry-New Holland and from a U.S. electronics company that prefers to remain anonymous. Once it became apparent that the research would have broad implications for public policy in the United States, we were able also to draw upon institutional support from the Andrew W. Mellon Foundation to UCLA. Finally, our work has benefitted and will benefit in the future from a generous endowment given to UCLA by George and Kimiko Nozawa to support U.S.-Japanese business studies. The spirit of that gift, like the spirit of this book, is to achieve greater understanding between these two nations. Without this joint public-private support, research of this sort could not take place. If this book makes a contribution to solving some of the problems of our society, then our debt is to these companies, foundations, and public sources that are willing to invest in social research.

About a year before I began work on the manuscript, I had my first conversations on the book with Ann Dilworth of the General Books Division at Addison-Wesley. On several occasions Ann visited my wife, Carol, and me, and we talked over the structure of the book. Ann supervised the editing of *Theory Z*, my first book, when she was editor in chief of the division. Though she is now Executive Vice President, she consented to edit personally *The M-Form Society*. I hope that every author will some day have the pleasure of working with an editor or publisher who has the skill, integrity, and grace that Ann has. If the book is effective, much of the credit goes to her.

After I had completed the first draft, which was written in the study above my garage, I took it to the Kona Village resort on the Island of Hawaii. There I handed it over to Dr. Thomas Hofstedt, then a professor of accounting at Southern Methodist University, a former neighbor, and a brilliant man. Tom is a rare person. He is the sort who can look you in the eye, tell you that your brilliant new book needs to be rewritten, and have you accept his advice. When I returned to UCLA, I received the same advice from two colleagues who had struggled through the entire first draft of 420 pages. These colleagues were Fred Weston, who is professor of economics, and Tom Copeland, who is associate professor of finance. John Young, president of Hewlett-Packard, also read the first draft and found several errors both of logic and of fact. Ralph Pfeiffer, chairman of IBM Americas/Far East, also scrutinized the first draft and offered many helpful criticisms. Their careful reading of the manuscript enabled me to see how to perform the job of reconstruction. I am also indebted to the several people who commented on parts of the first draft. These include Professor Andrew Van de Ven of the University of Minnesota; Dr. Robert Noyce, co-founder of Intel; Yoshiaki Shibusawa, executive vice-president of the California First Bank; Arjay Miller, formerly dean of the Stanford Business School; Ed Ferrey and Ken Hagerty of the American Electronics Association; Charles Angevine and the staff of the U.S. Embassy in Tokyo; Eric Lee of Senator Daniel Inouye's staff; Professor Oliver E. Williamson of Yale University; Akio Morita, chairman of Sony Corporation; and Masaya Miyoshi, managing director of the Keidanren.

Some people write in a steady, disciplined manner, a dozen or so pages each day. Not I. When I write, I write from eight in the morning until midnight or later, seven days a week until I am finished. I began writing the first draft on June 8, 1983, and completed it on Labor Day. The revisions were done by September 26. That was possible because the readers responded quickly and because my research team continued to provide assistance. Above all, it was possible only because my family put up with a summer devoted to writing. My sister, Carol, offered her encouragement and support throughout this project. Andy visited me in my room above the garage, bringing joy and relief into my days. Jennifer kept me supplied with Pringle's potato chips and kept me company as I wrote. Sarah brought her friends by to see how her father spent his days and nights, and she too kept at least some balance in my life. My wife, Carol, not only rendered me her love and support, she also listened to my arguments as I attempted to get each chapter straight. When we went out for an evening with friends, she gently reminded me not to talk on and on about my work. She managed the house while I was in Tokyo, Washington, and Minneapolis doing interviews and collecting data. She is the source of my equilibrium.

This book takes me into some waters that are unfamiliar to me. I am bringing the lessons of management to the problems of politics and, to some extent, finance. That sort of intellectual extension may be seen either as a laudable attempt on the part of the scholar to grow and to learn, or as an inappropriate breach of proper academic boundaries. Dean Clay LaForce has fostered an atmosphere at the Graduate School of Management at UCLA in which all are encouraged to learn and to grow. He has established a setting that allows for both rigor and creativity of thought, a setting in which I have been able to undertake my intellectual wanderings with a spirit of acceptance. I am indebted to him. I am indebted also to my hallway neighbors, those colleagues who have always been willing to engage in thoughtful conversation and to teach me about their specialties. Among those, the most helpful have been Jay Barney, Richard Rumelt, Bill McKelvey, Hal Mason, Tom Copeland, George Steiner, Fred Weston, and Victor Tabbush. I am grateful to each one, and I hope they will continue to teach me.

There is not space enough for me to list all of the others who contributed to my education in preparation for this book. The many people who helped us to arrange interviews and who themselves consented to interviews in Minneapolis, Washington, Tokyo, and other cities were invaluable. The many trade associations that we visited in the United States and in Japan are not mentioned here by name, nor are the several electronics companies, banks, and other organizations to whom I am nonetheless indebted. I hope that they will feel their time was well spent. I hope that they will find I was listening well to their lessons.

Finally, I am indebted above all to a few key scholars on whose work I have built my own. Alfred Chandler, Jr., of Harvard University, was the first to recognize the importance of the M-Form in business. Oliver Williamson of Yale University developed the general theory of organizational economics which I employ. Chalmers Johnson of the University of California at Berkeley wrote the definitive history of MITI from which I began. Mancur Olson of the University of Maryland developed the logic of collective action which stimulated my approach. This book attempts to point to some new directions, but it is oriented by their work.

preface

Last spring, I had a parking-lot conversation with a friend. It was one of those fifteen-minute delectations at the end of an evening, an opportunity for two ordinary people to plumb for just a moment the problems of civilization. It was the kind of conversation best held in the semi-darkness of the parking lot of the Chinese restaurant, where the dim light camouflages our commonness and permits us to discuss problems of state, to be for a moment Plato, Hobbes, or Adam Smith.

As it happens, my partner in this dialogue was John Doyle, a man who was trained as an engineer and who now serves as vice-president for research and development of the Hewlett-Packard Corporation, where he oversees the stream of invention that is his company's lifeblood. Five years ago, John was reading books on management, creativity at work, and productivity. More recently, he has been reading books on economic history. Like many of us, he has been wondering why we feel this persistent economic malaise, why we doubt the staying power of the business recovery that was underway by spring of 1983. Some of the books he has been reading are very good at detailing the woes of American industry; others have argued that our present state of economic decline is both inevitable and irreversible. John, however, has the mind of a scientist. He is a skeptic. He is skeptical of the idea that anything is inevitable, that anything is impossible, that any widely believed theory is correct. In fact, he observed as he finally headed for his car (an American product), "You know that most of the truly major inventions were impossible. At the time they were invented, all of the prevailing beliefs explained exactly why they would not work. After the invention appeared, the scholars developed new theories to explain its existence."

It was in that spirit that I sat down to write this book. Everyone knows that teamwork between business and government is impossible in America. Everyone knows that interest-group politics in Western nations are inevitable and that they are inevitably paralyzing to the nation. We have extensive theories in economics and political science that explain why this is so. Perhaps those beliefs are superstitious. Perhaps we can develop teamwork without giving up our freedoms. In this book, I describe the ways in which I believe we can achieve just such a state of teamwork.

My first book was titled *Theory Z: How American Business Can Meet the Japanese Challenge*. In that book, I used the example of teamwork in the Japanese company as a way to challenge the pessimism of those Americans who believe that teamwork on the job is not possible, that there must always be an adversarial relationship between manager and worker. The book consisted largely of my description of an American company, which I called Company Z. Company Z had on its own developed a very successful form of teamwork, a combination of discipline and support, of collaboration and individual effort, that has made it one of the great success stories of our time. What was interesting about Company Z was that it had many of the appearances of a Japanese company, although it was in every way American.

In this book, I once again return to the Japanese example, but this time to reveal that cooperation and teamwork are possible between business and government. Once again, my goal is not to suggest that we should emulate the Japanese, but rather to bring into sharp relief a clearer understanding of what we are and what we can be. The key is to use the Japanese example as the foil against which we see ourselves more clearly. Once again, I point to an extensive example of successful cooperation in America, this time in a study of Minneapolis, Minnesota.

When I sat down to write the final chapter of *Theory Z*, I intended to write a grand statement on what our government should do to go along with the efforts of our managers. It was only with all of the horses pulling together, I reasoned, that we would achieve progress. At the end of one week, I had made several starts but had written nothing that was sensible. I concluded that I had better learn something about the business-government relationship.

The great freedom of being a professor with tenure is the ability to choose to study anything at all that interests you. The great obligation is to choose to study something of importance to which you can make a contribution. I have spent the past three years working as part of a sixteen-person research team that has attempted to learn something about what the United States and other western nations can do to improve the quality of teamwork between business and government. It has been an exciting and rewarding intellectual enterprise for all of us, and I have attempted to communicate that excitement in this book. The time for mulling over our woes is past. It is time to look ahead, to establish the teamwork that we need: it is the time for action.

PART 1
THE M-FORM SOCIETY
what it is,
how it works

1

THE M-FORM
SOCIETY
why we need it

Your children and mine may never be able to look forward to the day when they will own two cars, a boat, and a three-bedroom house in the suburbs. American industry lost 16 percent of its share of world markets in the 1960s and another 23 percent in the 1970s. In 1980 the nation's total discretionary income was 1.2 percent less than in 1973.[1] We can reverse this trend of the past twenty years and regain our economic vitality, but to do so we must first throw off some old superstitions, overcome our pattern of adversarial relations, and establish a new form of teamwork between business and government. This book describes how we can go about that task of establishing teamwork. The lessons will come from the field of business management. Never before have we attempted to apply these lessons of our largest corporations to the problems of managing a society. The analogy is imperfect, of course, but we will find that the study of business organization provides some fresh insights into the problems of managing our society. In particular, the high-performing U.S. corporations are typically of the multidivisional form, or M-Form, and from these we will draw some lessons from which to design an M-Form society.

Economic Superstition

We believe, perhaps superstitiously, that our economy succeeds best when each company is left to behave as a narrow-minded maximizer of profit. The evidence of the past one hundred years, years of prosperity and of growth, has reinforced our faith in this belief. During the first sixty of those years, however, our economic system did not compete on a large scale with that of any other nation. Most of our commerce was domestic, and large-scale manufacturing was not highly developed anywhere in the world, so that relatively little of our economic growth depended on the success of our products versus those of any other nation.

During the past forty years, large-scale manufacturing has been highly developed, and trade has become important to us. Our success during this period was not due entirely to ingenuity and hard work, however. At the end of World War II, anyone who wanted to buy an airplane, a ship, a tractor, or an oscilloscope had to buy it in North America. Many of the industrial plants of Germany, France, England, and Japan had been destroyed. While those countries rebuilt, we supplied their needs and our industries flourished. We enjoyed forty years of an unprecedented industrial monopoly during which our companies earned monopoly profits, labor took home monopoly wages, and government extracted monopoly taxes. We scarcely noticed when the rest of the world began to catch up and offer competition.

Each of us can think of a company that has enjoyed a period of temporary monopoly. Often, a monopoly comes about when a company has a better product that is protected by patents. Other times it comes about through government regulation, as was the case with AT&T or with the U.S. airlines. When there is such a monopoly, the stage is set for superstitious learning. Under monopoly, the management can be remiss and the workers can be inefficient, yet the company will have greater sales and earnings each year. Everyone concerned will "learn" that they know how to run the business and make money. That learning, however, is entirely superstitious and bears no relation to reality. It is just as superstitious as the knowledge of a primitive tribe that if they perform a ritual each night, they will cause the sun to return twelve hours hence.

Superstitious learning is difficult to overcome. One member of that tribe, perhaps an intuitive scientist, probably said, "I'll bet that this ritual is unnecessary. I bet that even if we cut it out, the sun will come back." Probably one of his colleagues would agree, saying, "You're right. We should cut out this phony stuff . . . but on the other hand, why take a chance?" Over time, those rational beliefs that are most central to a community will take on an ethical and moral quality, which will serve to integrate those central beliefs into communal life more fully and which will protect them from change.

We have learned as a nation that each firm should stand as an entirely solo actor. We have learned also that firms will then sometimes exploit their freedom and take advantage of others, and so we have learned that government must prevent exploitation and so the two must be adversaries. We cherish the freedom and we accept the adversarial relations, because we have learned, over one hundred years of industrial success, that it works.

Political Superstition

We have also learned that interest-group politics are an inescapable fact of our pluralistic democracy. We understand that over time special interest groups will arise to represent the interests of the many segments of our polity. These interest groups serve a useful purpose, because they extend participation in government beyond the passive-citizen role of voting. Individually we cherish the opportunity to have our voices heard.

On the other hand, we observe that our nation seems to be caught in a political-economic gridlock similar to the notorious automobile gridlock of New York City: no one can move through any intersection, because no one is willing to stand aside. The entire system is locked into place, one huge, interconnected, and immobile grid.

Mancur Olson, a political economist at the University of Maryland, has recently argued that special interest groups will inevitably arise wherever there is political stability.[2] He thus describes an intuition about politics that many of us have believed but have not been able to articulate. When there is political stability, those who share common interests will find one another in order to press their common cause in the government. Over time, these interest groups will grow throughout the nation like weeds. Because each group will be unwilling to yield its self-interest to any other group even for a moment, they will all choke off the process of social choice that is necessary to focus the nation's efforts and to make economic progress. The result will be a political-economic gridlock.

According to Olson, history tells us that the only way to break this gridlock is to suffer a revolution or to lose a war. The European nations have gone through such traumas and have emerged with their interest groups scattered. As a result, each nation has been able to form a new consensus in a less selfish way and enjoy several decades of robust economic development. In time, however, the interest group politics return and the gridlock is reestablished. The result is a loss of economic vitality.

We believe that our form of pluralistic democracy works. It has distributed political influence broadly across our nation, and the many disparate groups do seem to coalesce when there is a national emergency, such as the threat of Sputnik or the need to develop an agricultural research and education system. Yet we observe that most citizens do not even bother to vote in national elections, we seem unable to address the high cost of health care, and we cannot fundamentally decide how to repair our social security system. Above all, we accept as fact the belief that adversarial interest-group politics are a necessary part of our democracy. Perhaps that belief is superstitious as well.

Lessons from Business Management

The study of business management has made great progress during the past ten or twenty years. One result that seems to emerge with some regularity (although there is some evidence to the contrary) is that among the largest companies, the high-performing type is the multidivisional form, or M-Form. It will be described fully in the next chapter. The M-Form company succeeds because it attains a state of balance between teamwork on the one hand and individual effort on the other.

In the M-Form company there are many separate divisions, each of which manufactures and sells a somewhat different product line. However, the managers of M-Form companies assume dual roles. On the one hand, each division manager is encouraged to maximize profits, make decisions, and behave as though he or she were a solo competitor in the marketplace. On the other hand, each division manager must also behave as though he or she were part of a team.

The ability to work as a team is particularly important in two instances: decision making and resource allocation. In the first place, the division managers will inevitably sometimes disagree on what kind of central computer should be purchased, which trucking company should be hired, or which division should develop a new product. If the managers meet together and confront one another, if they engage in a sustained dialogue and work out their problems, then they can make effective recommendations to the top management of the corporation. However, if they do not work as a team, each division general manager will sneak in separately to see the president and the corporate staff to plead his case in the hope of gaining advantage over the others. In that case, the corporate staff will balloon in size, top management will become more powerful, the company will become more centralized, division managers will complain about bureaucracy and inflexibility, and the company will suffer. They will, in other words, create a gridlock in which all are prisoners.

In the second place, every M-Form company provides some "free" central corporate resources on which every division draws. Those may be the research of the corporate laboratories or the skill of the corporate accounting staff. If each division manager sees himself or herself purely as a profit maximizer and not at all as part of a team, each will attempt to overuse those "free" resources and will resist being "taxed" to pay for them. In time, those essential common endowments will be depleted, and the company will wake up one day to find that a competitor has passed it by because the competitor has built up its endowments rather than using them up.

Our largest M-Form companies begin to resemble our nation. Of course, they are a good deal smaller and simpler, but they are instructive nonetheless. M-Form companies succeed only by stimulating the individual initiative and strivings of each separate division; they can be flexible and adaptable only if they are decentralized. But they must have teamwork rather than adversarial relations. The point is simple but important. In our nation, the leaders of our major industries, largest companies, and important trade associations and special interest groups are equivalent to the division general managers of an M-Form company. These middle managers of our society must retain their essential autonomy and independence if our society is to remain responsive and effective. But they must also work as a team. If they do not work as a team, each special interest will sneak in to lobby Congress or the White House in an attempt to seek advantage for itself. Its opponents will sneak in other doors in an attempt to block them. As a result, the bureaucracy will grow, the decision making in the nation will become more centralized, everyone will complain about too much government intervention and too much bureaucratic inflexibility, and all will be trapped in a political-economic gridlock that is of their own making. The successful M-Form company avoids these traps, and so can an M-Form society.

Social Memory

We all recognize the fact that each company in our society succeeds only because it draws on many social endowments that are "free" to the company. We have a system of private property rights, stable and honest government with peaceful succession of leadership, and nearly universal literacy. We need only compare ourselves to the less developed nations to see the importance of these social endowments to each company. In this book, we will look at the business–government relationship in Japan, and we will see that the Japanese have developed another social endowment, one which also benefits every company in Japan but which U.S. companies do not share. That endowment is a sense of teamwork between the several segments of the business community; between business, labor, and civic groups; and between business and government. Just as our companies could not be competitive without the social endowments of stable government and free public education, so they cannot be fully competitive in the world market without the endowment of effective national teamwork. The objective of this book is to describe how to establish that teamwork.

Teamwork sounds, however, like a potentially dangerous euphemism for something else. To business people, it raises fears of more government intervention. To others, it raises the specter of an all-powerful business elite running our nation. Is it possible to have teamwork of this sort, and is it desirable? In order to get at these questions, we must talk first about a new concept, the concept of social memory.

A nation has a social memory when it has the ability to remember—the ability to remember what group has been flexible in the past and what group has been unreasonably selfish. In order to have force, a social memory must also be enforced by a network of business, civic, and governmental associations that have the ability to grant or withhold cooperation to those interest groups that have shown themselves deserving of assistance or of punishment. A social memory is what was called in earlier times a sense of community, a sense of responsibility, a sense of civic-mindedness. This sense had little to do with altruism, however. Instead, it rested upon the fact that each person in a small town knew with certainty that his or her behavior today would be remembered and appropriately repaid tomorrow. In a mass society, the natural forces of community are absent. We must restore them, at least in some measure, and in a new way.

Why is a social memory necessary in a modern society, and what does it have to do with the economic vitality of a nation? The answer is quite simple. The task of encouraging the development of companies in an economy is similar to the task of encouraging the development of children in a family. We all understand that if our children attempt simultaneously to master algebra, Spanish, history, and physics, while also becoming adept at soccer, piano, flute, and social dancing, and meanwhile taking part in Boy Scouts or Girl Scouts and acting in school plays, they will end up being second-rate at everything. To excel, a person must focus. If we do not take the analogy to its ridiculous extreme, we can observe that much the same is true of a nation's economy. As an economy matures, some industries reach old age while other new industries are born. A new industry has certain needs for taxation, regulation, and export assistance, whereas a mature industry has quite different needs. Our nation has several hundred major industries, each with a unique set of needs. If we attempt to do a little bit to regulate or to assist each industry, we will end up making all of them second-rate in world markets. Instead, we must focus our legislative, financial, and educational resources on a few industries at a time.

Why is it that our steel and aluminum industries have languished for two decades while our government has done little to achieve the legislative changes or to overcome the labor-management conflicts that would help those industries? Why is it that U.S. shipping has shrunk to a shadow of its former world dominance, while the public and its government have stood by as silent observers? Is it that the technical issues are so complex that no one understands them? Is it that the barriers between labor and management are so formidable that no one can overcome them? It seems unlikely. If we as a nation would put other issues aside temporarily and for the next ten years use our legislative, financial, and educational resources to solve the problems of three or four industry groups, then we could accelerate those industries to full world competitiveness. We could engage in the necessary public debate and scrutiny and we could focus the eye of public attention on those few industries in a manner that would weed out the hopeless and force honest appraisal and change upon the others. We could alter the regulatory and legal apparatus in a way that would more effectively suit the needs and avoid the dangers of these industries.

Having accomplished that task, we could turn our attention to the next set of three or four industry groups, leaving the first set to continue on their own. Once an industry has accelerated to a higher speed, we could expect it to continue at that new velocity without continued infusions of public attention. In that manner, we could engage serially in the process of economic development, achieving preeminence in one industry after another.

This process of serial economic development implies a process of social choice. It implies that we as a nation will choose to focus the major portion of our attention and resources on a few industries and not, therefore, on others. In a democratic society, it is impossible to engage in the process of social choice without the support of those not chosen. But what group will support a choice that leaves them with an empty bag? No one. Not, that is, unless that group knows that their sacrificial support of today will be remembered and repaid tomorrow.

Only with a strong, visible, and reliable social memory will the citizens of a democracy submit to a process of social choice. Only with social choice can a nation focus its resources on its economic and social problems. Only with focus can progress be won. It is precisely this capacity to focus that accounts for the success of the M-Form company, and it is precisely this capacity to focus that we must develop in what can become an M-Form society.

The Industrial Policy Debate

From London to New York, from Singapore to Washington, the debate is over industrial policy. What most people mean by industrial policy is not clear, but in each case it refers to what the Japanese have done. Many observers have argued that the Japanese have squared the circle, that they have found a way to combine central planning with a market economy. It has been said that the Japanese government, headed by MITI (the Ministry of International Trade and Industry), targets industries for growth, directs the companies, subsidizes them, and then invades foreign markets.

How is it that the Japanese can target so flawlessly? How could they have targeted steel and then automobiles, computers and then machine tools, consumer electronics and then motorcycles? Is it, as some scholars have suggested, that they simply have smarter bureaucrats? Such an explanation strains the imagination.

Other observers have argued that the Japanese do engage in central planning under the title of industrial policy, but that they are not so flawless. They tried unsuccessfully to develop an electric automobile, a computer to rival the IBM System 360, and they overbuilt their aluminum, steel, and shipbuilding industries. Instead, these critics assert, the Japanese have convinced a sheepish public that they should accept below-market interest on their bank savings in order to subsidize targeted industries. Why would the public stand for that kind of treatment? Out of loyalty to the emperor and the nation, goes that equally unbelievable argument.

MITI publishes an English-language journal that presents its view of these issues. The issue of summer 1983 was devoted to correcting the world's view of industrial policy in Japan. The cover drawing was captioned "Japan's Industrial Policy" and featured an animal with the forebody of a lion, the hindquarters of a tiger, the wings of a swan, and the head and ears of a rabbit: a mythical beast. As we shall see in later chapters, the Japanese engage in dialogue and teamwork between business and government, but they do not engage in central planning.

It is fruitless to argue over whether the U.S. and other market economies should engage in central planning. We rejected central planning long ago, having observed its failure in the Soviet economy. The issue arises today only because we suffer from economic malaise while the Japanese continue to grow with vitality. It arises because many Western observers see Japan with Western eyes. To Western eyes, the only possible relationship between business and government is one of adversarial relations, and the only difference between nations is in who is on top. Looking at Japan through these lenses, we conclude that in Japan, the government must be on top; otherwise there could be no collaboration of the sort we see there. Thus, we conclude, the Japanese have found a way to engage in successful central planning. In this book, we will view Japan instead through the eyes of someone accustomed to studying the large firms of the United States, firms in which success depends not upon adversarial relations but upon teamwork. With this view, we will see that the Japanese have not engaged in central planning, and that the current debate over industrial policy in the West as currently framed is largely misinformed and pointless. Instead of arguing over who is going to be on top, we ought to be seeking ways to replace our political-economic gridlock with the kind of teamwork that has made our biggest and best companies successful.

The Research Behind This Book

In this book, I report the results of a three-year study of the business–government relationship in the United States and in Japan. The work was done by a group of graduate students led by UCLA Professor Jay B. Barney and me. Most of us worked full-time on this study for three years. Over that time, we interviewed more than two hundred people who are knowledgable on these issues. In Japan, we met with top officials and middle-level bureaucrats of the Bank of Japan, the Ministry of International Trade and Industry, the Ministry of Finance, the Economic Planning Agency, and with members of the Japanese Diet. We met several times with the staffs of the U.S. Embassy in Tokyo and the Japanese Embassy in Washington. We also visited with executives of Sony, Fujitsu, Hitachi, Oki, Mitsubishi Electric, NEC, and Toshiba, as well as bankers from Mitsui Bank, Mitsubishi Bank, the Long-Term Credit Bank, the Industrial Bank of Japan, and many others. We talked with top officials of the Keidanren; the Japan Chamber of Commerce; the Keizai Doyukai, the Japan Electronic Industries Development Association; the Electronic Industries Association of Japan; and dozens of others. In each case, an interview was conducted with two to eight members of the research team present, and an attempt was made to take verbatim notes. Many of these interviews were confidential and no direct quotes are reported from those. All of them, however, contributed to our ability to untangle the web of conflicting perceptions of how the Japanese manage the business–government relationship in a manner both competitive and collaborative.

Back at UCLA, the research team undertook several additional tasks. In order to understand the importance of ownership patterns in industry, we first constructed a list of all electronics and aerospace companies in the United States and in Japan that had publicly listed stock. We turned to public records to find basic data on all 814 of these companies and then made nearly 3,000 long-distance telephone calls in order to verify the data and to add new data. Then we turned to government-maintained lists of owners and recorded the name of each owner of every large block of stock in all 814 companies. Finally, we brought back from Japan piles of financial reports which we translated into English and then used to gain more detailed information. This work, which will continue for two or three more years, has so far yielded several insights and perhaps twenty-two working papers written for a technical, academic audience. In this book, I have attempted to distill the issues of practical importance to all of us, drawing upon the sense but not the technical intricacies of the research.

I only wish that each citizen of every nation could have shared directly in our experience. It was exciting, even arresting. What we saw was broad and deep agreement that our current approach to the public governance of business doesn't work, that our team's new thoughts on the subject held out some promise, and that change, though difficult, is possible. Who could ask for more? This book, I hope, will involve more of us in the challenge of creating political and social change that will enable us to take control of our destiny without losing a war or suffering a revolution.

A Call for Teamwork in America

There is a growing consensus that we must throw off our political and economic superstitions and move ahead in a different way. The 1983 report of the Business-Higher Education Forum was presented by a group that included Robert Anderson, the chairman of Rockwell International; David Saxon, the president of the University of California; Theodore Hesburgh, the president of Notre Dame University; and several other leaders. The report concluded: "We stand at the hinge of history, with an unprecedented opportunity to combine the lessons of our past with the resources of our future to revitalize the economy, create more jobs, and increase the standard of living. American society, through its seeming addiction to adversarial relationships, has created a formidable barrier to restoring the nation's competitiveness . . . very few institutions are capable of facilitating such cooperation. This major gap must be overcome."[3]

Another major report, this one by the bipartisan Fowler-McCracken Commision (fourteen members of Congress, seventeen members of the Reagan administration, and many others) sounds the same need to overcome our adversarial stance: ". . . our Commission members have identified . . . a need . . . to end the adversary concept between government and business—outmoded, counterproductive at best, even crippling in today's highly competitive world marketplace."[4]

The Democratic Caucus of the U.S. House of Representatives, a group chaired by Gillis Long and Timothy Wirth, adds: "Achieving economic growth will require a partnership among labor, small business, big corporations, universities, and government. . . . This need for partnership will require a lessening of the adversarial relationship between business and labor. Cooperation has always benefitted our country, from the building of the railroads to the success of the space program and is always more productive than confrontation."[5]

The call to action is clear. This book is about what action we can take and how. As a concrete way of considering these issues we will focus on the microelectronics and computer industries of the United States and Japan. Through the example of this heterogeneous industry, we will see the many ways in which our economic and political superstitions may be wrong. We will see some of the answers that may be practically available to us and how to initiate them.

By the year 1990, electronics will be the fourth largest industry in the United States. By the year 2000, it will rank second only to health care. In 1982, the electronics industries of the United States produced a net surplus (excluding consumer electronics) of $10 billion in our balance of trade. We cannot afford to let this future slip away from us. We must rise to the occasion and form the combination of teamwork and individual effort that will keep this and other industries healthy.

In February of 1983, the key members of the U.S. electronics industries and of our government met in Washington, D.C. to discuss the future of those industries. Most of us would think that such discussions go on all the time in Washington, that our government and business leaders are in constant dialogue over the needs of our industries. One keynote speaker was David Packard, the cofounder of the Hewlett-Packard Corporation and former deputy assistant secretary of defense. His opening words: "In my memory, this is the first time there has been any focused, public discussion of the whole range of issues that affect a prime national resource—high technology. . . . It's about time."

2

THE M-FORM SOCIETY
lessons from business management

The study of business management has something to contribute to the governance of our nation. It is true that the analogy is limited. Even the largest company is much simpler than the smallest nation. A nation cannot readily "fire" a citizen who does not fit, nor can it select from among its newborn only those few whom it would like to have as future members. Because each of us devotes only a fraction of our lives to our employer, we can tolerate some lack of democracy at work that we cannot tolerate in our government. In these and in many other ways, the problems of managing IBM or Procter and Gamble differ greatly from the problems that face those who govern a city, a state, or a nation.

Yet there are similarities that are great enough to warrant at least some comparison between the managerial problems of companies and of a society. In the recent past, our largest companies have become sufficiently complex that their problems have begun to resemble in some ways the problems of managing a nation. In the postwar year of 1949, only 30 percent of the 500 largest firms in the United States were diversified; that is, they did business in more than a single line of business. By 1974, the proportion of diversified firms had more than doubled, to 63 percent.[1] At the same time, several of these companies had grown to the point of employing more than 500,000 individuals, and AT&T, before its breakup in 1984, employed one million people.

Many of us have the mistaken belief that these large companies are governed at the top by an executive team that is single-minded in its agreement on what the company should do and how it should do it. Nothing could be farther from the truth. In fact, the top executives of a diversified company will find that the managers who run the furniture business understand relatively little about the problems faced by their colleagues who run the carpet or the textile divisions of the same corporation. Each business division will have a different manufacturing method, each will have different customers, and each will require a different number of years to achieve success in a new market. Moreover, each division will develop a different set of goals, values, and beliefs, and each will become to some extent a separate culture.

Typically, all of the division heads will want more of the corporation's funds and other resources than are available. The chief executive officer, who has the final decision-making authority, will have difficulty sorting out the various claims and determining what course is best. The successful companies have found a way to accomplish this task. They have found a way to structure themselves and to establish a combination of teamwork and of individual entrepreneurship that keeps the company healthy. Many management scholars have studied their experience and their successes in some detail, and some reliable patterns of success have appeared. These patterns can tell us something about how to govern a nation with its many independent interest groups and competing industries, its many claims against limited national resources, and its need to sustain at once a spirit of individual entrepreneurship and a spirit of teamwork.

We begin, therefore, with a brief look at business organization and management. We will review the basic forms of organization that large companies use, note their strengths and weaknesses, and observe that, for large, diversified companies, only one form is consistently successful—the M-Form. The central point of this exercise is transparent: in successful large companies, there is a balance between individual effort on the one hand and teamwork on the other. A large company cannot succeed if each division goes off entirely on its own; there must be some teamwork among divisions.

A large company also cannot succeed if no one is willing to make a decision or if the chief executive makes all decisions. In any large enterprise, there must be decentralized decision making, if for no reason other than that the chief executive is not omniscient and thus cannot know what is best for each division at each moment. Much the same is true of managing a nation.

The M-Form Hypothesis

In the study of very large firms, Professor Oliver Williamson of Yale University has made some particularly helpful observations.[2] I have drawn heavily upon his thoughts, although I have employed some of them in ways in which he might disapprove. Williamson has introduced what has become known in microeconomics as "The M-Form Hypothesis," from which the title of this book is drawn.[3] The hypothesis is that large companies of M-Form will, for reasons to be described below, be more profitable than large firms of any other type. In that analysis we will find some lessons that are applicable to the governance of our economy as well.

In the organization of large firms, only three elemental structures are possible: the U-Form, the H-Form and the M-Form.[4] Here I refer only to the underlying structure of an organization, what we think of more commonly as the lines and boxes that summarize, albeit grossly, who reports to whom. To describe an organization's structure is to oversimplify the subtleties of organizational life; every organization specialist understands that the people who inhabit organizations rarely see such clear divisions between responsibilities or units. Yet there are some substantial differences in how people behave within each form of organization.

The U-Form Structure

The most familiar form of organization is the U-Form, more commonly known as the functional organization. A simple U-Form structure may be depicted as follows:

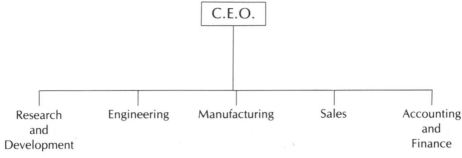

U-FORM ORGANIZATION

The organization is unified, or U-Form, in the sense that it can stand only as a unity. No subportion of the organization can exist on its own. Research and development by itself would have no product to sell; manufacturing alone would have no designs to work from; sales alone would be empty. More importantly, none of the subunits in a U-Form company can measure its performance in a clear or simple manner. No subunit has its own "bottom line;" it cannot be treated as a profit center. Because each subunit is wholly dependent on the others, the organization tends to be highly centralized. The chief executive cannot simply direct each department head to maximize profits as he or she sees fit, because no department has a measure of profitability.

As a result, the chief executive has no simple and complete measure of performance for each subunit and thus must rely on central control. If he or she were to specify that each department was to keep costs down but quality up, then arguments or differences of interpretation would arise as to what that means. In the accounting department, for example, costs can be kept to zero by firing the whole staff and doing no accounting; alternately, near-perfect accounting records can be kept by hiring fifty times as many accountants and buying a massive new computer system. It is obvious that neither extreme is reasonable, but it is not obvious just where in the middle things should be. Thus, the chief executive of the U-Form organization must stay close to the operations of each department, so that he or she can know when they should do more and when they should do less. He or she must be intimately informed about the details of each department. If the chief executive works hard and is well informed, he or she can do so, at least until the organization grows to middle size. However, because he or she must stay so closely focused on operating affairs, the chief executive typically fails to develop a long-run point of view and often loses sight of the larger direction and purpose of the organization. For these reasons, the U-Form organization tends to be a poor profit performer, except in the small organization.

The nearest thing to a U-Form society is a centrally planned economy of the Soviet type. It is one in which a central government apparatus directs the activities not only of each industry sector, but of each factory in some detail, working through a large bureaucratic apparatus. Rather than attempting to maximize profits, factory managers attempt to hit bureaucratically set targets. For several reasons which both political scientists and economists have argued over the years, such an economy will be grossly inefficient, as will any large company of the U-Form.

The H-Form Structure

The second pure organizational type is the H-Form, or holding company. In the pure H-Form, the corporate staff is very small and keeps only financial controls over the operating units. A typical (but imaginary) H-Form company would look as follows:

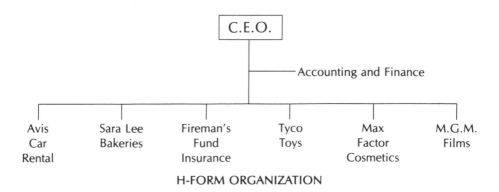

H-FORM ORGANIZATION

The critical aspect of the H-Form organization is that the operating units are in unrelated businesses. That is, the auto rental company and the cosmetic company share no factories, sales force, laboratories, or anything else in common. They are the opposite of the operating units in the U-Form company, in which the operating units, or departments, are wholly dependent upon each other. Here, each unit stands alone; it can be evaluated as a profit center or an investment center; its management can be directed simply to maximize profits and can then be left on its own. Because the chief executive of the larger corporation can tell at a glance which units are profitable and which are not, he or she has no need to inquire into the operating details of each business, and decentralization can be maximal. But if the top management of the parent company knows almost nothing about each unit, then why does the whole exist? Is this just an example of the "paper entrepreneurialism" Robert Reich of Harvard has criticized?[5]

Williamson and others have argued that the distinctive advantage of the H-Form is its ability to put money to its best use.[6] Ordinarily, a company will go to banks and to investors to obtain the money necessary to build a new plant, buy more delivery trucks, or continue research on a new product. If those "providers of capital"—those who provide equity and debt—do not know a great deal about the user of capital, they will give too much money to some and not enough to others, thus making the economy as a whole inefficient.

By comparison, the corporate office in the H-Form company knows a fair amount about each business, some of which it may have owned for two or three decades. It knows a good deal about the judgment, the quirks, the ability of the top managers of each unit, some of whom may have come from the corporate staff. The corporate financial staff has an unquestioned right to inquire deeply into the affairs of each unit, to look carefully at their most confidential future plans, to have information that even a trusted banker or outside investor can obtain only with great difficulty. If events begin to go awry, the corporate staff will know long before an outside provider of capital will know. Thus, the corporate office will have both better information and better control over each unit than the outside capital markets could. For these reasons, the corporation can serve as an "inside banker" and an "inside investor," deciding how to allocate capital among the operating units and doing so with more skill than any outsider could possess.

The H-Form is very nearly what a market economy aspires to be. In our idealized "perfect competition," each company acts on its own, attempting to maximize profits. There is a little bit of hierarchical control from government, but that is minimized. Capital flows are directed by the municipal, state, and federal governments to the housing industry, the health care industry, or the retail industry by arranging for subsidized mortgages, tax deductions for health care, or higher property taxes instead of higher sales taxes.

If in fact there are no common assets or social endowments on which each industry depends, then the H-Form will succeed. In business, a true conglomerate very nearly approaches a state of zero social endowments. The auto rental company in our example shares no common people or facilities with the bakery company, for instance. In a national economy, however, this is not so. In a national economy, the textile industry cannot prosper unless the garment manufacturing industry is also healthy. The machine-tool and robot industries cannot compete in world markets unless the semiconductor and computer industries are successful. None of these can succeed unless the education system is sound and the university-based research system is well supported. No industry can prosper unless the nation's health is good, its ethnic minorities are fully part of the democratic process, its system of laws are properly maintained.

If the nation is organized as an H-Form, then decision making is completely decentralized to each industry and, more fundamentally, to each company and to each individual. There is no social memory and no possibility of serial equity. If each actor simply attempts to maximize profit, then the perfection of the market (that is, a market with no social endowments at all) will guide the actor, as if by an invisible hand, to outcomes that are best for all. Much as we may strive for such a state, we need to recognize explicitly that our economy succeeds only with a great number of social endowments, that no industry or company can stand on its own, and that instead of completely decentralized decision making, we must have a more nearly balanced form. The answer is not a centralized and bureaucratic form of government regulation. That would take us to a U-Form, which is no better. The answer is a balance between centralization and decentralization: decentralization so that each firm can be left alone most of the time to attempt to maximize profit; centralization so that every firm will be prevented from abusing social endowments and encouraged to build future social endowments.

The M-Form Structure

The third form of organization, the M-Form, or multidivisional organization, is the high-performing type. The development of the M-Form organization has occurred during the past fifty years in Western Europe and in the United States, and has been described in detail by the Harvard University historian Alfred Chandler, Jr.[7] The true multidivisional organization is intermediate in its degree of centralization between the centralized U-Form and the decentralized H-Form. The pure form may be represented as follows:

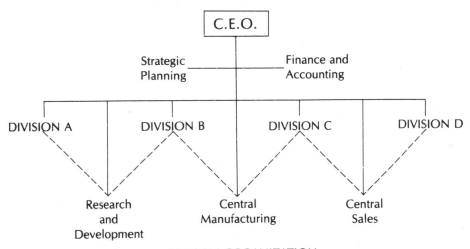

M-FORM ORGANIZATION

What is most important about the M-Form organization is that its operating units are partially interdependent. That is, each division makes a product or supplies a service that is distinctive and different from that of each other unit, but all share some common endowments such as technology, skill, or other important features. For example, Hewlett-Packard, which conforms nearly perfectly to the pure M-Form, is divided into nearly fifty semiautonomous divisions: one manufactures oscilloscopes, another hospital instruments, a third makes computers, and a fourth, hand-held calculators. Each division sells to a slightly different set of customers, each employs different manufacturing methods; but all share in common a base in the profession of electrical engineering, use some similar manufacturing methods, and most depend upon a continual process of invention from central laboratories to supplement their research. The reality of the corporation's businesses is that each is partially independent and yet partially dependent upon the whole. The formal structure of the M-Form reflects this ambiguous state and provides a means through which to attain a balance between autonomy for the divisions and central control over them.

The chief executive of an M-Form organization may ask each division manager to operate independently and to attempt simply to maximize profits. Each operating unit is sufficiently autonomous in that it is possible to calculate its sales, subtract its expenses, and thus to calculate its profits. Rather than having to know a great deal about just how happy the customers are, how rapidly new products are being developed, or whether the right people are being promoted within the division, the chief executive can rely to a considerable degree upon the much simpler financial measures of each manager's performance. However, if people take their "bottom line" measures too seriously, that is, if they attempt to maximize profits to the exclusion of all else, then trouble will emerge.

In fact, each division in an M-Form company is not truly autonomous and thus does not have an accurate picture of its performance reflected in the calculation of profitability. If each of the fifty division general managers attempts to maximize his or her divisional profits, then each will overuse "free" corporate social endowments, such as laboratory time and marketing staff. Each will be reluctant to increase his division's contribution to the corporate labs and will complain about the high corporate "tax" on divisional profits. In time, this attempt at local profit maximization will eat up the company's social endowments and everyone will wake up one day to find that a competitor has overtaken the company by investing more in the future.

The M-Form organization succeeds only if it maintains its balance. The individual strivings of division heads must not be reined in, but those individual efforts must have a collaborative rather than an adversarial climate within which to operate. The collaboration must never become dominant, however, or the advantages of autonomy and individualism will be lost and the organization will degenerate into a ponderous bureaucracy.

At the level of a whole society, an M-Form is headed by a government that governs but does not attempt to manage the industries and individual companies. That is, the government does not attempt to make day-to-day decisions for companies or to promulgate extensive bureaucratic and regulatory restrictions. Instead, the government attempts to create an atmosphere of balanced competition in which each firm strives to outdo the others, but in which all work as a team to resolve their differences directly. If teamwork is lacking in the middle management of an M-Form company, all the disputes will be passed up to the corporate office for resolution. In time, the power of the corporate staff will grow, the centralization of the company will become oppressive, and the division managers will complain about the excessive bureaucracy and staff interference without realizing that they have created the problem by failing to work as a team in the middle-management level. In a society, much the same may occur. If the top managements of companies and the leaders of industry do not work as a team to confront one another directly and settle their differences, then they will push the problems up to their government for resolution. In time, the government will increase in size and in power, centralization will follow, and the economy will become inflexible and inefficient.

The Forms of Governance: Markets, Bureaucracies, and Clans

Management refers to the making of operating decisions, whereas governance refers instead to the creation of a setting in which others can manage effectively. In a company as in a society, the task of the top management is to create an effective form of governance. In doing this, the chief executive may rely upon markets, bureaucracies, and clans.[8]

The objective of governance is to coordinate the efforts of individuals in such a way that each works to his or her highest level of ability. It is difficult to stimulate this high level of accomplishment, because all individuals the world over are self-interested. I take it as axiomatic that self-interest is universal among human beings; it is the mark of our humanity. Because people are self-interested, they strive to produce their best only if they know that they will be fairly compensated. In fact, each would prefer to be unfairly compensated if that unfairness were always in his or her favor, but that is not possible because there is in every society a norm of reciprocity. A norm of reciprocity is an agreement among the people of a community that if you do not return value received with equal value given, your peers will punish you. Without such an agreement to sustain equity, people would not be able to trust one another enough to engage in trade. Without trade, each of us would have to spend full time gathering our own food and erecting our own shelter, and society would not progress. As a result, a norm of reciprocity is universal, as sociologist Alvin Gouldner has observed, and each of us will work hard as long as we are guaranteed fair payment.[9]

But who determines what is fair? It is that process of guaranteeing equity of payment that constitutes the form of governance. There are three modes through which the norms of equity can be met, and thus three forms of governance. All three forms of governance grow out of a social agreement among the members of the community.

Those of us who live in market economies have, knowingly or otherwise, accepted the idea that when competitive conditions exist, whatever payment we receive is fair.[10] We may wish for more, but we agree that if there is competition, then whatever we get is, by communal moral standards, fair. However, if there is not free competition, if instead there is monopoly or restrained competition, then we will not feel that our payment, no matter how large, is fair. If competitive conditions are not met, then norms of equity cannot be satisfied, and both morale and effort will decline.

The second mode of governance is the bureaucracy. In a bureaucracy, each participant is an employee rather than a solo proprietor or contractor. Every company, hospital, or organization with employees is in this sense a bureaucracy rather than a market. A bureaucracy satisfies norms of equity when a superior is fair, well-informed, and distributes pay raises according to merit. Thus the bureaucracy satisfies norms of equity as does a market, but through a quite different mechanism. The great disadvantage of the bureaucratic form of governance is that it requires managers and other administrative overhead, which a market does not. The great advantage of the bureaucracy, however, is that it can achieve governance even under conditions of close teamwork and uniqueness; a market cannot govern under these conditions. If close teamwork is necessary or if the work you do is unique, then there is no other person to whom you can be compared and thus no competitive process through which to set your reward. In such a case, a market will not operate. In such a case, however, a well-informed boss can set a production standard or a budget, monitor your performance, and arrive at a judgment of how much reward you deserve. If that boss is evenhanded, and if the standards set are fair based on past performance, then the governance of a bureaucracy works.

The third mode of governance is the economic clan. By this I do not mean to suggest blood relations between employees. Rather, I want to suggest the permanence of a blood relation between fellow employees. In any event, even familial clans are rife with conflict and disagreement between family members, so perhaps they are not completely different from the industrial clan. A clan is an organization in which the members are bound together over a very long run. If the players on a professional basketball team are frequently traded, that team will not become a clan. A clan is also an organization in which the members understand one another. A society in which separate interest groups have little knowledge of one another is not a clan. If there is mutual understanding and the expectation of long-term involvement, the self-interested members of an organization will develop a clan.

The unique governance property of a clan is the way in which it achieves equity. In a market, equity is achieved on the spot. That is, in an auction, you pay money now for goods received now, and everyone agrees that equity has been achieved on the spot. In a bureaucracy, equity takes a little bit longer. You work hard for one year, receive a raise in pay or a bonus, and everyone agrees (if the bureaucracy runs well) that equity has been achieved. In a clan, however, equity is achieved serially rather than on the spot. That is, one clan member may be unfairly underpaid for three years before his true contribution is known, but everyone knows that his contribution will ultimately be recognized, that he will still be there, and that equity will be achieved in the end. This is what is meant by serial equity.

It is asking quite a lot for someone to continue to work hard for three years of underpayment, especially assuming universal self-interest. For that reason, a clan will emerge only if there is a strong social memory. As we discussed in Chapter One, a social memory is a set of people who will carry the memory of who has contributed value in the past and who has not. A social memory also requires that those who remember be capable of seeing to it that contributors are rewarded and shirkers punished in the end. A social memory must be able to satisfy the moral sense of equity.

Clearly, markets are the simplest and the most desirable form of governance, which accounts for our habit of idealizing markets in Western thought. If all forms of work and commerce could be governed through markets, we would be better off. There would be no large companies, no managers, and no need for business professors. Instead, each of us would be a solo entrepreneur with no employees, each selling our services each day in a marketplace. For a variety of reasons, however, markets cannot govern every aspect of economic life, and thus there are firms, also known as bureaucracies.[11] In some cases, the jobs in a bureaucracy are simple enough that people can come and go frequently without disrupting the flow of work. Standards are well known and easily communicated, and equity can be achieved even with high turnover. There is not quite enough similarity between jobs to permit market governance, but a bureaucracy works quite well in such conditions. However, if for any reason it is difficult to assess fairly the performance of a worker within a year or so, then the bureaucracy will be seen as capricious, inflexible, and unfair.[12] Norms of equity will be violated, morale will drop, and the organization will suffer. In that case, the only hope is to develop a sufficiently strong and believable social memory so that employees will await the long run to receive their just reward.

Markets, Bureaucracies, and Clans in an M-Form Society

As a society, the United States employs a curious mixture of forms of governance. We idealize an unrestrained market economy in which competition provides all the necessary governance to satisfy norms of equity. Then we observe that our markets are in fact imperfect, that companies will use all the free clean air and water that they can get, because they don't pay for it. So then we respond with the most bureaucratic forms of governance, writing extensive regulations to stop the exploitation of public endowments. The problem is similar to that in a large company. In an M-Form company, the divisions, as we have observed, may be told to behave as though they were independent competitors who should attempt to maximize profits. If they do so, however, each will attempt to overuse the "free" corporate endowments of central research, marketing, and so on. In order to stop this exploitation of corporate resources, the top management might resort to bureaucratic controls, perhaps allocating central staff time to each division or setting up an extensive system of transfer prices. Such a system is relatively commonplace in business, where it never works well. Both Alfred Chandler, Jr. of Harvard University and Oliver Williamson of Yale University, who have studied the M-Form company extensively, note that it works well only with a spirit of teamwork within the management. With a spirit of teamwork, each will use only as much of the common resources as he truly needs, and each will help to replenish those common goods. The reason is that the spirit of teamwork is supported by a social memory. The management must be stable, the memory of who has been exploitative must be long, and the means of achieving equity must be effective. In that case, the clan supplements rather than replaces market and bureaucratic forms of governance.

What we see as a nation, however, is a wild swing from market to bureaucratic forms of governance, with very little of anything that resembles a clan. The reason is that of the three structural forms, only the M-Form can use all three governance forms. In the U-Form organization, bureaucratic governance is the common form, but the teamwork of a clan is also possible. If the separate departments learn to work together, if the financial incentives emphasize teamwork, then the U-Form may employ both bureaucratic and clan forms of governance. A U-Form, however, cannot use market modes of governance internally. No department has a "bottom line," and thus the great advantages of market governance are lost to the U-Form.

An H-Form, by comparison, makes greatest internal use of market modes of governance. Each unit does have a bottom line, they share few common resources, and all compete against one another for infusions of corporate capital. An H-Form may also employ bureaucratic means of governance by setting targets and rules, particularly in the nonmarket areas of compliance with standards for affirmative action, product safety, and labor relations. But an H-Form cannot develop a clan. The individual businesses are too different from one another to be able to develop a common point of view, to understand or sympathize with one another's goals. Of course, some such commonality is possible, but each unit within an H-Form will be surrounded by other divisions and faced by a corporate staff that knows less about it than do the comparable units that surround a U-Form or M-Form competitor.

The M-Form structure can employ market, bureaucratic, and clan modes of governance. The units are almost autonomous and can attempt to maximize profit, thus bringing the benefits of market governance. At the same time, some bureaucratic standards and targets will be set by the corporate office. Finally, the commonality of technology, customer, or distribution system will enable the several divisions to develop a common outlook and understanding which assures each that long-run evaluations will be stored in a corporate memory and that as a result serial equity will be forthcoming. That is the reason for the general superiority of the M-Form. No one mode of governance can ever be complete. Because perfect competition never exists, markets can never govern completely. Because rules are inflexible and human beings fallible, bureaucracy can never govern completely. Because people are self-interested and individual tastes divergent, clans can never govern completely. Thus it is only the combination of all three forms of governance that can provide for the effective management of a complex enterprise.

A society is not a company. For one thing, most of the members of a nation are lifetime members. There is little turnover. As a result, the society develops over time a basic consensus on values across a wide variety of things, as Professor Andrew Van de Ven of the University of Minnesota has noted.[13] On the other hand, a society contains an immense variety of objectives, whereas a business is confined more narrowly to those objectives having to do with work. Many political scientists have focused on this theme, and many, such as Charles Lindblom of Yale University, see the conflict between interest groups as deep and irreconcilable.[14] Out of this form of analysis has come the point of view that sees interest group politics in the United States as irreconcilable and the ability to solve our problems therefore permanently impaired.

That is not my view. The view expressed in this book is that we can create the institutions of an M-Form society. We can create the units of social memory that will make social choice possible, which will break our political-economic gridlock. It is not a permanent problem, nor is it an intractable one. It is rather that the design of our form of governance has not kept pace with the needs of our society. We have a mismatch between the needs of our society to confront legitimate disagreements and to focus our scarce resources on the one hand, and the ability of our governance system to provide a social memory through which serial equity can be assured, and thus social choices taken, on the other.

Perhaps there are some lessons from the study of business management to be taken and applied to the management of a society. We cannot push the analogy too far, but we can cull from it whatever insights it provides. Above all, we observe in the study of management that a large organization cannot succeed without a combination of teamwork and competition. It would not be at all surprising to discover that a society must also have that combination of teamwork and competition to succeed. If there is a modern society that has developed a high level of teamwork across sectors of the society, it is Japan. If there is a modern society that has succeeded through healthy internal competition, it is the United States. We do not seek to relinquish what we have, but rather to improve upon it and to grow by learning more about ourselves. Like any college student who discovers himself by discovering other classmates who are very different, so we turn now to learn about ourselves by discovering the business-government relationship in Japan.

3
ELEMENTS OF
THE M-FORM
the role of
government and
trade associations

Several months ago, I was a guest speaker at the annual meeting of a U.S. trade association. The time was late winter, the place was Florida, the audience the 300 or so leaders of companies in the industry. I spoke one morning, after which the conferees adjourned for golf. The next morning they had another speaker, followed by tennis, and the third day another speaker, followed by fishing. Now, don't get me wrong; I am not against golf, tennis, or fishing, nor do I doubt the importance of informal contact in the building of relationships. Nonetheless, I said to my audience that morning: "While you are out on the golf course this afternoon, waiting for your partner to tee up, I want you to think about something. Last month I was in Tokyo, where I visited your trade association counterpart. It represents the roughly two hundred Japanese companies who are your direct competitors. They are now holding meetings from eight each morning until nine each night, five days a week, for three months straight, so that one company's oscilloscope will connect to another company's analyzer, so that they can agree on product safety standards to recommend to the government (to speed up getting to the market place), so that they can agree on their needs for changes in regulation, export policy, and financing and then approach their government with one voice to ask for cooperation. Tell me who you think is going to be in better shape five years from now."

That meeting crystallized my thoughts on the issue of industrial policy. First, I recognized with a clarity that I had not seen before that "industrial policy" in Japan is, above all else, the Western phrase for teamwork between competitors. I realized that Western executives either spend their time playing golf while waiting for government to solve their problems or else spend their time playing golf while waiting for the market mechanism to solve their problems in some mysterious and unseen way. I realized that, to these Western executives, the consistent and sometimes urgent focus that the Japanese have taken in developing their industries appears to be the result not of teamwork between companies but rather of direction from their government.

Second, I recognized that the debate on industrial policy as it has developed in the United States and in many European nations is misguided. The current debate focuses on the question of whether a single government bureau such as the Department of Commerce or a single government-labor-business council should have the power to set the future directions of industry. The debate is taking place largely because the participants in the debate believe, incorrectly, that the Japanese have directed industry from government.

In fact, the Japanese have instead permitted and encouraged their companies, large and small, to organize into many small associations, each of which serves as a forum for discussions on key industry issues. After each of these small industry groups reaches agreement, it must then attempt to convince the other industry groups that its position has merit. Only after a proposal has survived the scrutiny of other industry groups (many of which will oppose it, perhaps because they wish to push their own proposals instead) will the matter be taken up with government. At that point, government officials will engage in a typical business-government debate, but it will be a debate on an issue that has been carefully examined. More important, the debate will likely be a thorough one, because only a few issues will survive the inter-industry process and emerge at the business-government level. Rather than having to deal with thousands of proposals from individual companies, the government officials in Japan can focus their attention on a relatively small number of issues at a time and can give full and thoughtful scrutiny to each one.

Third, I concluded that the proper focus for the industrial policy debate in the United States should be on the question of whether or not we want our companies to get together to talk through their problems in private. If we change the antitrust law so that such discussions will become more common, we will increase somewhat the risk of collusive activity, such as price fixing. In addition, we might run the risk of diminishing the competitive strivings of each company, because collaboration may mean that each company knows what its competitor knows, with the result that all companies may slow down their drive to innovate, reduce their investment in research and development, and in the end weaken our industries. However, our companies presently have many hundreds of private associations and they do meet regularly, but they waste most of their time with golf and tennis. Since we already permit them to meet, should we not wish that they use that time productively?

More important is the fact that many of the problems faced by American industry cannot be remedied without changes in law at the state and federal level. As an industry changes, the legal structure that defines and regulates it must change. Unless the companies in an industry can agree on exactly what changes should be made, Congress will be faced with an impossible crossfire of claims and counterclaims, and the result will be political-economic gridlock. Unless we can develop the units of social memory that link the various industries of the United States together, no industry will put its cause aside in order to permit Congress to focus on another group. These are the pros and the cons of industrial policy that really matter.

In order to have an intelligent debate on industrial policy, we must begin with an understanding of the issues. Above all, we must begin with an understanding of industrial policy in Japan, because it is the Japanese economic success that has brought on the industrial policy debate in the West. It has become fashionable to refer to industrial policy with no mention of Japan, in large part because admiration for Japanese business success has become forbidden in many Western business and political circles. That bit of oversight, however, has impeded the development of an accurate understanding of the issues that are most central to the future development of our economy.

Whenever Japanese industrial policy is explicitly mentioned, MITI is mentioned in the same breath. MITI is the Ministry of International Trade and Industry, the government bureau that is most centrally involved in industrial policy in Japan. MITI is often described as an all-powerful force in economic affairs in Japan. Its staff has been characterized as a bureaucratic elite, the brightest and the most dedicated of civil servants in Japan and perhaps in the world.

I, too, have been impressed with the accomplishments of MITI and with the quality of the MITI staff. However, I approached my study of this government bureau with the suspicion that no central authority, no matter how effective, can successfully direct an entire economy. As a result, my research team extended its research beyond MITI to include the private business associations of Japan. These are the business associations with which MITI deals, the associations through which a single company must work before gaining a hearing within government circles. In essence, MITI and the trade associations of Japan together constitute a network that is the social memory, the community, of the Japanese economy. But it is more than a single-minded, pro-business social memory. It is one that takes at least partial account of the interests of consumer, labor, and civic groups by including them directly and formally in the debate about where business should go.

Let us begin by understanding the internal organization of MITI, which is both simple and accessible to the business community and to other interest groups. We will then turn our attention to the business associations of Japan, some quasi-governmental and others purely in the private business sector. As we learn about each of these separate institutions, let us not lose sight of the more important pattern of ties which knits all of them into a whole. That whole is what provides the balance between individual entrepreneurship on the one hand and teamwork on the other. It is what provides the lessons from which we can learn to fashion an M-Form society in the United States.

The Internal Organization of MITI

A young MITI official describes it as follows: "In MITI, we have little official power. We have limited legislative power, and few controls to use. It is as though we were walking a tightrope. We must be careful not to favor one industry over another or one company over another, because then we would lose the confidence of all." His view was echoed in a description from Pascale Buch, a visitor from the Ecole Nationale de l'Administration, Paris, who spent three weeks in one section at MITI: "The very area of its big collective offices, occupied by dozens of people, cluttered with papers, books and documents of all kinds, and enlivened by the constant ring of telephones and people coming in and out, symbolizes MITI to perfection. Nothing is kept back as personal or confidential; everything is shared and constantly accessible. In this regard, MITI seems to me to be the ministry of open doors: doors of all offices opening onto one another, but also a door open to the rest of the world, because in the corridors you cross paths not only with officials, but with journalists and even housewives, coming to do their shopping in the ministry's basement shops.

"In the office, there is a good-natured, family atmosphere that assures a feeling of equality and general understanding without, at the same time, really effacing hierarchical relations. It creates a curious mixture of conviviality and hidden authority, transforming the *kacho* (head of section) into not just a superior but the motivating force in the group. Day-to-day discussions are never formal and take place on demand, creating, if not a real democracy, at least the feeling of sharing a common destiny and task.

"This work bears little relation to the legend of the Japanese 'workaholic' and only a minority of officials stay late at the office . . . the days give the impression of great emptiness, because one spends the better part of the time waiting: waiting for a meeting to end, for a decision by a related section, for the outcome of a consultation process, with the interminable discussions it involves."[1]

MITI is the government agency charged with the responsibility of seeing to the successful economic development of Japan. It has enjoyed a broad public mandate since the end of World War II, which was to be expected in a nation whose economy had been devastated and in which there was clear public consensus that creating jobs was the first priority. MITI is one of twelve ministries and seven to ten agencies that comprise the executive branch of government. Because the system is parliamentary, the prime minister must be elected by the members of the Diet and must be one of them, but only a majority of the other ministers must be Diet members. Ordinarily, however, the minister of international trade and industry is a Diet member, and it is the administrative vice-minister who is the top-ranking career bureaucrat and the real power in MITI.

MITI is internally divided into seven bureaus, each of which is further divided into several divisions, as well as including three agencies, each in turn consisting of several departments (see Appendix VI–A). In addition, there is the patent office and the very powerful secretariat, which controls the MITI budget, personnel, and public relations. More interesting, perhaps, are the seven bureaus, of which three contain several divisions corresponding to major industrial groupings in the economy. For example, the Machinery and Information Industries Bureau is divided into a Cast and Wrought Products Division, Electronics Policy Division, Industrial Electronics, Automobile Division, and so on. The remaining four bureaus are not organized to deal with specific industries but rather to handle the common problem areas that cut across industries. For example, the Industrial Policy Bureau, often thought to be the most important, contains the Industrial Structure Division, the Industrial Finance Division, and Consumer Protection Division, and several others. Thus, a single company will have contact on a regular basis with representatives of both the industry-specific division and with several problem-specific divisions within MITI, and these divisions can be thought of as a matrix organization in which several different offices will share responsibility for each matter. The initial discussions on a new issue, however, will ordinarily be with the industry-specific division. As a consequence, a young MITI official (like any Japanese manager in business or government) must learn to coordinate with several other departments within MITI, as well as with the offices of the Ministry of Finance and perhaps others, if he or she is to accomplish a task and advance his or her career. This internal process of broad consultation and shared responsibility is a microcosm of the larger network within which MITI operates.

MITI is the smallest of the ministries in a nation that has successfully minimized government employment. During the postwar occupation years, government employment had grown tremendously, but public opinion and a concerted effort by business groups focused attention on the need for economy. As a result of these efforts over ten or fifteen years, the Japanese government (federal and local) spent during 1945–1975 only 30 percent of national income (compared to 40 percent for the United States, more than 60 percent in Denmark, Sweden, and Norway, and more than 40 percent for the rest of Western Europe). Although Japan has a very steeply progressive individual income tax, rising to a maximum of 75 percent in national and 18 percent in local taxes, total taxes in 1977 amounted to 19 percent of national income, compared to 28 percent in the United States and France, 37 percent in Britain, and 53 percent in Sweden.[2] It would be well to keep in mind the fact that, during this period, Japan devoted less than 1 percent of its national income to its self-defense forces, while the United States, as the peacekeeper for Japan as well as for much of the free world, devoted nearly 6 percent of national income to defense.

In a new book, *Policy and Politics in Japan*, T. J. Pempel feels that these moves for economy strengthened the government's ability to coordinate its various ministries and plans: "Particularly impressive throughout all of the Japanese policy cases studied is the apparent ability of the government to develop a relatively coherent and consistent set of policy objectives and to then concentrate attention and energy on their achievement. This would have been far more difficult had each government agency been allowed to follow its own narrowly defined priorities and interests. By forcing cutbacks in all agencies, the government forced most to examine their internal priorities regularly."[3]

However, as Pempel notes, the low level of government spending in Japan is due in large part to the fact that many services provided by governments in the West are provided by families and companies in Japan. For example, in 1968 a survey showed that of people over sixty-five years of age, 80 percent in Japan lived with their children, while the figures were 20 percent for Denmark, 28 percent in the United States, and 42 percent in Britain.[4] As for health and other benefits for workers, companies typically provide benefits that come from the state in other countries, partly out of a sense of duty to their workers and partly to forestall the development of adversarial unions.

Taking into account all of these caveats, the fact remains that MITI has accomplished a great deal with a very small staff. Indeed, MITI has succeeded so well that is has been elevated by some observers to superhuman and perhaps mythical status. Professor Chalmers Johnson notes in his history of MITI: ". . . the elite bureaucracy of Japan makes most major decisions, drafts virtually all legislation, controls the national budget, and is the source of all major policy innovations in the system."[5]

Professor Ezra Vogel, also an admirer of MITI, takes a somewhat more balanced view of the reasons behind the success of MITI: ". . . But Americans should not underestimate the capacity of qualified bureaucrats, working very closely with business leaders over a long period of time, to devise policies that give business a climate in which to make adjustments."[6] Vogel still indicates a belief that MITI initiates and business follows, although he gives emphasis to the coordinative role of the ministry staff.

A somewhat different point of view was expressed by a top official of the Keidanren during an April 1983 meeting with our research team: "It is unbelievable that people believe that MITI issues directives and everyone follows in line." It is understandable that a representative of the Keidanren would allocate most of the credit for past economic success to the independent actions of business, just as it is understandable that a MITI bureaucrat would tend to allocate most of the credit for past success to MITI.

A more balanced and perhaps more accurate view was described for us in an April 1983 interview with a middle-level MITI manager: "One way in which conflicts must be resolved between companies in the same industry is in the setting of standards. For example, there are three alternative specification categories for video disc products. . . . On this issue MITI is providing guidance to the industry. At this point, no consensus has been reached. It is clear, however, that some solutions will be better than others. MITI cannot force the companies or the public to accept one solution or another. One of the key divisions is between the Pioneer technology and the Sharp technology. . . . The issue will remain unsolved until it becomes clear that one type of technology is not only technically superior but is clearly more popularly accepted. The consensus has to be decided among the players and the public. It is then up to MITI to speed up the process and make the decision-making process smoother."

It is, above all, the role of intermediary that MITI fulfills. It is a critical role in the functioning of an M-Form society, but one that must not intrude into the market process. But what is there to keep energetic and zealous bureaucrats from overstepping those proper boundaries? There are the MITI discussion councils, through which the voice of business is expressed not as a cacophony, but as one coherent participant in a national dialogue.

The MITI Discussion Councils

As of 1982, MITI maintained thirty-eight advisory councils (see Appendix I), also known as discussion councils, since they discuss but do not vote, and because they are advisory only to the minister and his staff. These are among the key units of social memory. Most important among these is the Industrial Structure Council, the current name for the group initiated in 1927 by the Ministry of Commerce and Industry, the forerunner of today's MITI, which itself had been created in 1925.[7]

Today, the Industrial Structure Council consists of eighty-two members, of whom twenty-eight represent trade associations, twenty are chief executives representing their companies and industries, two are from trading companies, three are from government-affiliated organizations, one is a commercial banker, eleven are university professors, two are newspaper editors or publishers, four are major union leaders, three represent consumer groups, and eight represent diverse groups such as the National Governor's Conference, the National Mayor's Conference, and the Mitsubishi Research Institute (see Appendix II for a summary of the Industrial Structure Council and of the Aircraft-Machinery Council, and Appendix III for a detailed list of the Industrial Structure Council members). There are no civil servants or legislators on the discussion councils, although they are frequently consulted. Members are typically the top leaders of the largest trade associations, companies, and labor unions, and they are invited for two-year terms that are commonly renewed, with some members serving continually for ten or more years.

The Industrial Structure Council issues publications, the most recent of which was "The Vision of MITI Policies in the 1980s: Trade and Industrial Policy for the 1980s—Recommendations of the Industrial Structure Council." The document is broad-ranging and similar to the report of a typical presidential commission in the United States, touching on energy, high-technology, quality of life, trade, and urban problems. What is more important than the document, of course, is the dialogue preceding and following it.

Each council member makes a major commitment of time, as the task is an important one. Some reflections on the councils came from a senior MITI official in a January 1983 interview: "We want and must have diverse points of view on the MITI discussion councils. We have industry representatives, including banks and individual corporations, press, labor unions, women's groups, and consumer groups. Council membership terms are two years, but people are expected to stay on the council for three to four terms lasting a total of six to eight years. Members must generally spend three or four hours per session, two or three times a month. Twenty to forty members are on most councils, and two-thirds come to each meeting. There are study groups that present position papers to other subgroups within the council. As would be expected, outside forces influence the study groups.

"We spend a lot of time resolving conflicting interests in MITI. I can give you one recent example. The basic material industries are declining. The companies within these industries are in trouble. The companies want help. Unions want the government to support the companies. The relevant consumer groups also want the government to help. We want them to talk until they say everything there is to say about the subject. Saying everything helps them to feel better. So even after they have said everything they have to say, when there is a decision against them, they will concede that they have been fairly heard and the decision is perhaps acceptable to them. MITI attempts to summarize the views which have evolved and makes decisions based on its understanding of the emergent consensus.

"The council involved has thirty-four members and deals with issues concerning aluminum, petrochemicals, bar steel, and paper pulp industries. The council includes eight representatives from industry associations, four from labor, two from consumer groups, three or four journalists, three from the financial community, two mayors, and three or four professors (the remaining members represent companies in those industries). Labor wants jobs. The unions want government to force small companies into cartelization to save jobs. They also want exemption for their industries from antitrust litigation. The press and university economists were skeptical about loosening antitrust. The press saw it from the perspective of the constitution.

"Resolution on this issue required nine meetings. These began in August and lasted through December. After hearing the disparate views, no vote was taken. This is not our way. We did not want to take a majority position and force it onto the minority. After the discussions, when it was clear that no consensus was evolving, no

42 THE M-FORM SOCIETY

vote was taken. MITI then wrote a position paper that was reviewed by the members. They could have disagreed or made changes, but they did not. The final decision involves modest support from the government and a recommendation for continued discussions between MITI and the industry representatives. They are to discuss capacity problems without fear of being sued by the justice department (JFTC). If companies were to violate antitrust laws through this kind of cooperation, their group would be broken up, and the companies would be sued by the JFTC, as happened in the textile industry in the late 1960s. (During the twenty-five years from 1954 to 1979, the JFTC found various antitrust violations by trade associations on 269 occasions [Sec. 8-1-1 of Antimonopoly Law].)

"Sometimes people go directly to the prime minister to bypass the problems entailed in reaching a decision through discussion. It does happen in Japan sometimes. We at MITI have no way of preventing such dialogue. The prime minister will talk to the minister, who will then discuss it with the relevant ministry. The minister will listen but will seldom take the individual's interest over the interest of others.

"The only way to generate a good idea is to let everyone talk and then listen.

"We sometimes make changes as a result of union or industrial leaders informally influencing council members. In Japan, unions are honored and feel pride in talking to business and government leaders. We do have examples where one group will disagree with another group. You simply have to continue to discuss until there is agreement. We will not act until consensus is reached. If no agreement is reached, then the report to that effect goes to the minister. If an outlier does not like the discussion council resolution, the company must go its own way, and we can do nothing against it. Even if one or two companies do not agree, the total situation is improved because there is generalized agreement."

The central role attributed to these discussion councils and the role of MITI as intermediary rather than as central planner was seconded in a January 11, 1983 interview with Professor Miyohei Shinohara, who has served as a discussion council member on as many as five committees at once: "In the United States and Europe it is believed that MITI is powerful, but it is so only in certain situations and in certain industries. Sometimes MITI has problems adjusting the demands of different companies. MITI is not the leader, but the coordinator or moderator."

The Four Major
Business Associations of Japan

The work of the councils is done largely in the subcommittees, each of which reaches out to noncouncil members to create special-purpose task forces to collect data, debate issues, or offer opinions on various topics. At the same time that these grass-roots discussions are taking place, the senior council members, along with members of the Industrial Structure Council, will carry out direct discussions with the four major business associations which are part of the social memory and which span the nation. Of these, the Federation of Economic Organizations (Keidanren) is perhaps the most famous. Organized in August 1946, the Keidanren is a private, nonprofit organization that represents 110 major industry associations and the largest 812 corporations (as of 1982).[8] The organization does not have a large staff—perhaps fifty professionals—but it enjoys great prestige and is thought to have tremendous influence on both business and government circles. The Keidanren restricts itself to issues of national importance and cross-industry concern. Typically, it will not concern itself with the problems of any one industry, in part because to do so would cause internal dissension, in part because specialized industry associations exist for that purpose.

Recently, the Keidanren has focused anew on efficiency in government, although its traditional concerns are in the areas of antitrust, trade friction, and pollution.[9] On most tax matters, of course, the Keidanren comes out for lower taxes. In addition, the Keidanren maintains close relationships with MITI officials, just as U.S. bureaucrats must maintain ties with the industry groups they regulate, but in this case the usual topic is not regulation, it is economic development instead. The Keidanren is sometimes criticized by the press for its influence with the ruling Liberal Democratic Party, an allegation that has some foundation in the practice of having the Keidanren collect from its members campaign funds, which it then passes on to the leading members of the various factions, who themselves are constantly vying for power within the LDP. These political

leaders then distribute the funds among their followers, thus producing the sort of political "discipline" that is sometimes sought
after and other times denounced in the United States.

The real influence of the Keidanren stems from the desire of
its members to make it work. Although only companies and not
individuals may be members, it is typical that only the chief executive officer of a corporate member may be active. Usually, the
chairman of the Keidanren will be the just-retired chief executive
of one of the largest three or four companies, such as Nippon Steel
or Toshiba, an individual who is sufficiently respected to be able to
draw consensus out of the entire business community, sufficiently
energetic to bring great effort to the task, and sufficiently free as to
be able to devote nearly full time to it. Assisting the chairman are
ten vice-chairman, including (in 1983) the chief executives of Nissan
Motors, Sumitomo Chemical, and Hitachi. The work of the Keidanren is done in the forty-six standing committees and countless
ad hoc task forces (see Appendix V).

The Keidanren does not tell its members what to do, nor is it
paralyzed by disputes between its members, although major disagreements are common. It strikes a middle ground as a forum for
debate. Its members participate because they know that unless their
requests can pass the scrutiny and win the support of the members
of the Keidanren, they have no hope of success within MITI, the
Ministry of Finance, the Economic Planning Agency, or the Diet.
During this process of scrutiny, each company or industrial group
must lay out its requests (for tax changes, export loans, or whatever
from the government) directly before the leaders of other companies
and industries, look them in the eye, and make a convincing case.
The result, according to a vice-chairman of the Keidanren (in an
April 12, 1983 interview): "In Japan . . . there is much more transparency in business-government interaction and relations. This is
an important difference between the United States and Japan. The
reason for this transparency in Japan is the fact that the major players
are interacting with each other instead of using intermediaries in
the form of lobbyists."

Nonetheless, as the vice-chairman noted, not all conflicts can
be resolved: "Within the Keidanren are many conflicting elements
that are of equal status within the Keidanren and within Japanese
industry as a whole. A clear example of this would be the relationship among the automotive, coal, and steel industries. While many

disagreements are worked out over time, a basic conflict such as the one between Nippon Steel and the coal industry remains unresolved within the ranks of the Keidanren."

The Keidanren succeeds best when there is some social endowment to be had but which must be agreed upon and formulated in order to become a reality. Even then, however, the role of the Keidanren is only to promote discussion of the public policy alternatives. Another officer of the Keidanren noted that, "On the VLSI project it cannot be stated where the initiative for the effort began. But then the identity of who initiated the project is not important. It simply does not matter. There were unspoken positions in both the private and the government sectors that the VLSI was needed. The Keidanren simply helped to surface the existing positions . . ." The role of this unique organization, which combines big business with small, and one industry with another, is best summarized by another member: "I've worked in the Keidanren for twenty years. . . . The Keidanren has no formal power, so we must rely upon discussions. So our policy is to discuss an issue and then to discuss it some more."

The second major national business group is the Japan Committee for Economic Development (Keizai Doyukai). Four months older than the Keidanren, the Keizai Doyukai was founded in April 1946. Unlike the Keidanren, the Keizai Doyukai accepts only individuals rather than companies or trade associations as members, and it has grown from its original eighty members to slightly more than one thousand today. Membership in the Keizai Doyukai is considered to be an honor, only slightly less prestigious than membership in the Keidanren. The Doyukai principally conducts research through its small staff assisted by members and their companies, sponsors conferences and study trips to other nations, and carries out joint efforts to reduce trade friction with the Committee for Economic Development (CED) in the United States, CEDA in Australia, CEPES in West Germany, IDEP in France, PEP in England, and SNS in Sweden.[10] The Keizai Doyukai is headed by a chairman who presides over a board of two hundred trustees, who are top executives of the largest companies, many of them also members of the Keidanren. The work of the association is done through numerous committees and task forces, and their tasks commonly focus on topics broader than those of the Keidanren. Rather than focusing on coal or taxation, for example, the Keizai Doyukai will attempt to reach a consensus position on labor-management relations, the social responsibilities of business, the need for urban renewal, and the problems of education. Often, the Keizai Doyukai will serve to see what the sense of the business community is on issues that the Diet or the bureaucracy are considering for major new initiatives, and its relationships with government are close. In addition, the Keizai Doyukai maintains a close relationship with university professors, who ordinarily have distant or even chilly relationships with Japanese industry. University professors collaborate on many studies sponsored by the Keizai Doyukai, and some of these relationships have resulted in ongoing organizations such as the Japan Center for Area Research and Development (urban research), the Japan Research Council on Economics Education (for economics education in secondary school), and the Japan Greening Center (studies on increasing open, green space in urban areas). The Keizai Doyukai is an important complement to the Keidanren.

The third major national business group is the Japan Federation of Employers' Associations (Nikkeiren), which brings together 30,000 companies to deal with labor-management problems. The Japanese labor force is approximately one-third union represented, compared to approximately 18 percent of the U.S. labor force. Rather than being organized in national craft groups of machinists, electricians, or teamsters, however, most Japanese union members belong to a company union. These enterprise unions have the great advantage of permitting movement of a worker from one job to another within a plant without having to invade the territory of another union, as will often occur in some U.S. plants that cannot readily reorganize their operations because the seven or ten separate unions in the plant will not yield jobs to one another.[11]

There is, of course, no organization of employers in the United States that parallels the Nikkeiren, although there are similar employers' groups in some cities. Certainly it would be productive if the interests of employers could be gathered together and an association created that was capable of education, research, and most important, of carrying out a dialogue rather than a bargaining session with organized labor.

The final group in this major category is the Japan Chamber of Commerce and Industry. The Japan Chamber of Commerce and Industry is the headquarter organization of the 478 chambers scattered throughout Japan. Although the leaders of the chamber are the top executives of the largest companies, drawn from the same pool that supplies the membership of the Keidanren and the Keizai Do-yukai, the chamber is focused on serving the needs of small and medium-sized businesses, which in 1980 comprised some 5.8 million establishments, accounting for more than 99 percent of all businesses and 81 percent of all jobs. In small towns and rural areas that do not have chambers of commerce and industry, there are instead societies of commerce and industry, of which there were 3,852 in 1980. These societies are composed almost entirely of small businesses, and carry out a variety of activities for their members, but do not have the full range of chamber powers or services.

The Japan Chamber of Commerce and Industry, like the U.S. Chamber of Commerce, carries out many political activities in order to represent the interests of business generally and of small and medium-sized business in particular. Often, the chamber is unable to take a stand on major issues that find big business opposing small business, as is true for the U.S. chamber. In addition, both the U.S. and Japanese chambers carry out a large variety of educational, trade, public-relations, research, and other activities. Both also provide consultation services to their smaller members, as well as many other services. More than 100 of the Japan chambers maintain special offices to counsel small and medium-size business in danger of bankruptcy, helping them to avoid disaster or, if necessary, to arrange a relatively smooth dissolution of assets. The U.S. chamber has been creative in many ways, one of which has been to construct in its headquarters (which overlook the White House) a complete television broadcast studio, from which it operates a private network, broadcasting talk shows, analysis, and business news to members.

In Japan, the real focus of action of the chamber is within the 478 local chambers, of which the Tokyo Chamber of Commerce and Industry is the largest. The Tokyo chamber was established in March 1878 by Eiichi Shibusawa, a financier who is often credited with bringing modern capitalism to Japan (the U.S. chamber was established in April 1912 under the guidance of President Taft).[12] Today, the Tokyo Chamber of Commerce and Industry has offices in each of the 23 wards of Tokyo, with its 34,264 members organized into 28 standing committees.[13] What is most interesting about the chamber, however, is that it has some quasiofficial ties with the government, which makes use of the chamber in place of a separate bureaucracy to carry out certain functions.[14]

For example, a 1978 law provides for loans to small business in order to avoid bankruptcy, these loans to be granted by the government-run Small Business Corporation, which maintains offices throughout the nation. However, the Small Business Corporation does not have the staff and does not wish to increase its bureaucracy in order to evaluate loan applications, so the evaluations with recommendations are instead performed by the chambers of commerce and industry, the societies of commerce and industry, and by the prefectural federations.[15]

Beginning in 1973, the People's Finance Corporation, wholly owned by the national government, initiated a general system of providing subsidized loans, which require no collateral and no guarantors, to small business. The loans are available to manufacturing businesses with no more than twenty employees and to service businesses with no more than five employees, and may be for sums up to $15,000 for equipment and $15,000 of working capital with terms of four years and three years, respectively. The loan applications may go only to the chambers of commerce and industry, whose 3,320 "managerial instructors" across the country carry out the investigation. Screening and final recommendations are by the chamber members and staff.[16] In order to accomplish this public-private cooperation, a 1953 law (the Chamber of Commerce and Industry Law) gave official status and recognition to the chamber, although it remains an exclusively private body, just as the U.S. chamber is.

Small Business in Japan

Small business activities in Japan are coordinated through a close relationship in every town between the chambers of commerce and industry, the societies of commerce and industry, the prefectural federations, and the offices of the three government banks that specialize in loans to small business. At a national level, these activities are coordinated by one of the three agencies of MITI, the Small and Medium Enterprise Agency, which was established in 1948 by the government of the Allied powers. In addition, the voice of small business is heard through four MITI discussion councils devoted exclusively to the affairs of this sector, including the Small and Medium Enterprise Policy Making Council, the Small and Medium Enterprise Stabilization Council, the Central Small and Medium Enterprise Mediation Council, and the Small and Medium Enterprise Modernization Council (see Appendix I).

It is through several avenues that the interests of small and big business are reconciled in Japan. Big business is represented largely by the Keidanren and the Keizai Doyukai, but small and big business come together in the Japan Chamber of Commerce and Industry. Big business dominates many of the thirty-eight MITI discussion councils, with small business dominating four, but the differing interests of both parties must be reconciled in the deliberations of twenty-one standing committees of the Industrial Structure Council, which is the highest level discussion council of MITI. More importantly, because membership on these councils is for a long term and because the same institutions tend to be represented even after one member retires, they are an important unit of social memory, in which big business will remember its debt to small business and vice versa.

The structure works well as a whole. In 1963, for example, special legislation was passed by the Diet to assist small business in those industries that were in greatest difficulty. Staff work was performed by the Small and Medium Enterprise Agency of MITI, information was gathered with the assistance of the chambers, societies, and federations, and deliberations were held within the Small and Medium Enterprises Modernization Council. The result: as of 1980, there were 46 programs covering 168 industries and providing government loans and loan guarantees tailored to the needs of each. Not only that, but because the bulk of the work is done by private associations rather than government bureaucrats, Japanese government employees comprise only 9 percent of the labor force, compared to 14–20 percent for the nations of North America and Europe.[17]

This close cooperation between government and small business in Japan stands in sharp contrast to the situation in the United States. In both nations, small business is a potent political force, accounting for 81 percent of jobs in Japan and for 53 percent in the United States.[18] In the United States, the strength of small business has been expressed most obviously in an active antitrust policy of the U.S. Department of Justice. In Japan, small business has preserved small retail and wholesale businesses, thus creating what many U.S. business people criticize as a byzantine distribution system that constitutes the principal nontariff barrier to U.S. economic success in Japan. However, it seems clear that in Japan, small business has a more comfortable relationship with both government and with big business than is true in the United States.

The Industry Associations of Japan

No nation can focus its resources and achieve economic growth unless its people can arrive at a consensus on who goes first and who must wait. In any such social choice, there will be a difference of self-interest between big business and small, between one industry and another, between one city and another. So far, we have seen that the Japanese have developed over a period of time a series of institutions that have the capacity to bring together these disparate parties. These institutions include the 7 bureaus and 3 agencies of MITI, the 38 MITI discussion councils, their 185 standing committees and hundreds of ad hoc task forces, the 812 corporate members and the 110 trade association members of the Keidanren, over 1,000 members of the Keizai Doyukai, the 30,000 corporate members of the Nikkeiren, the 478 local chambers of commerce, of which one, the Tokyo Chamber, has 34,264 members, the 3,852 societies of commerce and industry, and the 47 prefectural federations of commerce and industry, each of which brings together several thousand members. But all of these bodies are primarily coordinative. They do not themselves develop the initiatives that result in a JECC, a VLSI Research Association, or a tax change. That work is done in the industry associations, of which there are two kinds, general and specialized.

The General Trade Associations of The Electronics Industry

The Electronics Industries Association of Japan (EIAJ) is one of the 110 general trade associations that holds membership in the Keidanren. The EIAJ was founded about thirty years ago, at the end of the Allied occupation. Today, the EIAJ includes 600 companies that manufacture consumer appliances, industrial apparatus, and electronic components, such as semiconductors. Only manufacturers may join, because others in the industry such as distributors and raw-materials suppliers will often have interests directly opposed to those of manufacturers, although these allied companies may participate as associate members. Foreign manufacturers in Japan are welcome. The association itself has a modest-sized staff organized into five departments, those subdivided into a total of twenty-two sections. The members are organized into more than 200 committees that gather information, attempt to develop common industry positions on legislative issues, and run trade shows.[19]

The EIAJ, which is housed in the building of the Tokyo Chamber of Commerce and Industry, plays a critical role, but one that is typical of trade associations. The trade association serves as a neutral ground on which the companies in an industry can engage in a continual dialogue. Thus they can approach a legislative issue on which the member companies initially disagree, express their positions, and search for a compromise. Each company has an incentive to stay at the table and keep talking, because the influence of the association as a whole will be much greater than that of any single firm. This is true in part because public opinion causes both politicians and MITI officials to avoid the appearance of favoring one company, but also because the bureaucrats have learned to deny individual requests for assistance, knowing that to respond would be to invite an unmanageable flood of special requests. Because a major association such as the EIAJ has close ties to the government, with the director often a former MITI official, the bureaucrats both understand and trust the association not to abuse its access to government nor its right to private meetings. In this sense, the EIAJ is a quasigovernmental body, a place in which private firms are permitted to talk together without fearing illegal collusion (the EIAJ has no lawyers on its staff), but one that is explicitly the advocate for the special interests of one industry. The EIAJ also carries out the more typical association tasks of research, standard-setting and operating trade shows, but its distinctive contribution is as a unit of memory.

If one major corporate member opposes a position that other members wish to endorse, the EIAJ staff will visit the company and attempt to win its compliance. Ordinarily, this request will succeed, although the association will not attempt to find a consensus on issues that are so divisive as to be impossible.[20] Presumably, that compliance is forthcoming because the company that gives way knows that its support today will be remembered tomorrow. The same social memory operates at a higher level. The Keidanren staff offers a hypothetical example: "Suppose that the EIAJ wants a tax credit. Suppose that the EIAJ brought up such a proposal to the government and the government turned it down. Then the EIAJ might come to the Keidanren, and ask to make it into a more general tax proposal. If the Keidanren's other members find this to their advantage, a committee on taxation will be made up, and a proposal approved by the Keidanren. If the board of directors makes a decision to support, then the Keidanren will take it to the government. Sometimes, however, the government might disagree with the Keidanren."[21] In this process of constrained self-interest, members are not expected to give up on an important point, but they will be willing to lend their support to an issue on which they have no opinion or which they oppose only mildly, because they know that their support today will be remembered tomorrow.

At the same level of industry associations is JEIDA, the association of computer makers. JEIDA and the EIAJ have many members in common, which is important because the memory of past assistance or harm will reside in not one but two (in fact, dozens) of locations, and because repayment for past assistance can be provided in any of several associations. If you asked me for a favor of political support in our association, and if we had in common only this one association, I might deny your request for no other reason than the unlikelihood of the occasion ever arising for you to repay me. If, however, we were linked together in MITI discussion councils, Keizai Doyukai study groups, Chamber of Commerce and Industry committees, and membership of fifteen different trade associations, I would know that the day will come for reciprocity, and thus I would be more willing to yield my self-interest to you right now. Below JEIDA and the EIAJ lie the specialized trade associations, which are the grassroots of the social memory of business in Japan.

The Specialized Trade Association of the Electronics Industry

The Electric Wire and Cable Makers Association consists of 169 companies, mostly medium-sized and small, many of whom sell their products to the members of the EIAJ. The manager of the research division of the association describes their political activities as follows: "After a consensus is made within this trade association, we bring the matter to the EIAJ to cooperate with us, since we consist only of makers and users of wire and cable. In order to make decisions fair to everyone, we have to account for the equipment maker's needs (their customers). MITI has set up this kind of policy, that is, accounting for everyone's needs. Our association can't go directly to MITI because this would be regarded as the interest of the wire makers only and MITI would not want to give special assistance to us only; that is why we go through the EIAJ."[22] The process ordinarily involves several steps: "In the first stage, in order to form a consensus with MITI, a member company and the trade association head will meet with MITI. But in the final stage, only the staff of the EIAJ meets with MITI. Our particular trade association is making a proposal to MITI for what we would like to get, but the EIAJ is an intermediary between us and MITI. This takes away some of the burden from MITI."

The Japan Electric Measuring Instruments Manufacturers' Association (JEMIMA) established also at the end of the occupation, today includes 118 corporate members of the 250 in the industry. The association's members put in a great deal of time: "We have over six hundred meetings a year. In these meetings, several topics such as standardization, public relations, and so on are discussed. If there is a consensus, then this trade association acts with MITI. It would be rare for a member company to act directly. The communication channel from MITI to each company [60 percent of JEMIMA members have fewer than 300 employees] is through this trade association. In each committee there is an association staff person present. If a member company disagrees with a position, we will reason with it and the other members will try to persuade the company to agree. It will take a long, long time to reach final agreement on anything. The process goes like this:

"We meet from nine A.M. to ten P.M. for one week. Sometimes this goes on for three consecutive months. This is quite different, apparently, from the United States. Sometimes, MITI officials will come to the meetings."[23]

The same kind of process occurs in the Japan Institute of Office Automation (800 corporate members, most of them small or medium-size), the Communication Industries Association of Japan (200 member companies), and other associations throughout not only the electronics industry, but all industries. The MITI staff attends these meetings, keeping informed through contact with executives and association staffs, suggesting new issues to journalists in order to find out what public reaction to a new policy might be, and remembering those impressive few who might someday be nominated to a MITI discussion council. The work is done by the younger, junior MITI staff who share notes between sections in frequent meetings and study groups.

The Process of Policy Formulation

Once it appears that industry groups have begun to focus on a particular issue, the various study groups and subsection chiefs within the MITI bureaus and agencies will begin discussions. They will attempt to reconcile conflicting ideas within the division and to arrive at a position consistent with the division's general mission and outlook. Once consensus has been achieved, the division chiefs will bring the matter up among themselves in their and other bureaus. Again the process of debate will begin, this time with the objective of seeing to it that one division is not unfairly advancing the interests of "its" particular industry. The bureau chief will take responsibility for consulting other bureau chiefs, in order to ensure their support and to see to it that all activities within MITI are coordinated.

At about this time, the appropriate MITI discussion council may be asked to create a task force to consider the proposal. The chairman of the council may appoint from among his or her council members a task force chairman or ask a committee chairman to take on the job or approach the MITI section chiefs who began the project initially, asking them to recommend knowledgeable association staff, industry leaders, and academics with whom they have had contact. From this group, many of whom may not be members of a discussion council, the task force chairman will appoint a team.[24]

After this point, discussions will occur at several levels. The MITI minister, vice-minister, and bureau chief will talk with the MITI discussion council chairman and members, the heads of the Keidanren, the chamber of commerce and industry, the chief executives of the major companies to be affected, and the leaders of the political parties. At the next level down, the bureau chief and division chief will talk with the committee of the discussion council, the Diet members, the trade association leaders, and the directors and general managers of the relevant companies. One level after that, the MITI division chief and section chief will talk with the subcommittee or task force of the discussion council, the staff of the trade association, and the general managers and department heads of the companies. And at the bottom level, where the work actually gets done, the MITI section chief, subsection head, and staff will work with the task force of the discussion council, the general and specialized trade associations, and the section chiefs of the companies involved. In addition, agreement must be forthcoming from other government agencies. If and when all these parties find a way to reach consensus, a proposal will be forwarded to the Diet for legislative action, or action will be taken directly.

There are two kinds of sponsorship of bills in the Japanese Diet, those sponsored by the government and those sponsored by Diet members. During 1975–1980, the government sponsored an average of 104 bills per session, while members introduced an average of 51. The success rate for member-sponsored bills averaged 18 percent (most were of the pork-barrel variety), but the government bills, almost all of which had gone through a process like that described above, averaged a success rate of 80 percent, which is not in the least surprising.[25] Faced with a process as all-encompassing and thorough as that we have just seen, it is unlikely that a bill could survive with major technical or political flaws, and faced with a constituency that had put so much work into a bill, it is unlikely that any legislator of any nation would ignore or oppose it, except with very good reason.

A similar process of consensus making is also used to gather support for major nonlegislative programs, such as the Fifth Generation Computer Project. In this process, it is clear that the staff of MITI does indeed walk a tightrope, that they must in addition be well-informed, patient, and fair to all sides. However, it would be ridiculous to assert that MITI is an agency of central planning, that it somehow works its will upon this vast network of organized representatives of business both large and small, that Japan has resorted to central planning. Most critical of all is the capacity of the constituency of a few hundred large companies and more than eight million small businesses to deal with one another. Clearly, they make no attempt to reach one grand consensus. Rather, they have organized into units initially small enough to share common interests, to pursue these common interests, to regroup into larger associations that still share those areas of self-interest at that higher level, and to meet finally in national forums that again attempt only to find common ground among self-interested parties. It works only because each party has an incentive to yield his self-interest, at least in minor ways, so that someone else may achieve his or her goal. The incentive is that all parties know that their sacrifice today will be remembered and repaid in the future. No one has to depend solely upon the beneficiary of his or her cooperation to remember and repay; the memory is firmly and reliably lodged in several units of social memory, and repayment or retribution is a certainty. But even with this social apparatus in place, the system does not always work.

The Government Funding Process

Whether new legislation is involved or not, a MITI-sponsored program will often call for a commitment of government funds. If the funds are modest in amount, they may be allocated directly out of the MITI budget. If the sum is large, the funds will come from other sources within the government. In either case, the Ministry of Finance will have to concur (See Appendix IX for a summary of these sources). Although proposals ordinarily come from the associations to the MITI staff and, if necessary, to the MITI discussion councils, then to the Ministry of Finance, it is the staff of the Ministry of Finance (MOF) that casts a cold eye on each proposal and subjects it to careful scrutiny. Several alternate funding possibilities exist, but the largest among these is the Japan Development Bank (JDB), which appears to be roughly the model for the new proposals in the United States for establishment of a new Reconstruction Finance Corporation or its equivalent.

The JDB is an independent domestic bank ordinarily used to provide funding in those areas of national economic development that have been identified as high-priority. During the 1950s, for example, the JDB provided financing to the electric power and steel industries, which were basic to all future economic growth. During the late 1950s and early 1960s, funds were also used to promote economic development on the side of Japan facing the Japan Sea, a region that was undeveloped compared to the Pacific coast of Japan. During the late 1960s and early 1970s, urbanization and air and water pollution control became important policy areas, and the late 1970s saw the rise of energy independence and electronics as major claimants upon these funds. Similar national and municipal financing schemes develop, often on an ad hoc basis, for development of housing, corporate relocation, and other socioeconomic purposes in the United States, but no program as large and permanent as the Japanese system exists here.

The JDB extends loans for periods of about five years and will provide up to 40 percent of the total estimated investment in an industrial project, according to the JDB staff. The bank has very strict demands for collateral, requiring title to machinery, plants, and other physical assets in order to secure its loans. Ordinarily, the JDB will extend loans only to companies with a capitalization of at least 100 million yen or with more than 300 employees. Smaller businesses that do not qualify for JDB loans may apply to the People's Bank or to other similar government financing banks.

The JDB was the major supplier of loan funds to JECC, the computer-leasing combine, and supplies funds to similar projects in every industry. It should be clearly understood that JDB funds are loans rather than grants or contracts, and that the bank expects to get its money back, with interest. In the electronics industry, the JDB staff deals mostly with three trade associations, the EIAJ, JEIDA, and JEMIMA. The bank staff will often attend meetings of these associations as well as of the general associations of other industries, and it will sometimes participate in Keidanren meetings. The consequence of this close rapport between the JDB, MITI, and MOF is that when a consensus is reached on what to do, money is available with which to do it. The 1982 report of the U.S. Comptroller General on "Industrial Policy: Japan's Flexible Approach" summarizes the result: "According to JDB officials, the Bank's primary aim is to implement the government's economic policy goals. Those goals, generally defined in the multiyear economic plans, are translated by the JDB into specific loan programs in consultation with MITI. The correlation between JDB loans and economic policy goals is striking; in the first phase of postwar industrial development close to 85 percent of JDB loans went to the four basic industries targeted by the government for reconstruction."

Perhaps most remarkable of all is the fact that other industries, by implication, had to wait their turn while this low-cost financing went to only four industries. It is that sort of ability to engage in social choice, undergirded by social memory, that accounts for the success of the Japanese in economic development. If a similar development bank were begun in the United States and fell prey to normal political pressures, its resources would soon be depleted with no noticeable gain to the nation as a whole. The activities of the JDB involve, in essence, the creation of social endowments, which in the long run will benefit the economy generally, but which can be realized only if the whole of an industry—including major manufacturers, their suppliers and their distributors—can be rehabilitated or accelerated to a new level of international competitiveness. The JDB has value only as one part of a broad system that searches for a broad consensus, develops that consensus into plans, and then finances and launches those plans.

In 1983, the JDB had a lending budget of approximately $525 million. Of this, one-fourth was provided by repayments to the bank of previous loans, and the remainder was provided by the Fiscal Investment and Loan Program (FILP). FILP provides annually about $900 million of funds for loans and equity investments by the national government in three areas: (1) policy implementation financing (JDB, Export-Import Bank, and others); (2) public investments (Japan Housing Corp., public works, and so on); (3) local governments (equity investments, loans, and public works). FILP itself receives its funds from several sources: the postal savings accounts of individual savers, some welfare pension accounts, other national pension accounts, postal life insurance and annuity accounts, sale of government bonds to private financial institutions, and a few small items from the general budget of the national government. In essence, these monies are being held by the government for savers and future pension recipients, and it is loaned by the government back to the private sector to develop those industries and local needs that will throw off major externalities but that a single firm will not undertake. As long as FILP does not stray from this charter, it provides an essential national need. It attracts funds by offering tax-deductible interest to savers and other providers of funds, and thus can offer to them below-market rates of return (which are at market rates after taxes are considered). It can then turn around and offer below-market rates of interest on loans to the private sector while still maintaining the value of its capital. FILP has thus become a serious competitor to private financial markets, and many critics observe that both FILP and the JDB have tended to operate in industries in which private banks could do the job better, as a consequence of normal bureaucratic expansionist tendencies.

In part, the JDB came to play an important role only because Japanese financial markets were devastated after World War II, but it has come to be a major part of the allocation of industrial capital in Japan.

When Consensus Fails

When consensus is lacking in the private sector, MITI's ability to provide guidance is greatly limited. Such a case was that of an attempt to reorganize open-arc electric furnace steel production after 1978. Before 1978, the Anti-Monopoly Law (1947) of Japan had permitted the formation of cartels to permit companies in a seriously depressed industry to agree to orderly production cutbacks and plant closings in order to avoid widespread bankruptcies during periods of economic recession. However, that provision required prior approval by the Japanese FTC under strict rules and specified that the companies in the industry, not MITI, must seek such relief.[26] The companies typically preferred to fight it out on their own, refusing to close down idle plants and thus producing a market solution, but one having the consequence of high unemployment and negative impact on some cities and towns. After the oil shocks of the early 1970s, the energy-intensive industries such as electric-furnace steel making and aluminum making became permanently depressed in Japan, leading to the 1978 Law for Temporary Measures to Stabilize Designated Depressed Industries.[27]

Under this 1978 law, the MITI minister was encouraged to use "administrative guidance," or jawboning, to persuade the companies in these two industries, as well as others, to agree to mutual closing of certain plants under a MITI-approved plan. In the electric steelmaking industry, the smaller firms agreed to such a plan, but the largest, most efficient producers refused to go along, planning instead to increase their capacity with new, energy-efficient plants. In the end, although discussions continued, complete industry agreement was never reached. The smaller makers formed a limited cartel on their own that benefitted them despite the absence of the big companies.

In 1924, Japan Ford Corporation was founded, followed by Japan General Motors in 1925. By 1929, the two companies produced between them 30,000 automobiles annually from parts imported from the United States, and held 85 percent of the market.[28] During the 1930s, Toyota and Nissan came into being, the government took an interest in this new domestic industry, and laws were passed first taxing the import of auto subassemblies and then prohibiting them. Ford and General Motors were driven out of Japan. World War II left the industry devastated, but soon after the war, Toyota and Nissan were back in business and joined by Isuzu. In 1951, Prince joined the industry, followed by Hino and Mitsubishi. By 1958, total production was 330,000 automobiles.[29]

By 1960, with Toyo Kogyo, Mitsubishi, Daihatsu, Fuji, Isuzu, Toyota, and Nissan all producing passenger cars, MITI was worried. The bureaucrats understood the economies of scale in mass production and wanted to see an export market develop. With so many companies, they felt that no Japanese maker could become efficient enough to match Renault, Ford, Fiat, or General Motors. Eugene J. Kaplan describes the events: "At a 1961 meeting of the Industry Structure Advisory Council, MITI revealed a proposal to organize passenger car producers into groups based on the car's basic design type. Three groups—regular passenger cars, minicars, and specialty cars including sportscars—were defined. A firm's entire production would be limited to one group."[30] The auto producers were, understandably, enraged—except for Nissan and Toyota, who would have emerged the survivors and who, presumably, had been in on the planning. The idea died once and for all, the industry continued on its competitive track, and the industry has developed quite well, despite the strategic analysis of the MITI bureaucrats.

Creating Balance in the M-Form Society

The boundary separating MITI from the major trade associations is so thin as to be invisible at times. MITI staff will often visit meetings at the Keidanren or the chamber of commerce, and those visits are often reciprocated. Yet the MITI bureaucrats have not become captives of industry, nor do they often intrude into the private affairs of business. The relationship is one of balance. At times, it is true, MITI has been criticized as the ministry owned by business, and at other times MITI has angered the business community by attempting to take a more prominent role than is appropriate. On the whole, though, those two types of errors suggest an effective relationship.

Without that close relationship in which businesses confront one another directly under the watchful eye of government officials, the intermediate form between centralization and decentralization would not be possible. Without that sustained dialogue or the public recognition of the legitimacy of collaboration between firms and industries, the Japanese would have to resort either to a bureaucratic form of governance or to an atomistic laissez-faire market. Instead, they have constructed the institutions of which the U.S. Business-Higher Education Forum has spoken and for which the Democratic Caucus has called—institutions capable of cooperation. It is within this framework that social capital is allocated and within which social endowments are created while the public interest is protected.

It should be clear by now that perfect competition cannot exist in a modern economy and that market governance alone will therefore fail. However, market forces should be preserved whenever possible. We turn next to a consideration of one of the most important of markets, the market for capital. It is through this most simple of markets that we will see most clearly the importance of striking a balance between market, bureaucratic, and clan mechanisms of control. It is also in the next chapter that we will see how the structure of capital markets in the United States has become seriously distorted.

4

ELEMENTS OF
THE M-FORM
the role of
the banks

Our research team visited the offices of Tohmatsu, Awoki & Company, the largest firm of public accountants in Japan and an affiliate of Touche, Ross International, a U.S. firm. We talked with five of the senior partners in Tokyo, who said, "You must understand that in Japan, no one cares what the earnings are. For that reason, the job of the C.P.A. is fundamentally different than in the United States. Of course, everyone cares whether the company is making money, but they don't care about an accountant's official statement of how much money the company has earned last year. The people who own the company know so much about its affairs that no accountant can add anything more. Instead, the job of the accountant is to assist them in knowing how to get information on a regular basis."

Much the same should be true of an entire economy. An economy can use its financial resources well only if those who provide capital know a greal deal about those who use capital. The allocation of capital in the United States is in many ways the most critical element of the industrial policy debate. Experienced lobbyists and business people, as well as legislators and bureaucrats of even the shortest tenure, understand that the industrial policy debate is only so much talk unless it has something to do with money. As a result, much of the debate has focused on the question of whether or not there should be a new kind of government bank in the United States, a bank with massive financial resources. Proponents of the development bank argue that without such a new bank, industrial policy will be hollow. Such a bank would be able to direct capital to those cities and those industries that have been targeted for aid. Critics of the idea argue that a U.S. development bank would be torn apart by normal political pressures and would end up making massive mistakes and wasting public funds. Why is anyone even talking about the possibility of a new U.S. development bank? What is wrong with our current banking system, with our current equity markets?

Again, if we are to have an intelligent debate, we must begin with some understanding of the facts. Again, it will be instructive to turn to the M-Form example and then compare the financial decisions within a single company to the financial decisions that occur within our economy as a whole.

In any well-run M-Form company, the top management knows better than the accountants how well each division is doing. They know the people in the division, they know its customers, they know how well its new-product development is doing. As a result, the top management can be both demanding and patient—demanding when the division is not working hard enough or intelligently enough, patient when its short-term results look poor but its long-term prospects bright. Without intimate knowledge, however, the top management of an M-Form company cannot provide that kind of wise governance. If the top management is poorly informed about a division, it will rely for its judgment on the relatively crude accounting measures of performance. If the division is not doing well but the market is expanding, the top management will pour capital into what looks like a winner on the books, only to discover later that it has made a mistake. If the division's sales or profits are down, the top management will clamp down, not knowing that it may thereby be killing off an important future market. Without intimate knowledge of each division, an M-Form company cannot succeed.

An economy is far more complex than a company, no matter how large that company. As a result, we do not even attempt to decide at the state or national level how much capital should flow into one company rather than another. Instead, we leave that task to our banks, our securities markets, and to the many other participants in our financial markets. Despite these differences, the basic principles of management in the M-Form company have some application. If our nation is to allocate capital properly to those companies that can provide the greatest future economic growth and prosperity without drawing down our social endowments, those who provide capital must be well informed about those who use capital. If we fail to husband our resources—if we squander our savings and our national wealth—our future will be a poor one indeed.

Within the financial markets, it is the banks that play a pivotal role. Banks have been the largest financial institutions for the longest time. They have often been criticized and rarely praised. Much of that criticism is unfair. If banks in the United States have not fulfilled our expectations, it has been largely because we will not let them. The important role that banks can play in the creation of economic vitality is evident in Japan. Indeed, David Packard noted in his speech before the high-technology conference that ". . . a recent study done for Congress on U.S.-Japanese competition in semiconductors stated that capital costs were the greatest single factor that helped the Japanese in their recent incursion into the U.S. market."[1]

The strong link between financing and economic success was underscored in a December 14, 1981 *Business Week* special report: "It was their superior financial clout that enabled the Japanese in 1979 to make their first big splash in the chip market. They did it in memory chips, which represent not only the largest-volume products but also about 30 percent of the value of the total chip market, the most hotly contested segment of the semiconductor business. And this is the market where Japanese companies are in the lead today.

"It all began during the mid-1970s recession, when U.S. semiconductor suppliers were obliged to cut back sharply on capital spending. But during the same period, the big Japanese producers—especially NEC, Hitachi, and Toshiba—continued to invest heavily in new production capacity. By 1979 the demand for so-called 16K dynamic RAMs—the latest generation of memory circuits . . . had picked up to the point where it overwhelmed the capacity-limited output of U.S. suppliers. The Japanese slipped into the gap and picked up all the orders that U.S. vendors could not meet. By the end of that year, the Japanese producers had grabbed 42 percent of the market for 16K RAMs." How different the story might be today if those U.S. makers had been supported by financial sources who knew them well, could see the need for continued investment even during a recession, and could have provided the growth that the Japanese bankers were able to provide.

Why doesn't our banking system work as well as theirs? It is because we have encumbered our banking system with old laws that no longer are necessary and that in fact do great damage to those industries that must borrow in order to remain healthy. In particular, we prohibit U.S. banks from developing an intimate and even forceful relationship with the companies to which they lend, with the result that they remain at arm's length from their corporate borrowers. At arm's length, no one can manage a long-term financial relationship properly. In this chapter, we will see both the evidence of that failure and the reasons for the greater efficiency of the Japanese banking system.

An M-Form Analysis of Banking

It is with some trepidation that I attack the basic organization of banking and, by extension, of capital markets in the United States. The study of banking and of financial economics is a field that has attracted many of the finest academic minds. Nonetheless, banking has not been subjected to an organizational analysis such as a student of management (rather than of economics) might apply.

Our superstitious ideology of perfectly competitive markets is nowhere as evident as in the field of finance. Professors of finance and bankers are fond of repeating the litany that "capital markets are efficient." The litany stems from a very specialized academic meaning that has been transformed into a misleading aspect of our economic superstition. When an academic says that "capital markets are efficient," he means only that the markets in which people buy equity stock or make loans are not completely stupid. That is, capital markets take account of whatever information is available. The efficient markets hypothesis has been powerful in demonstrating, for example, that no investing theory or approach will enable you or me to make large profits by speculating in stocks, because other potential buyers of those same stocks have instant access to any public information that may suggest how the company's profits will rise or fall in the future. In this sense, the capital markets are perfectly informed at each moment to move capital efficiently to those companies that can make best use of it. But what happens if all investors are equally poorly informed? Is the market "efficient"?

Over time, the average citizen has come to believe that the litany means that capital markets work perfectly, that bankers and investors know exactly whom to lend to and in what amount. Recent events in Latin America, Poland, and in the oil-drilling industry have exposed the fallacy of that belief. In each of those instances, many of the largest and most highly regarded of U.S. banks extended large loans that may now never be repaid. Clearly, they are not perfectly informed. As a result, many of us who believe that capital markets are efficient also have come to believe that bankers are not only imperfect, but that they are almost perfectly imperfect. Bankers are in fact just like other human beings. If they systematically err, the reason must lie in an inappropriate structure of banking.

The ideology of perfect competition in capital markets suggests that the movement of money from one company to another works best when individual and autonomous lenders and investors are left to compete freely for the best opportunities, and individual users of capital are left alone to compete freely for the cheapest sources of capital. Therefore we should require no bureaucratic nor clan forms of governance between the providers of capital and the users of capital. Markets will provide all the governance needed.

Certainly, if there are any pure markets at all, they must be the markets for capital. In capital markets the rules of disclosure guarantee that all relevant information is made public, all potential buyers and sellers have access to the same information, and competition abounds. Equity is achieved on the spot, and a dissatisfied stockholder or lender can simply sell his stock or loan portfolio in another secondary spot market. That is the received wisdom.

Equity Markets

Capital markets may be divided roughly into two subcategories, the market for equity and the market for debt. Typically, the equity investor takes a greater risk than the debt provider, because the equity investor is considered to be a "residual claimant" who gets his money back only after the employees, suppliers, debt holders, and everyone else has been paid. Thus investors will not buy the relatively higher-risk equities issued by a company unless they are also offered a risk premium, or higher rate of return, than that paid to the debt holders. Moreover, it is ordinarily felt that the more debt a company has, the riskier it is to an equity investor, so that the higher a company's debt ratio, the greater will be the risk premium demanded by equity holders and thus the higher the company's cost of equity. The greater the risk to the provider of capital, the higher will be the risk premium.

Consider the organization of equity markets in the United States. Our big businesses, which employ 80 percent of our labor force, typically have their shares owned by tens of thousands of investors. These investors freely buy and sell shares on the stock exchanges based on publicly available information, but how good is that information? An individual who owns one hundred shares of stock in the Ford Motor Company has never met the executives of the company in which he or she owns shares, has probably never visited a Ford plant, and knows almost nothing at all about the company. Harold Demsetz, a UCLA economist, has observed that the buyer of shares is aware of this limitation and takes it into account, so that the small investor is not unfairly penalized by this system.[2] However, the small investor and the company itself are penalized in another and very significant way.

If the investor knows little about the company or its managers, he cannot be expected to evaluate the company's long-run needs to invest in new technology, to train people, to keep loyal and experienced employees on the payroll even through a sales slump. Instead, that poorly informed equity holder knows only that earnings will probably go up or down over the next few quarters and will buy or sell on that short-term information. It is that poorly informed owner who initiates the short-run pressures on and the short-sighted decisions of managers.

On the other hand, a great deal of stock in major U.S. firms is held by a few large shareholders, such as insurance companies, pension funds, and bank trust departments. Certainly they must have the clout and the ability to gain access to such intimate knowledge and thus serve as better-informed owners. In fact, these large institutional shareholders are considered to be trustees who hold the shares for the benefit of their annuitants, pension beneficiaries, or trust beneficiaries. Under current law, if a trustee takes any action that causes a loss in the principal held for a beneficiary, and if that action was unreasonably risky, the beneficiaries may be able to sue successfully the trustee to recoup those losses. As a result, our large institutional holders of equities have an incentive to be passive shareholders and to sell off their stock at the first public sign of weakness in a company. That, of course, exacerbates the short-run pressures on managers.

Equity markets work well only if the equity holders are well informed about the company. The major equity holders must know the company well, know its executives personally, and be able to provide wise and farsighted guidance to the managers of the company. Our current equity markets do not make this possible. In Japan, by comparison, banks are permitted by law both to own equity and to provide debt to manufacturing and other companies, with the result that the banks play the role of the well-informed holder of equity. U.S. law prohibits our banks from owning equities in nonbanking businesses. The unnaturalness of that law is apparent, because U.S. banks constantly attempt to evade it by establishing bank holding companies that can and do hold such equities, although banks are careful not to overdo it, lest they arouse the regulatory bodies. This area of law needs desperately to be reviewed and modified.

Debt Markets

Consider now the market for debt. In fact, there is a market for debt only when a loan is first made. A company can shop around to find the bank from which it would like to borrow, and banks can shop around to find the companies to which they would like to lend. Once a loan has been made, say, to Chrysler or to International Harvester, however, the bank is stuck with it. Very rarely can a bank "sell" a loan to another bank (with the exception of home mortgages and other such high-volume commodity loans). In the United States, banks are not only stuck with those loans (in many cases, of course, quite happily) but are severely restricted in the amount of influence they can bring to bear over the debtor. That is, once a loan is made, there is no longer a market mode of governance between borrower and lender. Neither, however, is there a bureaucratic relationship, because the bank is not allowed to have legitimate hierarchical powers over the borrower. A clan relationship does not develop because the bank and the borrower have different goals: the borrower wants to maximize returns to the equity holders and just meet bank payments, and thus will be inclined to take business risks that may have gigantic future payoffs; the bank wants only to get its money back and have the borrower grow a little bit, but it is against many business risks because such risks may fail and endanger the bank's loans. If the risk succeeds, the bank does not participate in that gain; it only gets its money back (with interest).

Banking law in the United States restricts banks from exercising effective governance over borrowers. Thus neither market, bureaucratic, nor clan governance is possible between borrower and lender. The consequence is that the bank faces great risk in making business loans and thus must charge a higher risk premium or rate of interest and is unwilling to allow a corporate borrower to rise to a debt ratio as high as is commonplace in Japan.

Managing Capital Markets

Capital markets in the United States are vastly imperfect. They are imperfect because the strictures of U.S. law prevent the providers of capital from being well informed and from exercising governance over the users of capital. The result is to penalize the users of capital. This happens because those who provide capital are well aware of their inability to be well informed and to protect their interests, and thus withhold capital while simultaneously charging a high-risk premium for the capital they provide.

The assertions are strong, but the evidence is compelling. Our research team is performing a detailed analysis of the banking system of Japan, led by Professor Jay Barney. The team has used a variety of statistical techniques to estimate the effects on cost of capital of many details of the pattern of concentrated shareholdings in Japan. Here we will review only a few of the most critical of these results.

Financing the Electronics Industry: Debt versus Equity

In June 1980, the Chase Manhattan Bank published a report titled, "U.S. and Japanese Semiconductor Industries: A Financial Comparison," commissioned by the Semiconductor Industry Association, one of the more active and effective of U.S. trade associations. The problem: "The U.S. semiconductor industry believes the ability of the Japanese semiconductor companies to employ considerably higher debt ratios regardless of business and economic conditions places U.S. semiconductor companies at a disadvantage in raising capital."[3] The conclusions of the study match those argued here: "In the U.S., loans to highly levered corporations entail a greater degree of risk than in Japan. The close affiliation of banks and corporations in Japan mentioned earlier makes the potential credit risks more manageable by giving lenders and borrowers a common interest. To the extent that a [main] bank and its affiliates own a significant interest in shares of a borrower, the bank has a continuing voice in establishing corporate policy and direction. Additionally, lenders who are outside the Keiretsu (financial group) can take comfort in the knowledge that members of the Keiretsu typically provide financial assistance or loan guarantees if required. During periods of financial difficulty, the principal Keiretsu bank may even subordinate its position to that of other lenders.... The Japanese and U.S. financial systems differ dramatically in another respect. Because of the influence which the Japanese government has on the lending practices of the private banking system, priority is given to designated "key" industries in obtaining bank financing.... In summary, the economic and financial system in Japan provides corporations with a decided advantage over U.S. companies in obtaining capital at lower cost."[4]

Two primary issues are of interest. First is the lower cost of capital to Japanese companies, and second is the higher debt ratio of Japanese companies. Let us consider each in turn. The Chase Manhattan study estimated the weighted average cost of capital for each of several U.S. and Japanese semiconductor companies. The companies are not strictly comparable, because the typical U.S. semiconductor firms in the study are specialty houses that manufacture only semiconductors, whereas the Japanese semiconductor makers are exclusively part of integrated computer makers for whom semiconductors account for only part of the business. Thus the Japanese companies are larger, more diversified, and present less risk to a lender or investor.

The weighted average cost of capital (WACC) reflects the cost to a company of obtaining debt as well as the cost to the company of attracting equity. Ordinarily, equity is more costly to obtain, because it entails greater risk to the provider of capital. In estimating the WACC, the Chase Manhattan study was not able to take into account the effect of compensating balances, which our study did. If we combine some of the results of the Chase Manhattan Study with the more refined measures of cost of debt from the UCLA study, we obtain the following results:

Cost of Capital for Selected Companies[5]

Company	Cost of Equity* (%)	Cost of Debt (%)	WACC (%)
U.S. Companies			
Advanced Micro Devices	21.4	12.0	17.7
Fairchild Camera	19.6	12.0	15.5
Intel	17.7	10.8	16.8
National Semiconductor	19.8	11.7	17.5
Motorola	16.5	10.8	13.8
Texas Instruments	18.1	10.8	16.5
U.S. Average	18.85	11.35	16.30
Japanese Companies			
Hitachi	18.2	9.14	13.76
NEC	19.0	8.8	10.84
Toshiba	17.1	8.3	12.1
Mitsubishi Electric	19.5	13.4	15.34
Fujitsu	19.7	6.76	11.09
Japanese Average	18.70	9.28	12.63

*Market method. See Appendix VIII for an explanation of the method used.

Even taking into account the compensating balances, it is clear that Japanese semiconductor makers enjoy a large advantage over their U.S. competitors in the cost of capital, with an overall cost of 16.3 percent for the U.S. companies compared to 12.63 percent for the Japanese. The cost of equity is not the same as the returns earned on equity investments, but rather is an index reflecting the risk attributed to the company by investors. The results here show that the Japanese and U.S. stock markets appraise the level of risk attached to these companies at nearly identical levels, with an average U.S. cost of equity of 18.85 percent, compared to 18.70 percent in Japan. What is surprising is that Japanese investors do not demand a higher equity return on these companies, even though their average debt amounts of 68 percent of total capital, a level that would be very risky to a U.S. investor. By comparison, the U.S. companies described here rely on debt for only 51 percent of their capital.

The big difference is that debt is less risky and thus carries less of a risk premium in Japan, with an average cost of debt of 9.28 percent as opposed to the 11.35 percent in the United States. Because debt carries less risk, it is less costly than equity in both economies, and because the Japanese companies can carry far greater debt than American companies, their advantage is multiplied. Finally, the use of debt benefits the shareholders, because interest payments on debt are deducted before the computation of corporate income taxes (corporate income tax in Japan is a maximum of 42 percent of profits but 32 percent on profits paid out as dividends, whereas the maximum U.S. rate is 46 percent whether paid out as dividends or not.)

Skeptics and academics will observe that these results are less than compelling, because U.S. and Japanese firms operate in different capital markets. It may be that other features of those capital markets, features missed by my research team, are more important than the ones I have described. That kind of skepticism is well placed and should be examined through more research. However, the preliminary results of the analysis performed by Professor Jay Barney of our research team shows that even if we limit our study to Japanese companies, we find that the more of the company's stock that is held by a few banks, the lower is the borrower's cost of capital. There is much yet to be learned, and the questions are of the utmost importance.

But, some will ask, how can we imagine U.S. banks lending to companies that are 70 percent debt? If that is a critical requirement of the Japanese system, it will not work here. In fact, the debt ratio of Japanese companies tends to be overstated for a variety of reasons. First, we have seen that Japanese companies commonly hold stock in other companies, stock that they value on their books at the purchase price of fifteen or twenty years ago and that is worth many times what is indicated on the books. Second, Japanese accounting practices tend to undervalue some important assets. Third, the tax system in Japan encourages deductions and reserves for a large variety of special categories.[6] The *Bank of England Quarterly Bulletin* has estimated that if we adjust for all of these conditions, the average debt of Japanese companies will be approximately 55 percent, somewhat but not dramatically higher than similar ratios for other industrialized countries.

An M-Form Banking System

The most important fact, however, is that Japanese electronics companies have access to more capital at a lower cost than do U.S. companies. In other words, their capital markets are more efficient than ours. That superiority rests on the structure of Japanese capital markets. The structure of Japanese capital markets closely resembles an M-Form. In the first place, banks have not only the limited rights of a creditor but also the broader hierarchical rights of an owner to oversee the companies to which they lend. The relationship between banks and companies is dominantly a market relationship in which banks compete against one another for corporate business. That market governance is typical of an M-Form structure. In addition, however, banks also have the rights of bureaucratic governance over those companies. Finally, banks are also large shareholders who cannot easily dispose of their stockholdings without bringing about a drop in the value of those shares. Consequently, banks have a long-term interest in the health and risk-taking of their debtors and develop clan forms of governance. It is the balance between these market, bureaucratic, and clan forms of governance in the M-Form structure of financial markets that accounts for their effectiveness in Japan.

As a Mitsubishi Bank manager explained it, "Nowadays, many

of these stockholdings are 'hidden assets' that could be sold at a big gain but rarely are . . . These 'hidden assets' are hard to liquidate; if we sell, it has a big negative impact on the company, and it would be hard to extract the full value of the stock in one sale. If a sale is necessary, as when the stockholding limit was lowered from 10 percent to 5 percent, the bank asks the company to recommend a trusted, stable buyer, and the company suggests the right time for the transaction. . . . Conflict of interest is not a problem, because 5 percent is not large enough to really exert control, and the total of a bank's stockholdings are never more than the bank's capital, so the depositor's funds are not really put at risk."[7]

In the second place, the banks and government of Japan recognize that capital is among the most precious of social endowments and must not be squandered. Because the capacity of government to direct capital flows is extremely limited, the market mechanism is allowed to function without much interference from government. But because capital is necessary to create social endowments, government maintains an intermediate form of collaboration with the banks that is typical of an M-Form structure. Let us examine these effects.

In the United States, it has become a commonplace that the shares of large corporations are held by a large, diffuse body of investors. The problem was raised by Berle and Means in 1932 (in *The Modern Corporation and Private Property*) as being potentially serious, as indeed it has become.[8] In the United States, anyone who owns 5 percent or more of a publicly traded company must file a report with the SEC, and thus we can compare the total of shares held by these over-five percent owners in the two countries. In our study, the U.S. companies, on the average, had 16 percent of their shares held by such large shareholders, while for the Japanese companies the average was 28 percent. However, the difference is more striking when we compare the largest companies only. For the 20 largest U.S. companies in our study, the average holding by large shareholders was 7.5 percent of each company's stock, and for the 20 largest Japanese companies the figure was 23 percent. Having a few large shareholders is far more common in Japan. Of our 585 U.S. companies, 306 had no single shareholder with 5 percent or more, while among our 135 Japanese companies, all but 6 had at least one such large shareholder.

The large shareholders in the United States tend to be individuals who founded a company or their estates, while the large holders in Japan are banks, insurance companies, and other manufacturing companies. A typical pattern of shareholding is exhibited by the ten companies of the Mitsubishi Group, as of 1974.[9] The Mitsubishi Bank, lead bank to the group, owns 2.2 percent of Mitsubishi Trust Bank, 5.8 percent of Tokyo Marine, 5.8 percent of Mitsubishi Heavy Industries, 7.9 percent of Mitsubishi Corporation (the trading company), 3.4 percent of Mitsubishi Electric, 7.7 percent of Asahi Glass, 3.0 percent of Kirin Beer, 5.7 percent of Mitsubishi Chemical, and 4.4. percent of NYK. In return, those companies own a total of 26.9 percent of the stock of Mitsubishi Bank, as well as holding stock in one another, so that control effectively resides within the group, among a small group of ten owners.

Clearly, there are many important shareholders whose holdings are just under 5 percent. In Japan, these are routinely reported data, but not in the United States. Thus, it is not possible to compare fully the importance of major shareholders. However, we can describe the situation in Japan. If we consider all shares in our electronics companies held by banks, insurance companies, and other manufacturing companies, whether their holdings are above or below 5 percent, we find:

Proportion of Equity Held
in 135 Japanese Electronics Companies

Banks	12.09%
Insurance Companies	7.9
Other Manufacturers	17.0
Total	36.99%

Most important among these shareholders are the banks. Ordinarily, a company will have sizable blocks of its stock held by each of five or six banks, with each bank having a stockholding in proportion to the amount of business it does with the company. For example, in 1978 these were the bank holdings of stock in some Japanese computer makers:[10]

Bank Shareholdings in
Computer Manufacturers (as of 1978)

Manufacturers	Bank	Percent Held
Fujitsu, Ltd.	Dai-Ichi Kangyo Bank	9.5
	Industrial Bank of Japan	3.6
	Tokyo Trust and Banking	2.1
	Total	15.2
Hitachi, Ltd.	Industrial Bank of Japan	2.3
	Sanwa Bank	2.2
	Dai-Ichi Kangyo Bank	1.9
	Fuji Bank	1.9
	Total	8.3

These patterns will change soon, because a new regulation limits banks after 1987 to no more than 5 percent of the equity of a company, down from the previous limit of 10 percent. In most cases, however, this new limit will not have a major impact on shareholding patterns.

The critical importance of this equity position of banks is that the bank has a direct property right to know a debtor company well, to influence it if necessary, and to force a change in its management in extreme circumstances. Akio Morita, the co-founder of the Sony Corporation, which is one-third owned by U.S. investors, comments: "The Mitsui Bank is our lead bank and is an important owner of our shares. Although we do not rely heavily on debt as most other Japanese companies do, still we have a close relationship with our bank. The treasurer of our company came to us from Mitsui Bank, as did some of our other financial managers. As a result, the bank has very good information about our condition. In any eventuality, the bank is there to protect the interests of all of the shareholders, the customers, and the employees of Sony. For example, if the bank decides that as chief executive officer I am not doing my job right, it can push me out." As a result of having the powers of a property owner, the Japanese bank can and does monitor closely the affairs of each company to which it makes a loan. That is not to say that the bank attempts to make daily decisions, but rather that it can more easily obtain detailed information and act to control the company if necessary.

In like manner, the stock of city banks in Japan is concentrated in the hands of several major industrial firms, typically the loan customers of the bank. For example, 27 percent of Mitsui Bank stock is held by ten companies, including Mitsui Life Insurance, Toshiba, and Toyota Motors. The other hundred or so major shareholders added to these own a total of approximately 60 percent of Mitsui Bank's stock. Thus the number of shareholders is large enough that no one shareholder can force the bank to make unsafe loans to prop up an owner's failing business, but small enough that the bank's owners can be well informed about the bank's policies and thus not exert unreasonable short-term profit pressures on the bank. In a sense, the city bank is like a farmer's cooperative bank in the United States, except that the members of the cooperative are large industrial firms rather than small farmers. The cooperative is able to attract savings from depositors and put them to high-yield uses that deliver adequate rates of return to savers and create new industries and jobs for all. Savers in rural areas put their savings into local banks or savings associations that can participate in the financing of industry by buying bonds and other financial instruments issued by the city banks. Thus the city banks have the expertise to scrutinize and to support the needs of major capital-intensive industries, and they put to use the savings of the public in that purpose.

The Structure of Banking in Japan

The structure of banking in Japan is quite different from that in the United States, and there is little reason to think that either country will move to adapt to the other's method within the foreseeable future. The United States has approximately 14,000 banks, with an even larger number of savings associations, credit bureaus, and other financial institutions. In Japan, there are 86 commercial banks, including 13 major institutions, the city banks, with 2,409 branches among them across the nation; 61 local banks with a total of 4,335 branches confined to one or two prefectures per bank; and one foreign exchange bank, which also operates as a city bank. In addition, there are 3 long-term credit banks, which specialize in loans over five years to companies and accept no ordinary deposits like yours and mine; and 7 trust banks, which must separate their trust and other banking activities as in the United States. In addition to these, however, there are 1,156 financial institutions that make loans or guarantee loans to small business through their 9,250 branch offices; another 7,761 financial institutions that provide loans to agriculture, forestry, and fisheries; as well as 11 official government banks and 17,209 post offices accepting individual savings accounts and offering tax-free interest up to a limit.[11] It has, understandably, been argued by some that Japan, with half the population of the United States, is overbanked. However, we should not forget that the Japanese save far more than do the citizens of any other industrial nation, perhaps because saving is so safe and so convenient.

Banking in Japan has not always taken this form. In 1918, there were 2,033 banks, but the government has consistently encouraged mergers, bringing the number down to 1,445 in 1928, to 663 in 1932, and 69 by the end of World War II.[12] The principal motivation, apparently, has been to allow only banks sufficiently large and strong so that bank failures are unlikely, because the failure of even one small bank tarnishes the reputation of all banks and thus raises doubts in the minds of potential savers about the wisdom of saving in banks at all.

In its broad outlines, the Japanese banking system serves a straightforward and clear purpose and it is supported by an ideology of financial economics which is quite different from that held by U.S. scholars and bankers. Our research team interviewed bankers and officials of the Ministry of Finance and of the Bank of Japan during January of 1983, and arrived at the following interpretation of their banking system.

Equity markets, in which people buy and sell shares of stock, always have a tendency to produce diffuse ownership of that stock. The result of diffuse ownership is that the owners of the company's stock have a difficult time becoming well informed about a company, and thus are not likely to provide appropriate governance to the company they own. The smaller the company and the less well known it is to the public, the less informed the owners will be and the more detrimental diffuse ownership will be. On the other hand, there must always be equity markets. Therefore, equity markets should be restricted to the largest, best-known and most stable companies. The venture capital necessary for medium and small businesses and for emerging industries should instead be provided by banks. Banks can gain the expertise to be able to scrutinize the needs of borrowers with some skill, and can determine who is a good bet for successful growth and who is not. Banks cannot do this perfectly, but they can do it better than thousands of individual shareholders can.

The objective of any financial system is to encourage millions of small savers to save as much as possible and to channel those funds into the businesses that will create the most future jobs and prosperity for the nation, thus creating social endowments. If these small savers are allowed to invest in equities of unstable companies about which they know very little, or if they deposit some of their money in an unstable bank and lose part of it; they will save less in the future. It is therefore the responsibility of MOF and BOJ to see to it that only sound companies enter the equity markets and that banks never fail.

As a result, the Bank of Japan must maintain a close relationship with the major banks. They do this in the form of "window guidance." Once every three months, officials of MOF and BOJ meet with representatives of each of the thirteen city banks, the long-term credit banks, and major government banks to listen to their plans for total loans over the next few months. In some cases, the BOJ officials may ask a bank to cool its lending plans down in order to avoid creating inflationary pressures or other problems. But no bureaucrat would ever think of even implying that loans to one specific company should be approved or not. On a monthly basis, these MOF and BOJ officials meet with groups, including all banks, in order to hear their plans and their needs.

On the regular visits to city banks, the bank examiners ask for detailed information concerning the bank's strategy against other banks, although the examiners would never indicate approval or disapproval of any strategy. Some bankers accept this close relationship, as one observed, because, "Guidance aids the economic growth of the whole country, so it is worth it to mind MOF in the long run." Other bankers take a different view. As one said, "Window guidance may be a good thing, but for us bankers it's a pain in the neck."

The primary importance of window guidance is that the Bank of Japan can open or shut the window of credit availability to the city banks. As a result, the city banks are responsive to and can shape the national consensus on economic development, and will be ready to make loans (at market rates) available to those new industries or developmental areas that have been agreed upon for economic development. This kind of national coordination is possible only if the bulk of industrial capital comes from the banking system rather than through the equity markets, which cannot be so readily engaged in a dialogue. One consequence is that individual savers do not have the option of putting their money into the wide array of instruments providing higher returns to U.S. savers, such as money funds and mutual funds. In effect, the individual saver is thus subsidizing economic development by accepting lower current returns than he or she could get in an unrestricted market. However, savers accept this system because they understand that the result of this subsidy is the creation of social endowments, such as more jobs and a healthier economy. Thus, the total returns to the individual saver are not just the passbook interest on savings, but include also the ability to find employment in a properly financed company that has well-informed providers of capital and can provide lifetime employment and good wages.

On the other hand, the report of the U.S. comptroller general reflects a quite different interpretation of that same system.[13] As I interpret the report, it sees the same facts but applies to them a different ideology and perspective that grows out of the very different institutional structure of the United States. In this view, the Japanese government took control of the banking system after World War II, when there were no savings and thus no credit. The Bank of Japan loaned money directly to the city banks, which they in turn made available to industry. As a result, the Bank of Japan and the Ministry of Finance obtained very strong control over the major banks. In order to consolidate this control, the government prohibited the development of new major banks with national branch systems. As the Japanese economy prospered, more capital became available. In order to maintain control in this new situation, the Japanese government kept interest rates to industry artificially low, which guaranteed the nonmarket situation of more demand for credit than was available. In such a situation, rationing will take place, and thus the MOF and BOJ were able to ration credit among the city banks. No city bank could prosper unless it received credit from BOJ and MOF, and thus the city banks had to be responsive to the policy initiatives developed by government.

In this manner, the Japanese government was able to direct capital flows into those industries targeted for development. The system worked because the government allowed free markets to operate at the local level by refusing to meddle in decisions about which company should receive funds or how much, thus leaving the market system to operate. At the policy level, the government did not rely on bureaucrats alone to determine which industries to target, but rather listened through its discussion councils to the trade associations, citizens groups, and labor unions. Whenever these disparate groups reached consensus on the need for a major economic thrust, it was obvious that real opportunity lay there and that economic progress of a major sort could be achieved. Thus government was able to seek out areas of consensus and direct capital flows into those areas, creating social endowments for the economy and allowing the marketplace to pick winners in specific companies. In the years since the mid-1970s, however, it has become more and more difficult for the Japanese government to ration credit. Outside nations have insisted on being able to borrow (usually by issuing bonds) in Japan in order to take advantage of the low interest rates or to protect themselves from exchange-rate fluctuations, and the Japanese government has been politically unable to resist these pressures. However, those outside companies do not typically contribute to the creation of positive externalities in Japan and may not in the future be willing to sacrifice their short-run self-interest in favor of a broader and longer-run interest. Thus, the structure of capital markets and of banking in Japan will certainly change over the next several years. Just how that change will proceed remains to be seen.

The historical development of the Japanese patterns of equity holding and of banking stems from the pre-World War II Zaibatsu, which were often family-dominated holding companies from which the present-day Keiretsu, or loose financial groups, have evolved. Also of some interest is the financial role played by the Sogo Sosha, or nine major trading companies, which act like quasibanks in financing the smaller and medium-sized businesses of Japan to enable them to sell their products overseas. A brief review of the Zaibatsu and of the Sogo Sosha is included as Appendix X to the book.

Does the U.S. Need an M-Form Banking Structure?

To observe that the Japanese banking system approximates an M-Form and to argue that Japanese companies benefit from a lower cost of capital does not necessarily mean that the United States should do the same. Indeed, the evidence is that Japanese companies are relying less and less on debt financing in recent years, and several moves are underway in Japan to encourage diffuse stockholding through more active equity markets. We have an imperfect banking system, but perhaps it's as good as we can make it. There must be some very good reasons why we don't permit banks to own stock in nonbanking businesses, and perhaps they really don't need to.

These are the questions that any thoughtful citizen will ask. I cannot provide definitive answers to them, but I can share with you the results of my research into them.

Why Do We Prohibit U.S. Banks from Owning Equity in Other Businesses?

Many observers believe that the exploitation by banks of small investors during the early 1900s led to the prohibition against banks owning equities in nonbanking businesses and that these prohibitions were laid down in the Glass-Steagall Act of 1933. That interpretation is wrong. In fact, it was the National Banking Act of 1864 which prohibited bank holdings of such equities. The Glass-Steagall Act resulted from the criticism that banks at the time were selling equities to customers that were so unsound that the banks themselves would never own those same equities, even if they could. Indeed, if banks had been required to own any equities that they also sold to customers, the abuses of the 1920s could never have occurred. These key events bear some further elaboration.

The National
Banking Act of 1864

In 1900, John Jay Knox wrote a history of U.S. banking that describes the National Banking Act of 1864.[14] Knox, who had served for seventeen years as deputy comptroller and as comptroller of the currency, described the congressional hearings of 1863 on the problems of the U.S. Treasury. The Civil War was at an end and the U.S. Treasury had been depleted. In addition, some large banks of the time issued their own banknotes or currencies, with the result that there was no single U.S. currency in universal use. The congress solved both problems with the National Banking Act of 1864. The atmosphere was one of emergency in financial circles, and the act was not the result of patient and careful deliberation but rather of emergency stop-gap measures.

The act placed a tax of 10 percent on all private bank currencies in order to discourage their use, and then allowed banks to obtain the national currency only by buying U.S. government bonds. In order to move all available capital into the U.S. Treasury, the act also forbade banks from buying bonds issued by the separate states. In one move, a national currency was created and the U.S. Treasury was replenished.

The act of 1864 did not explicitly prohibit banks from investing in shares of nonbanking businesses; neither did the act explicitly grant that right to banks. However, it was clear that such investments would draw scarce capital away from the U.S. Treasury. In 1865, a federal court held that because the law did not explicitly grant to banks the right to own nonbank equities, they were therefore forbidden to do so.

Banks widely ignored this ruling during the ensuing decades, either by forming bank holding companies that owned both the bank and other nonbanking businesses, or by requiring that those who owned stock in the bank must also own stock in specified nonbank companies. In many cases, the investing was done through a security-dealing affiliate of the bank. These securities affiliates not only invested the bank's own funds in other businesses, however; they also engaged in the business of underwriting equity issues. In an underwriting, the underwriter agrees to buy, for example, 100,000 shares of newly issued stock in the XYZ Company at a price of $6.00

per share. The underwriter then hopes to sell those shares to the public at $6.25 per share and thereby earn a profit. In the eyes of the investing public and of the congress, little distinction was made between a bank that sold equities to the public and a bank that bought equities for its own account.

The Glass-Steagall Act of 1933

In 1921, the United States had more than 31,000 banks. By 1933, the number was down to 18,000. (Today it is approximately 14,000). The failure rate for banks was higher than for any other business during those years. As Susan Kennedy, an economic historian, describes it, Herbert Hoover left the presidency and Franklin Roosevelt entered it in 1933, with the banking system of the United States on the verge of total collapse. Only bank holidays in thirty-four states kept their banks from wholesale failures.[15] Nearly all of the banks that closed were small; most had only the central office and no other branches. Clearly, something had to be done to save the banks.

Something also had to be done to limit the scope of their activities. The great stock market crash of 1929 was blamed, rightly or wrongly, largely on the banks. At the time, banks were permitted to engage in all financial activities, including accepting deposits, making loans, managing other people's funds as trustee, and underwriting new issues of stock for companies as well as government bonds. There was no Securities and Exchange Commission at the time, no FDIC to insure depositors, only a weak and decentralized Federal Reserve System. The problem, in particular, was that banks were lending often-large sums of money to individuals for the purpose of speculating in the stock exchanges. That activity benefitted the bank twice: once through the interest received on the loan, and a second time through the fees earned by selling the shares of stock. Because the loans were secured by the shares of stock, which seemed immediately convertible into cash, and because the share prices continued to rise, the banks continued to lend on this basis. Then it all came unglued.

Several long-time abuses of banking came to light. In some cases, wealthy individuals or companies had taken over control of banks and had made unwise loans to themselves. In other cases, bank officers had subverted laws on the books to make loans to themselves so that they could participate in the wild speculation.[16] As the economy began to unravel, some bank officers blatantly lied to shareholders about the real distress of the bank. The public lost its former confidence in banks and in bankers and demanded reform. One reform centered on the separation of commercial banking (accepting deposits and making loans) from investment banking (arranging new issues of stock and long-term bonds for companies). The banks opposed this attempted reform, since by 1930 they or their security affiliates accounted for 54 percent of all new securities issues.[17] The Senate conducted long hearings on the Glass bill, with the banks opposing the reforms every step of the way. Then in January 1933, the Senate acquired a new counsel, Ferdinand Pecora of New York. The Pecora hearings, as they came to be known, were sensational.[18] They included the full range of congressional drama in public testimony, down to the self-made man on the stand, now in rags, who had lost his entire fortune through bank-financed speculation and still had no idea what had happened to him. Pecora captured the emotions of many Americans, who, like that man, had no idea what had happened to them and who, like the poor man, preferred to ignore the role that their own greed had played in their downfall.

The Pecora hearings so galvanized public opinion against the banks that they had no choice but to yield on almost every front. Investment banking and commercial banking were separated with the passage of the Glass-Steagall Act of 1933, with most of the large banks choosing to remain in the commercial banking business and separating their investment-banking affiliates into independent companies. Moreover, banks agreed to erect the so-called Chinese Wall between their trust departments and their commercial banking departments, so that trust officers could not invest pension funds they managed in the stock of companies to which the bank had loans, in order to rescue such a company.

There is no question that the times were frenzied. In 1931 alone, 2,298 banks closed their doors. In 1932 another 1,453 followed. It was hardly a time for cool debate or surgical precision in legislation. It is not surprising that we threw the baby out with the bathwater.

On June 16, 1933, President Franklin D. Roosevelt signed the Banking Act of 1933, which reorganized the laws regarding branch banking, tightened restrictions on bank officers, strengthened central control of the Federal Reserve System, abolished interest payments on checking accounts (this was to be reversed in 1982), created the Federal Deposit Insurance Corporation, and forced the separation of investment and commercial banking.

The very brief review does not conclusively establish the assertion that banks in the United States should be permitted to own equities in nonbanking businesses. However, it should make us wonder whether there is any good reason today for such a prohibition. If not, then the law should be amended so as to give this freedom to banks. That is not to say that banks will rush to buy equities. Indeed, banks have been largely silent on this aspect of bank regulation. It is more likely that, over a period of years, the largest and most expert banks will find that they can more effectively serve those corporate borrowers in whom they hold equity positions, that those borrowers will place competitive pressure on banks to buy those equities in order to get the loan business, and that a different banking relationship will evolve over time.

But is that different relationship really necessary? Isn't it already possible that a U.S. bank has ready access as a lender to all of the information that it needs about a borrower? Doesn't a U.S. bank already have more power than it needs to protect its interests and its depositor's funds by exercising control over a corporate borrower who gets into financial trouble?

The Governance Rights of U.S. Banks

Surely, one might think, a major bank such as the Bank of America or Chase Manhattan is well equipped to look after it loans, even to the largest corporations. Even though the bank has no equity and thus is not an owner, certainly the law must permit it to protect its loans and thus its depositors, and surely such a large institution is possessed of the expertise to do just that. Unfortunately, the rights of creditors in general and of banks in particular are not clear in this regard.

The problem crops up most often in bankruptcy cases. Here, we often find that the bankrupt company has been in trouble for some time and that its banks may have taken steps both to help the company and to protect the bank's position. Apparently, the bankruptcy courts have not been able to achieve clarity on what the rights of a bank are, but the underlying legal theory is not complex. In general, a bank may take whatever steps are necessary to protect its loan to a client company in distress, but the bank may not completely dominate and control that subservient company, nor may it take any actions that will improve the bank's status in comparison to other claimants.[19] For example, when the retail company W. T. Grant was in bankruptcy proceedings during the late 1970s, its banks had claims against it totalling $650 million. Many of the bank loans were secured by physical assets of W. T. Grant, and the banks should have been paid back in full before other creditors were paid. However, the bankruptcy trustee argued that in attempting to protect themselves, the banks had so tied up W. T. Grant's assets that it was no longer able to operate, thus harming the company and its other creditors. In an analysis of the case, Margaret H. Douglas-Hamilton observes, "The trustee based its argument that the banks dominated and controlled Grant on the fact that a person who was a director of Morgan Guaranty Trust Company, Grant's lead lending bank and agent for the other banks, as well as Vice-Chairman of the lead bank's holding company, served on Grant's Board of Directors and on its Executive and Audit Committees."[20] The result was that the twenty-six banks, led by Morgan, agreed to an out-of-court settlement of their claims, in which some of the assets pledged as collateral were not paid to the banks but to other creditors with prior standing, and some creditors who should have come after the banks were paid before them. In another case, a bank loan agreement was declared invalid because upon receiving the loan, the borrowing company handed to the bank the resignations of all its executives and directors and gave the bank power to appoint all new officers and directors.[21] If a bank is judged to have dominated and controlled a debtor corporation, then the bank may be held liable for the claims against that subservient company, as in a 1922 case.[22]

However, the rights of banks to protect their loans are broad, as affirmed in *Chicago Mill & Lumber Co.* v. *Boatmen's Bank.*[23] In that case, the bank had its assistant cashier, who gave orders and supervised the mill manager, elected president of the lumber mill. After the mill went bankrupt, another of its creditors sued the bank on the grounds that it was acting like an owner and thus was liable as though the mill were a division of the bank. In that case, the court ruled that the bank was within its rights to take those steps in order to protect its loan, and that it had not dominated the mill.

The law is murky on this issue, but one thing is clear: any bank manager who attempts to influence directly and deeply the management of a debtor company runs the risk that a court will judge the bank to be in dominant control. If that happens, then in effect the bank's supposedly low-risk debt has been converted into high-risk equity. In such a case, the bank has the worst of all possible worlds: it takes the risk of other equity holders that it may lose all of its money, but unlike the other equity holders it has no chance ever of making a large profit on the equity position.

As a consequence of these and other legal decisions, banks are understandably reluctant to attempt much control over companies to which they lend money. Instead, the bank must attempt to be well informed but keep an arm's-length relationship. However, suppose that the bank learns that a company to which it has loans is in trouble. What can it do? It cannot remove the executives, it cannot intrude too deeply in the company's affairs, and it certainly will not find a ready buyer for its loan. And suppose that the debtor starts to slip into trouble and the bank asks for more detailed information, which the debtor is reluctant to supply. The bank can threaten to withhold future loans, but to do so may jeopardize the loans already made. It can go to court to seek information, but that may be too late and will certainly be costly. The bank does not have the right of a property owner to waltz in, sit down with the treasurer, and look at anything that it pleases, which an owner may do.

Compare this to the typical response of a Japanese bank to a client in trouble: "The bank will send a director to an ailing firm. If the director succeeds in revitalizing the firm, he or she is a hero and is guaranteed a top position in the bank. If one bank pulls out its person before the company is rejuvenated, another bank will step in. If this director concludes that changes are necessary for the corporation's management practices, he or she will recommend them. The perspective as an objective third party who is not involved in daily affairs of the company lets this director perceive necessary changes better. The bank might also recommend that a supplier make certain changes that are necessary to revitalize the company . . ."[24] Often, the main bank will have guaranteed loans made to suppliers by smaller banks, so that the main bank has balanced incentives in such cases, on the one hand wanting the supplier to lower costs to the company in distress, but on the other hand not wanting the supplier to be abused. Other creditors will give way to the main bank, which is most at risk and which can in effect unilaterally slow payments to all creditors.

Bankruptcies in Japan are currently occuring at the rate of 11.93 for every 10,000 businesses per year, with 99.7 percent of all bankruptcies among small and medium firms. The rates are about 15 percent lower than in the United States. Perhaps the closer relationship between the providers and users of capital accounts for this difference.

Who Owns American Industry?

It is paradoxical that the United States, which highly prizes its system of private property rights, has unintentionally created a system in which no one owns American industry. There is in most cases no individual or institution who has both the right and the power to behave like an owner, to become intimately informed about a company and to provide guidance to its management. There is no owner who can be understanding and patient when investment over the long-run is appropriate, no owner who can be demanding and tough when the management goes astray.

In an age in which we must have large companies in order to engage effectively in research, development, and production, it is not possible for an individual or family to own most large companies. We need instead to develop institutional owners that can combine the savings of millions of citizens and act on their behalf as the owner of General Motors, RCA, and Citibank. It will not be a perfect system, just as the Japanese system is not perfect. But without some form of concentration of ownership, we cannot have effective capital markets or a proper guidance of industry.

That is not to say that we should encourage our banks to run our companies in a directive and centralized manner. That is not what happens in Japan, and it is not the practice of an M-Form organization. What is called for is a free flow of information between the providers and users of capital, and the capacity of the owners to exercise their rights over the companies they own. If banks and large companies in the United States had forty or one hundred owners instead of five thousand, then we would have better informed governance of both kinds of institutions.

The issue, of course, is not limited to the electronics industries. Every business, large and small, needs capital. Many a small business complains that its bank has never taken the time to get to know it well and thus cannot appreciate its problems or provide the proper financing. But if that same small business will switch banks in order to borrow an additional few thousand dollars or to save a loan fee, then what incentive does a bank have to take the time and trouble to get to know that customer well? If there is to be an effective, long-term relationship between the provider and user of capital, there must be some sort of bond between them, some kind of asset held hostage to both parties, assuring them that neither can escape the long reach of serial equity.

PART 2

THE M-FORM
IN ACTION
microelectronics
in Japan and
the United States

5

THE FRUITS OF COLLABORATION
the rise
of the Japanese
computer industry

What are the fruits of collaboration? We have described the process of collaboration in America's best companies, those of the M-Form. From that example we have drawn the lesson that both teamwork and individual effort can be emphasized within the same company. We have observed that much the same process that characterizes our M-Form companies also describes the business-to-business and the business-to-government relationships in Japan. We have seen that each company in Japan expends great effort and time in maintaining a confrontive dialogue with other companies. We have seen that both government and business spend time in the dialogue that is far beyond anything familiar to us in the United States. We have observed that even the banking relationship in Japan relies upon more than simple market governance and includes, in addition, both bureaucratic and clan features, thus bringing banks and their borrowers into more intimate contact with one another. What does all of this effort at teamwork produce?

One answer is that it has produced a successful automobile industry. Another answer is that it has produced a successful machine tool industry. Yet another answer is that it has produced successful motorcycle, robotic, and consumer electronics industries. Most significant of all, however, it has produced a successful microelectronics and computer industry, the industry that more than any other will be the bedrock that will determine the overall health of the economies of Japan and of the United States, of the United Kingdom, France, and Germany, of every major industrial nation, for the next several decades.

Twenty-five years ago, the Japanese were not a factor in the world computer industry. Then, as now, the United States was the world leader, but the emerging contenders were in France, Germany, Canada, and the United Kingdom. Over the intervening years, the U.S. computer industry continued to lead, developing its success largely without government guidance or assistance. In other nations, particularly in France and in the United Kingdom, however, governments took an active role in attempting to propel their new computer industries to world competitiveness. Today, although there are some distinctively strong computer companies in European nations and in Canada, U.S. companies continue to lead and the major competitors are from Japan.

Perhaps no single issue in foreign trade arouses stronger emotions than does the computer industry, whether the discussion is taking place in Silicon Valley, California, or on Silicon Island, Japan. Perhaps no single industrial issue has been subjected to more misinformation, misunderstanding, and mistrust, on both sides of both the Pacific and the Atlantic oceans. Certainly, it is critical that we understand it with some clarity, because no industry is more important to our future prosperity.

As we learn about the development of the computer industry in Japan, let us again keep a firm grip on our objective, which is to see the whole fabric of economic development. To many Western observers, this story is the most threatening of all. It is not threatening in the sense that we fear the loss of our computer industry to the Japanese. There is little danger of that. It is threatening because it defies some of our most deeply held political and economic beliefs. We believe that the U.S. computer industry has in the past and will in the future succeed largely because our market economy leaves each company alone, thus inviting the spirited competition that produces rapid technological advance. In Japan, it may appear that the successes of the computer industry have come about largely through joint research and development.

We must be careful not to perceive as black or white that which in fact is many shades of gray. It is not the case that the U.S. computer industry has grown entirely through independent and unaided entrepreneurship. Every U.S. computer company depends critically upon a large university-based education and research effort that is funded primarily by state and federal government. Every U.S. computer company owes a debt to the early breakthroughs in technology which were achieved largely through federal government purchase contracts. It is equally incorrect to view the Japanese success as one of government-sponsored or subsidized research. Although the Japanese have engaged in many more joint research efforts than have companies of other nations, the vast majority of the research and development as well as all of the product design and manufacturing has been done by each company working entirely on its own.

That is not to say that the United States and Japan are no different when it comes to their computer industries. Indeed, the chief reason to study the Japanese computer industry is to learn more about just how it has profited from a combination of teamwork with competition. As we see these striking examples, however, we would do well to remember that although it is different from what we do in the West, it is not altogether different, not so different that we cannot profit from it. If we can learn how to achieve more teamwork not just in the computer industry but also in the textile, garment, steel, automobile, and housing industries, we can guarantee our future prosperity. Let us not miss the forest for the trees. Let us attempt to understand, through this one example, how to achieve that combination of teamwork and of competition that is necessary across our nation.

The Birth of Japan's Computer Industry

Japan, Inc. is perhaps best known and most feared for its successes in developing a computer industry that came from nowhere to rival the largest firms in the United States. In the 1960s, IBM held 70 percent of the market for large-scale computers (mainframes) in Japan. By 1982, the Japanese industry had developed to the point that IBM's share had declined to about 40 percent and Fujitsu, a Japanese company, sold $2.1 billion of all kinds of computer equipment in Japan to IBM's $1.9 billion.[1] By 1978, there were thirty-two

Japanese manufacturers of business computers, with more entering each month.[2] Although it is widely agreed, even among the Japanese, that their computer technology has been a "me too" copy of the industry leader, IBM, there are signs that the Japanese are now striking out on their own and may move ahead of the United States industry in some respects.

In their 1983 book, Feigenbaum and McCorduck describe Japanese plans for the fifth generation: "In October 1981, when Japan first let the world at large know about its plans for the Fifth Generation of computers, the Japanese government announced that over the next decade it planned to spend seed money of about $450 million (participating industries are expected to match, or perhaps double that amount) and would eventually involve several hundred top scientists in this project. Their goal is to develop computers for the 1990s and beyond—intelligent computers that will be able to converse with humans in natural language and understand speech and pictures. These will be computers that can learn, associate, make inferences, make decisions, and otherwise behave in ways we have always considered the exclusive province of human reason."[3]

If in fact these levels of research and development investment are reached, this project will consume $450 million of public funds and $900 million of company funds, a total of $135 million per year for ten years on a single, albeit many-faceted, research project. To appreciate the scale of this commitment, consider that in 1982, IBM reported a research budget of $2.1 billion and Xerox a research budget of $565 million, Hewlett-Packard $424 million, Westinghouse $230 million, and Apple $38 million.

How has the Japanese industry come so far so fast? It has been argued that the Japanese have succeeded by keeping out U.S. computers through tariff and nontariff barriers. There is no question that U.S. makers have been treated unfairly, but that protectionism does not explain why the Japanese have succeeded at developing their own industry while other countries such as the United Kingdom and France have failed. It has been argued that the Japanese have succeeded by copying IBM. But that explanation does not satisfy, because other computer makers in the United States have failed at that same strategy.

To understand the Japanese achievement in the computer industry, it is important to look at the five generations of computers.

They can be summarized as follows:

First Generation:	Electronic Vacuum-Tube Computers
Second Generation:	Transistorized Computers
Third Generation:	Integrated Circuit Computers
Fourth Generation:	Very Large-Scale Integrated Computers (VLSI)
Fifth Generation:	Knowledge Information Processing Systems (KIPS)

The world computer industry began in the United States with the introduction of Mark I, a first generation computer developed by Harvard University and IBM. The first commercial computer, ENIAC, (which used 18,000 vacuum tubes) was produced by Sperry Rand in 1946. The Japanese industry began approximately ten years later, with a relay system machine produced by the Agency of Industrial Science and Technology (AIST), followed by a vacuum tube machine produced by University of Tokyo scientists in 1953. However, these machines were experimental only and never became available for sale. In 1954, the first U.S. computers were exported to Japan. At the time, there were five major Japanese companies manufacturing sophisticated electronic products: NEC, Fujitsu, Hitachi, Matsushita, and Toshiba. The five companies approached MITI and asked for support in accelerating the development of the domestic computer industry. MITI responded by initiating a dialogue. MITI organized the Research Committee on the Computer in 1955, bringing together MITI officials, prospective manufacturers, the government-owned telephone company NTT, and university scientists. This private-public discussion group offered a number of suggestions, and its deliberations led to a flexible government response, which recognized the need to arrange special conditions if this new industry were to develop.

These special conditions were formalized in a new 1957 law, "The Law Concerning Temporary Measures for the Promotion of the Electronics Industry." The law contained several provisions which provided for a cooperative form of competition, and it was to remain in force for only seven years, although it was subsequently renewed for another seven years. The key provisions: first, an Electronics Industries Section was created within the MITI bureaucracy to focus specifically on the new industry; second, a new Electronic Industry

Deliberation Council (later renamed Electronic and Machinery Industries Council to accommodate the electronics-machinery interface found in robotics) was created alongside the other MITI discussion councils. Like the others, this discussion council included about forty industry representatives, bankers, university scholars, and electronics trade association heads. Third, the act provided for research and development subsidies and loans to the industry. Fourth, the act gave MITI the authority to temporarily exempt any portion of the industry from the Anti-Monopoly Law, an exemption that has never been used, but which clearly signaled to the industry an atmosphere of collaboration.[4] Thus, the law created governmental units that could listen to and be influenced by the industry, provide financial assistance, and suspend antitrust enforcement.

Japan Enters the Second Generation

Meanwhile, the Japanese computer industry had begun to develop collaborative efforts on its own. A joint transistor project funded by AIST was completed in 1957 (the transistor had been invented at the Bell Labs in 1947), and in that year two Japanese-produced computers were installed. By 1959, computers had been introduced by NEC, Fujitsu, Hitachi, Toshiba, and Oki. By 1961, Matsushita and Mitsubishi were in the market. During this period (1957–1961), the total government subsidies to the industry amounted to less than $1 million.[5] However, during this period a consensus was reached among all parties that future emphasis would shift away from the television and transistor radio industries to the new computer industry. The consumer-electronics companies were not happy about this change, but they accepted it.[6]

During the early 1960s, several U.S. companies were selling their computers in Japan: IBM, Sperry-Univac, NCR, Burroughs, and Control Data Corporation.[7] Twenty-thousand computers were in place worldwide, 14,000 of them IBM. Thirteen Japanese companies were preparing to compete with them. Two of the American companies, IBM and Sperry Univac, wanted to establish manufacturing subsidiaries in Japan, which the Japanese industry did not want. The Japanese government refused entry, enforcing their refusal under the Foreign Investment Law of 1951, which required government authorization (no longer in force) for foreigners to bring capital into Japan.[8] IBM circumvented this restriction by gathering surplus yen funds from other companies in order to establish IBM Japan, a wholly-owned subsidiary of IBM, and went into production. MITI retaliated by refusing to allow IBM to import either the machinery needed to build computers or computers for sale. Finally, a truce was reached with the agreement that IBM would make available some of its patents in exchange for royalty payments, and the company was to be limited in the kinds of computer equipment that it could import for sale in Japan.[9] Other electronics and computer makers were allowed to begin manufacturing in Japan, so long as they did so through a joint venture, at least 51 percent of which was owned by Japanese. During the 1960s, Hitachi formed licensing agreements with RCA, Mitsubishi with TRW and Xerox, NEC with Honeywell, Oki with Univac, and Toshiba with General Electric.[10]

Financing
the Computer Industry: JECC

In addition to needing a developing computer technology, the Japanese makers faced a major challenge in locating financing. In 1961, there were a total of 170 computer systems installed in Japan. Of these, 79 were Japanese and 91 were imported. However, of the 8 large computers installed, all were imports. The Japanese were at the time competitive only at the low end of the industry.[11] This dominance of the imports in the important big computers was due mostly to the superior quality of the U.S. imports, but it had also to do with the practice of U.S. companies to lease rather than sell the big machines. In 1961, 71 percent of the imported machines were leased by customers rather than being bought outright, whereas 28 percent of the Japanese machines were leased.[12] Customers typically preferred to lease large mainframes for two reasons: first, a large mainframe might require a cash outlay of $20 million or more if purchased but a payment of only one-fiftieth of the purchase price each month if leased; second, new computers were being developed so rapidly that once purchased, a machine might soon be obsolete. In the United States, the computer industry was already fifteen years old, and the practice of leasing was well established. The computer companies had sufficient capital to be able to incur the expense of building a machine, leasing it, and receiving payment little by little over several years. In Japan, the companies could not afford to stretch payments out over several years.

In the United States, banks and other lenders had enough experience with financing the leasing of computers to be willing to make a loan either to a maker or a user, taking the computer as collateral, and thus financing the industry. In Japan, the computer industry was so new that no bank had enough experience to be able to make such a loan. A Japanese bank did not know whether a mainframe would hold its value for five months or five years, and thus it was too risky for them to make a loan of five or six years with the computer as collateral. In a sense, the private capital markets in Japan failed. The risk in this new industry was so great that no bank could prudently put up the money necessary to support the industry. On the other hand, it had become evident in the discussion councils between business and government that this new industry was potentially so large and so important to the future of the Japanese economy that it must be developed. In a sense, the Japanese public would be the future beneficiary if the computer industry developed successfully, producing jobs on a massive new scale, and thus it made sense that the public should bear part of the financial risk in the start-up of this new industry. The new industry would be a major social endowment from which many segments of the economy would benefit.

It was with this logic that the seven Japanese computer makers approached MITI for assistance in arranging financing so that Japanese-made computers could be leased to customers.[13] After discussion between the several industry groups, MITI, and the Ministry of Finance, all parties agreed to the formation of the Japan Electronic Computers Corporation, or JECC. JECC was a computer-leasing corporation owned by the seven Japanese makers, who provided one-half of the initial capital, with the other half provided in the form of a loan at below-market rates from a government bank, the Japan Development Bank.[14] The companies were able to raise additional money through loans from banks, whose risk was greatly reduced by this explicit government support of the industry.[15] A company would build a computer, set a monthly lease fee, and then sell the computer to JECC for 90 percent of the full retail price. JECC would then turn around and lease the machine to the end user, who would make lease payments to JECC. If the user returned the machine, then the maker had to take it back and refund a pro-rata sum to JECC. Thus JECC accepted part of the risk, with the companies taking part of the risk.

In the early years, JECC accounted for nearly 100 percent of all computer leasing by Japanese makers in Japan, thus providing a source of capital without which the industry could not have begun. However, JECC was not an entirely harmonious arrangement of private firms enjoying a government handout. Over its first ten years, JECC had an annual compound growth rate of 65 percent. With such growth, the member companies were often required to contribute additional capital, with each of the seven companies contributing an equal amount. However, some companies were making far more use of JECC than others, thus causing the smaller participants to complain that they were in effect subsidizing the bigger users of JECC, who were their direct competitors. These smaller users complained to MITI, which refused to intervene. As in any M-Form, the central authority (MITI) was limited to the role of helping the firms reach a consensus if possible. Sometimes a consensus cannot be found. The friction became so great that Matsushita, one of the smaller users of JECC, finally quit the cooperative. In 1965, the member companies agreed to adjust capital contributions to correspond to market shares in JECC.[16] The Japan Development Bank later on refused additional subsidized loans, and thus JECC also turned to Japanese and foreign commercial banks, trust banks, and life insurance companies for loans.[17] In 1969, in order to conserve its limited funds, JECC discontinued leasing of the smallest computers, which accounted then for 20 percent of its volume and which could most easily be financed by the companies on their own.

JECC was, strictly speaking, a private corporation requiring no government approval nor special legislation to get started. It was not initiated by the government, nor was it imposed upon the industry by MITI. Instead, it was an entirely private effort, initiated by the industry in an uncomfortable but necessary act of temporary cooperation. On the other hand, JECC was successful only because the whole network of governmental, business, and other groups involved in the industry associations, discussions councils, and political bodies agreed to support it.[18] The successful application for an initial loan from the Japan Development Bank relied upon the agreement of technical and financial experts within MITI and the Ministry of Finance. JECC was staffed by many former MITI officials, thus assuring the public that the consortium would not stray far from its permissible boundaries. Finally, steps were taken to ensure that companies would not continue forever to rely on government subsidy. JECC was constructed so that the stockholding companies could not receive any dividend payments. Thus, as the Japanese industry developed, JECC began to earn profits that the companies could not reclaim as long as JECC existed thus creating the desired incentive for the member companies to leave JECC and rely on private financing as soon as possible.[19]

IBM Ushers in the Third Generation: System 360

Despite its stresses and strains, JECC was succeeding nicely. Then in 1964, IBM introduced the System 360, the first of the third generation, integrated-circuit computers. The 360 was so superior to anything else on the market that it forced both U.S. and Japanese companies out, including Matsushita, RCA, Xerox, and ultimately General Electric. In Japan, customers began returning their mainframes to JECC in large numbers. In 1966, JECC took back 25 percent of its leased computers, with another 30 percent returned in 1967. IBM was shipping nearly 1,000 System 360 computers per month worldwide. The Japanese industry was in chaos, and it appeared that a new industry would be stillborn. Also in 1964, General Electric acquired the largest European computer maker, Machines Bull of France. According to a U.S. Department of Commerce report (Kaplan, 1972, p. 90), these two major events caused the Japanese to realize that no domestic computer industry could survive except at a very large scale. The superstition of atomistic R & D was gone. IBM had relied upon the U.S. government as a steady customer to allow it to undertake extensive R & D and the Japanese saw that they too needed some form of public-private teamwork in order to build their new industry.

The Japanese government mobilized assistance in several ways. MITI proposed to the Ministry of Finance a special measure to allow companies a deduction amounting to 10 percent of each company's sales to JECC, in order to compensate for the massive losses from the repurchase of machines that the companies had to buy back from JECC according to the original agreement.[20] This provision was enacted in 1968. In 1969, the deduction was increased to 15 percent and later to 20 percent. More recently, the deduction has again been reduced.[21] More important but less known was the support of LASDEC, the Local Authorities System Development Corporation, part of the Ministry of Local Automony. LASDEC coordinates the computer needs of the 3,000 cities, towns, and villages of Japan, more than 90 percent of which use computers for one purpose or another. LASDEC adopted the practice of leasing its computers exclusively through JECC, thus shutting IBM out of a major customer source and providing a use for the obsolete Japanese-made equipment.[22]

At this point in the history of the Japanese computer industry, it was not at all clear that a viable domestic industry would evolve. The seven Japanese makers had been reduced to six, all of whom were essentially copying IBM. The leasing problem had been solved through an intricate form of public-private cooperation, but then IBM had once again taken the industry by surprise with yet another superior product. The Japanese had responded with protectionist measures that closed IBM out of several markets, but no one could have thought that protectionism alone would carry the industry for long.

In a nutshell, the problem was this: in the Japan of the 1960s, there were not more than a few hundred scientists capable of working at the forefront of third-generation computer technology, and these were distributed among forty to fifty companies, with the result that no one company was at "critical mass" with respect to scientific ability. Tilton (1972) has compiled a list of the thirteen major semiconductor developments in the world during the period 1951, when Western Electric produced the point-contact transistor, until 1963, when IBM produced the Gunn diode. Of these thirteen developments, twelve came from U.S. industry, with only one, the tunnel diode, pioneered in Japan (by Sony in 1957).[23]

The M-Form Reacts: JEIDA

To solve this problem, the industry turned to its primary private association, the Japan Electronic Industry Development Association, or JEIDA. JEIDA had been founded in 1958 by the major Japanese electronics companies, for the purpose of advancing research in the industry. The 1981–1982 *Guide to JEIDA* lists twenty-eight subcommittees on subjects such as "Technology of Software," "Research on Future Office Systems," and "Research for Medical Electronic Equipment Systems." The 26 directors include the presidents of Mitsubishi Electric, Toshiba, NEC, Hitachi, Fujitsu, Yokogawa Electric, Sony, Sharp, TDK, Yamatake Honeywell, Matsushita, and other industry leaders. The director was a former official of MITI. Like other specialized associations within electronics, JEIDA coordinates closely with the Electronics Industries Association of Japan, EIAJ. The EIAJ is a slightly older association which deals not only with computers but with all electronics manufacturing. The EIAJ counts 600 corporate members, organized into 200 subcommittees on various specific topics. If an issue affects many sectors of the electronics industries, it will be taken up by the EIAJ. On more narrowly focused issues, the specialized associations such as JEIDA will take the lead, coordinating with the EIAJ.

Following the shock of the introduction of the IBM 360 mainframe in 1964, JEIDA became extremely active. Its members, most of whom were also members of the MITI Electronics Industry Deliberation Committee, precipitated debate within government and the public. In 1966, the Electronics Industry Deliberation Council of MITI issued a report expressing consensus among all parties that the computer industry in Japan should be developed, that all efforts should be made to help it succeed, and that it could indeed be successful.

The M-Form Reacts: AIST

Soon after the creation of JEIDA in 1958, the Japanese Diet had passed a new law, the Mining and Manufacturing Technology Research Associations Law of 1961. This law allows any three or more companies to apply for certification as a research association.[24] A similar law seemed likely to be enacted in the United States by 1984. Certification permitted the members of the research association tax benefits regarding rapid depreciation of tools, equipment, and other materials needed for the research, conferred upon the association an aura of legitimacy, which enhanced the likelihood of securing future government research grants and contracts, and provided a nonofficial but nonetheless effective antitrust immunity. Certification was the province of the Agency of Industrial Science and Technology (AIST), an arm of MITI formed by the Allied Occupation Forces in 1948. When a research association is approved by AIST, it is still possible for an excluded company to bring a private antitrust suit against the association or for the Japanese Fair Trade Commission (JFTC) to bring a criminal antitrust suit. It is the fear of such private and public suits that has deterred many U.S. companies from engaging in just this kind of joint research activity. In Japan, however, the interpretation has so far been made by the JFTC that the 1961 Research Associations Law, by its nature, closes no one out from participation (no Japanese company, that is). In addition, although no bureacratic rule or law specifies who may have access to patents produced by such associations, it has been customary for MITI to apply pressure on research associations to make all of their patents available to any domestic firm at a reasonable royalty. For these reasons, the approximately sixty associations that have been formed since 1961 have enjoyed tax benefits and no antitrust suits.[25]

In 1968, the Keidanren created a Committee on Data Processing, in which the computer makers could explain their needs to other industries, hear their questions and criticisms, and solicit the support of other industrial groups. At the same time, 160 legislators of the majority Liberal Democratic Party established the Dietmen's Federation for Promotion of the Information Industry, to carry out dialogue with the new Keidanren group.[26] Meanwhile, the U.S. Department of Justice opened a massive antitrust case against IBM on January 17, 1969, and kept at it until January of 1982, when it was dropped as being "without merit." For thirteen years, IBM was competing with one hand tied behind its back.

We must also note here the great advantage of the U.S. system of free enterprise, a system that gave birth to a uniquely capable company, IBM, that singlehandedly not only competed against but consistently outperformed the combined efforts of six Japanese companies supported by their government. Finally, one is forced to ask whether a closer form of business-government cooperation and cooperation between competitors would help or hurt an IBM. If IBM had known that its efforts, the fruits of its research and development, were to be shared with a consortium consisting of General Electric,

DEC, Honeywell, Burroughs, and NCR, would its efforts have been as strenuous and its results as great? The Japanese claim has always been that its companies collaborate only on basic research and then compete ferociously against one another on product development, manufacturing, sales, and service, thus serving the customer well. One might argue that the U.S. government does much the same, providing vast tax benefits and outright grants to U.S. universities, which work closely with all computer companies to develop new research, following which the companies compete on product development and the later stages of work. We should also note the important role of the U.S. government as a major customer of IBM in its early days. The question is an important one, and the answer is not clear. Up until now, however, we have taken it for granted as an article of faith that no cooperation should be permitted, that it is best in the long run if we keep companies apart from one another and away from government collaboration. The history of the computer industry in both the United States and in Japan should at the very least cause us to reexamine that belief.

The Structure of the Japanese Computer Industry in 1970—Survival Is the Issue

By 1970, it was clear that the Japanese computer industry was in trouble, despite the several efforts described above. The special seven-year law enacted to help the industry that was passed in 1957 and renewed in 1964 was due to expire in 1971, and the time was ripe for new legislative action. The concern of the government was that foreign companies, particularly U.S. companies, would take over the Japanese computer industry. The concern had arisen for good reason. During the 1960s most of the Japanese makers had concluded technical licensing agreements with U.S. firms: Hitachi with RCA (1961), Mitsubishi with TRW (1962) and with Xerox (1969), NEC with Honeywell (1962), Oki with Remington-Univac (1963) and with Remington Rand (1969), and Toshiba with GE (1964). Only Fujitsu, the sole computer specialist among Japanese makers, had no foreign license agreements.[27] More threatening to the Japanese had been the purchase of stock in Japanese makers by large foreign firms. By 1970, ITT owned 12 percent of NEC, GE had 10 percent of Toshiba, Westinghouse held 4 percent of Mitsubishi, Sperry Rand had 49 percent of its joint venture in Oki, Phillips owned 30 percent of Matsushita, Raytheon 33 percent of New Japan Radio Company, International Rectifier 33 percent of International Rectifier of Japan, Texas Instruments 50 percent of a joint venture with Sony, while NCR held 70 percent of NCR Japan and IBM held 100 percent of IBM Japan.[28] Other foreign computer companies were active in Japan but did not have manufacturing there.

By 1970, it was also apparent that foreign government pressures would force a change in Japanese laws restricting the purchase of Japanese companies by foreigners. The Japanese government feared that as soon as liberalization occurred (it began on February 24, 1975),[29] foreigners would rush in to take over the new industry for good. Thus the new law had the purpose of quickly forcing the existing Japanese makers to divide the segments of the computer industry among them, so that each company could become the efficient producer of a narrow range of equipment.

In 1971, MITI urged the companies to form a four-group structure as follows: (1) Fujitsu, (2) Hitachi, (3) NEC-Toshiba, and (4) Oki-Univac-Mitsubishi.[30] However, the companies refused to go along with the bureaucrat's plan. The companies each felt ready to compete with foreign makers. Their only desire was for additional government subsidies to underwrite their research and development. In essence the position of the companies was, "Just give us the money and leave us alone. We know what to do and you don't." The government response, however, was approximately, "Not so fast. It's not clear that you know what to do. Show us a plan that will convince us." JEIDA became the focal point of discussion. It is important to note that JEIDA was a critical institution, because it was owned and run by its member companies but had as a director a former MITI official. Thus the government felt that discussions within JEIDA would be responsible, the companies were able to take the initiative, and the public was reassured that the discussions would not involve illegal price-fixing or other inappropriate behavior because they would occur under the watchful eye of a former government official whose future influence depended on his present trustworthiness. The JEIDA director, clearly, was on the spot to be impartial.

Up through 1970, the U.S. Department of Commerce report (Kaplan, 1972) estimates that the total government support of the industry through loans, subsidies, and tax savings amounted to less than $25 million.[31] With the introduction of the IBM 370 series (in 1970), it became clearer than ever that joint research and development was the only way, and that government investment in the new industry was essential.

The Japanese Makers Form Three Groups to Match the IBM System 370

By the end of 1971, the Japanese makers had agreed to form three groups for the purpose of engaging in joint research and development. While MITI hoped that each group would concentrate on a different sector of the market, the firms had no intention of doing so, each intending to compete with the other five across the board. The groups:

1. Fujitsu with Hitachi (40 percent of the market)
2. NEC with Toshiba (40 percent of the market)
3. Oki with Mitsubishi (20 percent of the market)[32]

Each group received a total of approximately $250 million in interest-free loans for research and development over the period 1972–1976.[33] The pairings were designed to promote ease of technical integration.[34] The objective was to produce a computer system competitive with the IBM System 370, an upgraded version of the previous System 360. By 1976, Oki-Mitsubishi had produced its COSMOS series, NEC-Toshiba the ACOS series, but Fujitsu and Hitachi were unable to overcome their competitiveness toward one another and never jointly produced their intended M series.[35] Instead Fujitsu independently brought out its M–180–2, and Hitachi fought back with its M–162 and M–200. However, the other two pairings also engendered bitter struggles between old competitors who now had to cooperate with one another. As with the previous joint efforts, such as FONTAC, DIPS, PIPS, and the supercomputer, this joint activity had the result of moving the Japanese industry ahead in the development of semiconductor devices. IBM remained the world leader by perhaps a margin of six or seven years, but back in the early 1960s, the lead had been twelve or fifteen years.

In these joint projects, the three teams did not form joint laboratories. Instead, the scientific work was done separately by each company in its own laboratories. Then, through discussion groups and meetings, the work was disseminated to the other partner. Ultimately, the results were fed back to the research association, the governing body representing all six companies. The idea was that the joint work was to be confined to basic research, which each company then had to develop into actual products, with the result that the basic work would be available and beneficial to the entire industry. Of course, each company attempted to keep private the important portions of its research, and much of it was not revealed to the research association.

By 1975, NEC and Toshiba had announced ten types of their ACOS 77 system, Mitsubishi and Oki had six types of the COSMOS, and Fujitsu and Hitachi had announced six types of the M series.[36] All of these were basically equivalent to the IBM 370. In March 1977, IBM responded with price cuts of 30 percent on the 370 system and 35 percent on main storage, while at the same time announcing the new 303X series.[37] At this point, the largest Japanese machines were competitive with the largest IBM machines, but the IBM machines had the price advantage. Amidst this intense competition, it seemed that the Japanese were closing the gap.

The Japanese continued to rely on JECC for financing of computer leases. The Japan Development Bank had loaned $112 million to JECC in fiscal 1974, $155 million in 1975, $158 million in 1976, and $203 million in 1977. The total of loans to JECC from 1971–1980 was $2.4 billion. Most of the benefit was to Fujitsu, which accounted for 43 percent of JECC leases while NEC accounted for 30 percent, Toshiba 13 percent, with Oki and Hitachi at about 6 percent each and Mitsubishi at 2 percent.[38] Fujitsu and NEC proposed that the six JECC members increase the cooperative's capital by $18 million in 1977, but the other four, quite understandably, refused.

Forming the VLSI Research Association: The Fourth Generation

The race was on to develop the fourth generation computer. One of its key components would be the memory unit, which was to be the 64K RAM, a large step ahead of the 16K RAM then in use. The competition was all the more intense following the liberalization measures that had just been enacted. At the end of 1975, quotas on the import of computers and peripherals were eliminated and capital investment by foreigners for computer manufacturing was liberalized. In 1976, controls were lifted on the import of foreign software into Japan and on the investment by foreigners in the software industry. The Japanese makers hoped that they were strong enough to survive this increased competition, but it was not yet clear that they could.

On July 15, 1975, all parties agreed to the formation of a new joint research and development venture that was to become the most celebrated of all such attempts in the Japanese computer industry. Beginning in 1976, the VLSI (Very Large Scale Integrated Circuit) Research Association was formed under the 1961 Mining and Manufacturing Technology Research Associations Law. The association began with capital contributed by the five companies: NEC, Toshiba, Hitachi, Mitsubishi, and Fujitsu. These five were the owners of the association. In addition, NTIS, which was owned by NEC and Toshiba, cooperated by sending researchers, as did CDL, which was owned by Hitachi, Mitsubishi, and Fujitsu. The other participants included scientists from the Electro Technical Laboratory of AIST, and some cooperation from the government telephone company, NTT. The idea was that all parties except for NTT would collaborate in sending scientists to a joint research laboratory, which would focus on basic research. These results would then be passed to the two group laboratories, NTIS and CDL, each of which would competitively attempt to develop the basic research into usable technology. Finally, this technology would pass to the five computer makers, who would go all-out in a computer war against one another and against the foreign competition.

In its brief outline, the VLSI Research Association sounds again like Japan, Inc. marshalling its forces to beat the world. It sounds like the kind of cozy cooperation between competitors that can be achieved only in a unique society of homogeneous businesspeople who place loyalty to country above commercial self-interest. It sounds like an attractive idea for developing an industry, but it doesn't sound as though it could succeed in the adversarial, skeptical, individualistic West. Let us examine this important example more closely.

Building Consensus for the VLSI Research Association: The First Steps

In early 1975, JEIDA organized a small discussion group to consider the problems of very large scale integration of semiconductor devices. By that time, it was clear to all concerned that the key to successful competition against IBM lay in the development of this technology. All six of the computer firms, including Oki, were hard at work on figuring out how to make a 64K RAM, as was NTT, the telephone company, and the Electro Technical Laboratory of AIST.

The issue was summarized by the JEIDA staff in a January 13, 1983 interview: "The background of the VLSI project is that Japan was behind the United States and wanted to catch up. Discussions took place in committees and subcommittees (of JEIDA), to which department heads of individual companies belonged as members. There were many suggestions, and one of them was to have a VLSI project. . . . JEIDA was at the center. There were discussions with MITI. . . . Most relations were with the Industrial Structure Council. It has an Information Industry Committee that takes positions about the strategic direction of the information industries in five years and which prepares reports on certain topics. This committee decided that VLSI was a good project."

Professor Shoji Tanaka of the University of Tokyo, a member of the JEIDA discussion group, suggested that the various parties collaborate on VLSI research. The companies resisted, preferring subsidies to each company without government interference or the requirement of collaboration.[39] In particular, the experiences of the recent past in developing ACOS, COSMOS, and the M series had been bruising, and the companies had no desire to be brought again into close collaboration. Indeed, some of those involved in the discussions had vowed never again to collaborate with certain competitors. On the other hand, it was apparent that the funding for VLSI research would have to be on a scale much larger than that of any previous such project, and the government was unwilling to make direct subsidies to companies perceived by the Japanese public as large and rich. The MITI officials, supported by NTT, which was a major customer of all six of the computer companies, insisted that a large subsidy must take place through a joint laboratory, if for no other reason than to give the appearance of synergy, thus justifying in the public's mind the large cash outlay. In addition, there were some critical areas of research in which no single company had enough scientists to be able to move ahead quickly enough to keep up with IBM.

In the end, the JEIDA discussion group members agreed to the formation of a joint laboratory, in a series of talks led by Dr. Yasuo Tarui, of the government's Electro Technical Laboratory. The members of JEIDA had meanwhile been carrying out simultaneous discussions with the Committee on Data Processing of the Keidanren in order to secure the support of other industry groups, and with the Dietmen's Federation for the Promotion of the Information Industry, in order to achieve political support. Each company also carried out extensive talks with members of the MITI staff, expressing its desires and concerns.[40]

There were several important disagreements that had to be resolved. The Dietmen's Federation felt that, "To develop Japan's computer industry, what is needed is a unification of firms, not division into five companies." The companies, on the other hand, desired no collaboration at all. The compromise was a design in which some of the research would be done at CDL, some at NTIS, and some in a joint research facility. Between MITI and the companies, there was disagreement over whether the research should focus on the development of a production-volume 64K RAM, which the companies favored, or on more basic research that would lead also to the 256K and the 1,000K RAM of the future. This disagreement was further complicated by an insistence by each company that it would not give up its hard-won know-how, or expertise at product design and manufacturing, to any competitor. The companies wanted direct subsidies without collaboration, so that each could work on the 64K RAM, an immediate problem, without the danger of losing its know-how to competitors. MITI, backed by Dr. Tarui, favored basic research with collaboration. In the end, direct subsidies were understood by all to be politically impossible, and once collaboration had been accepted, no company wanted the research focused on the 64K RAM only, because to do so would inevitably endanger individual expertise.

Finally, there were the issues of NTT and of Oki. NTT possessed the most advanced VLSI laboratories at the time and felt that it had little to gain by joining the association. The companies could not pressure NTT into joining, since it was a major customer for all six.

Oki, on the other hand, wanted to remain in the association, since it had potentially a great deal to gain. As one Fujitsu manager commented, "Of course, to some extent each firm wanted to get the most technology while contributing as little as possible to the project. . . ."[41] The other five companies wanted to exclude Oki, which they felt had little to contribute, and so Oki was left out. (According to a *Fortune* Magazine story of August 8, 1983, Oki became the first Japanese company to test the 256K chip. The company did it on its own.)

After a year of discussion, the framework was set. On July 15, 1975, official authorization was granted to the VLSI Research Association, in December its budget was set by the Ministry of Finance, and on March 30, 1976, the new organization set up quarters temporarily on the twenty-ninth floor of the Kasumigaseki Building, in the heart of downtown Tokyo. The small initial staff included Masato Nebashi as executive director, a former MITI senior official, and Dr. Yasuo Tarui, who came from the Electro Technical Laboratory. They were joined by two other former scientists from ETL, and work began.

Setting Up the Joint VLSI Laboratory—An Exercise in Constraining Self-Interest

The first problem was the recruitment of 100 scientists from the five companies plus the ETL. Everyone feared that some companies might send lower-quality or inexperienced scientists, thus attempting to shirk their responsibility. If one company did so, then all the others would retaliate in like manner, and the project would be doomed before it began. In order to deal with this problem, Dr. Tarui, who was director of the joint laboratory and the top scientist, simply announced that he would personally interview each scientist who was sent to the joint lab. He did not imply that he had the right to choose nor that he might refuse anyone; he simply let it be known that he would be familiar personally with the qualifications of each and every scientist. In the context of the many overlapping joint efforts between companies, the simple knowledge that Dr. Tarui would serve as a memory of who had sent its best and who had not, was sufficient to deter any thoughts of sending unqualified scientists.[42]

Having acquired 100 scientists, Mr. Nebashi now needed a place in which they could work. Each of the two groups of companies, the NTIS group and the CDL group, proposed its own laboratory site. The debate on this issue apparently was fierce, with neither side willing to give in. Finally, faced with an impasse, the companies turned to JEIDA, asking the director of their association to make a decision, by which all promised to abide. The director of JEIDA performed some analysis, certainly engaged in a good deal of corporate politics, and selected the then-vacant Kawasaki laboratory owned by NEC. NEC, Toshiba, and Fujitsu all had their own laboratories or factories in Kawasaki, so that both the NTIS and CDL groups were close by, although the location was slightly more convenient for the NTIS group.

The next issue had to do with the formal reporting structure of the joint laboratory. At the top were the executive director, Mr. Nebashi, and the laboratory director, Dr. Tarui. As for the companies, there were several layers of committees. The topmost was the executive committee, which included the presidents of all five companies, and which met two or three times each year.[43] At the next level was a council, consisting of vice-presidents or executive directors from each company. At the lowest level were two committees, the Technology Committee and the Operations Committee, each consisting of division general managers (just below the level of vice-president) from each of the companies. The Technology and Operations committees worked closely with the laboratory scientists, and their chairmanship became the subject of heated debate. As Nebashi described the situation, "Because of the respective goals and strategies of the five companies, the debate between the association members was fierce, and the decision a difficult one. . . . In the end, a former bureaucrat, myself, was appointed as chairman of both committees, and I fulfilled those responsibilities for four years [the entire life of the joint laboratory project]. That was how strong the concerns about protecting corporate interests were."[44]

The research topics were divided by the committees into six subjects: 1) micromanufacturing technology; 2) crystal technology; 3) design technology; 4) process technology; 5) test evaluation technology; and 6) device technology. Subjects 4, 5, and 6 involved both basic research and product development. The basic research issues were to take place in the joint lab, with the development researched separately by NTIS and CDL, and final product development in all cases to be done by each company on its own. Subjects 1, 2, and 3 involved basic research only and thus were done entirely in the joint lab.

The division of the laboratory into six projects conveniently allowed for the appointment of six department heads, one from each of the five companies, and one from the Electro Technical Lab. The lab itself consisted of one large room, which was partitioned into six separate rooms. At first, there was little cooperation between scientists, despite the fact that scientists from each company shared each room. During the first year, the scientists tended to spend at least some time with their colleagues back at their home company laboratory, and there was little communication between the six lab projects. Once or twice a month, meetings were held to promote communication between the lab sections. Twenty scientists of the NTIS group in the joint lab and twenty from the CDL group were invited. A group of researchers would present their work, followed by discussion. It was a terribly formal means of communication, but necessary due to the lack of trust between the companies.

The ownership of patents was another major point of contention. Over a series of ten meetings, the patent ownership rights were finally settled in 1980, after the project had ended and the joint lab had been disbanded. Indeed, it is remarkable that the companies embarked on the joint research without having clear, prearranged rules governing the ownership of patents. The problem was not as critical as it might have been, however, because the project began with the agreement that all parties would have equal use rights to any patents, and it was the right to use the patents that mattered most, with ownership being as much a point of pride as anything else. In general, any patent that the government scientists developed alone was held by the government, the few government business patents were owned jointly by the research association and by the government, and any patent on which government scientists had not worked was held by the research association.

One final problem lay in the motivation of the scientists. First, performance evaluations were conducted by the management of the joint laboratory, but were turned over to each scientist's company, which made final decisions on pay. Each scientist remained on the payroll of his or her company, and most were rotated out of the laboratory after two years, in keeping with the standard corporate practice of job rotation. Finally, Nebashi notes, "In the mind of the transferee, the anxiety that 'I might be forgotten by the parent company' becomes a problem. Thinking that the best way to dissolve this kind of fear would be to retain close contact with the parent company, we held all of the meetings for the executive committee, council, committees, and committee sections at the lab's Kawasaki location. I think it lent special emotional support to a researcher when, after a conference, the directors and the president of his company took a tour of the lab."[45]

Despite these efforts at teambuilding, the walls between companies and between lab sections remained thick. Nebashi finally resorted to "whiskey operations," taking small groups of scientists out for drinks in the evening, then defining and solving the problem areas that had been revealed the night before. After three years of work, the walls began to come down. By then, each section had made enough progress that it had important results to share with the others, and trust between companies had grown to the point where some openness was in order. Conversations between sections were formally held each Saturday, and in the evenings, conversations would go on late into the night.

Success: 500 Patents and a Healthy Computer Industry

The VLSI Research Association was conceived as a four-year project, and it was completed on schedule in 1979. The joint laboratory was dissolved, and the scientists returned home to their companies. Nebashi, the executive director, took a position as an executive at, of all places, IBM Japan, and Dr. Tarui, the chief scientist, took a post as a professor at Tokyo University of Agriculture and Technology. The project had consumed a total of approximately $308 million between CDL, NTIS, and the joint laboratory. Of this sum, $132 million was a government subsidy in a form of loans, with the remaining funds provided by the five companies. The government loan funds call for repayment beginning in 1983, after a postponement of three years. Repayment is made according to a schedule specifying that profits from computers using the lab's output must be shared with the government for five years, from 1983 to 1988. Typically, however, the five-year period is used for product development, so that products are not sold in large numbers until after the five years are up, and repayment is usually a small fraction of the loan.

The project applied for a total of 1,000 patents, and former members estimate that from those applications, ultimately 300 to 500 patents will be approved. Of those applications, 59 percent represent the work of an independent inventor, 25 percent were made by several inventors from the same company, and 16 percent were made by inventors from several companies or the Electro Technical Laboratory. Whether the project yielded truly significant joint scientific achievements is not clear. Many observers agree that for several reasons, the project was a success. First, the timing was good: everyone recognized in 1975 that within four or five years, VLSI would be a key competitive issue. Thus the problems were close enough to be solvable, but far away enough to be challenging for any one company to solve alone. Second, the joint laboratory stayed away from attempting to invent useable, commercial products, thus avoiding the inevitable refusals to share know-how. The joint laboratory was limited to basic research, with applied research done at CDL and NTIS, and final commercialization was handled by each company on its own. Finally, all agree that a major impetus was the perception of IBM as a technically superior competitor, one so highly regarded and even feared that no one company could imagine successfully overtaking it without help.

The success of the VLSI Research Association is best measured by its impact on the competitiveness of the Japanese mainframes in the marketplace. By 1978, the third year of the joint project, the basic technologies for the 64K RAM had been mastered and trial production was started. Fujitsu and Hitachi each announced new versions of their M series, which exceeded the capacity of the largest IBM model available at the time, the 3033.

The fourth generation of computers had entered the marketplace, but the Japanese and IBM were nearly simultaneously introducing models based on the same main memory component, the 64K RAM. At about this time, NEC and Mitsubishi announced new models that were also competitive with the IBM 4300, followed quickly by Fujitsu. According to the magazine *Electronics in Japan*

(1979/80), the new models by NEC and Toshiba were 1.5 times faster than the IBM 4331, while Mitsubishi and Oki put out two models that possessed, respectively, two and four times the processing capacity of the IBM 4341. Just two years later, Fujitsu replaced IBM as the largest seller of computers in Japan.

IBM remained the largest and most successful computer company in the world; it was still the most highly respected and most emulated of all computer companies. However, the Japanese computer industry, which had once been ten years behind the competition and which had nearly been destroyed by the introduction of the IBM System 360, had now approached the world's leading company. The gap was down to perhaps a matter of months, not years.

The story does not end here. Now, it is true, the greatest excitement in the computer industry is over the development of smaller computers and the personal computer, but major new developments are still coming in the large, mainframe part of the industry. The Japanese firms, despite their differences, are continuing to find ways to work together.

In July of 1979, a new research association, the Electronic Computer Basic Software Technology Research Association (ECSTRA), was formed. Its members include the same five companies, plus CDL and NTIS. This research association again will benefit from the large tax benefits that draw all research associations together, again principally in the form of extremely rapid depreciation on equipment needed for the joint research. ECSTRA is budgeted at approximately $206 million, of which half will come from the member companies and half from the government. ECSTRA will have an effect on approximately 1,500 software companies that have sprung up in Japan since the Information Technology Promotion Agency first provided seed money for such start-up firms in 1971. More importantly, the results of ECSTRA's work can be disseminated rapidly throughout the software industry by the university-based centers sponsored by the Ministry of Education, through the training programs of JIPDEC and its Information Technology Institute, and by the companies themselves. The new technology, once developed, will not sit on a shelf. Because the new technology has been planned, developed, and executed by a broad array of private and public institutions, the process of dissemination is built in to the process of invention.

The Fifth Generation Project

Then, there will be the Fifth Generation. The Fifth Generation of computers will replace the von Neumann architecture of all present and past computers with a fundamentally different approach. According to the official description of ICOT, the Fifth Generation's project, "The design philosophy behind conventional, von Neumann computers was based on configuring systems of maximum simplicity with minimal hardware, because in von Neumann's day hardware was expensive, bulky, short-lived, and consumed a lot of power . . . The key factors leading to the necessity for rethinking the conventional computer design philosophy just described include the following: (1) Device speeds are approaching the limit imposed by the speed of light; (2) The emergence of VLSI's substantially reduces hardware costs, and an environment permitting the use of as much hardware as is required will be feasible shortly . . .''[46] The Fifth Generation computer will be able to understand not only numbers, but words as well, with a vocabulary of 10,000 words and 2,000 grammatical rules, and a 99 percent accuracy in syntactic analysis. The Fifth Generation computer will be able to understand spoken language by multiple speakers at three times the normal rate of speech, have a vocabulary of 50,000 words and an accuracy of 95 percent, leaving 5 percent to be corrected by humans. Many observers are skeptical that these goals can be achieved, but even a partial success would put the Japanese makers not just even with, but probably ahead of the rest of the world, should they make their target date of 1990.

The organization of the Fifth Generation project reflects the lessons of the past in organizing joint research projects. First, the project began with an announcement of discussions in 1978. After three years of discussions among all parties, MITI announced a first phase of three years, 1981–1984, funded entirely by the government with $45 million. The preliminary studies had been funded by JIPDEC at an approximate cost of a half-million dollars.[47] The Fifth Generation project was lodged in April 1982 within a foundation, the Institute for New Generation Computer Technology (ICOT). At the end of 1982, the project employed approximately forty researchers and was located in an office next door to the staff of the old VLSI Research Association in downtown Tokyo (the VLSI Research Association's Kawasaki lab had been vacated at the end of the project in 1979). The plan calls for the companies to spend approximately two dollars of their own money for each dollar of government money over the ten-year period 1981–1990, with a total expenditure of $1.35 billion, or an average of $135 million per year, a vast sum by comparison with any previous project.

It is not likely that the Fifth Generation project will threaten the basic viability of the U.S. or any other computer industry. It would be grossly inappropriate to regard the project as a threat to the world computer industry. If any of us should react to this project with concern, however, that concern indicates a belief that the Japanese form of cooperative competition works. If it works, we should be learning from that example.

Collaboration Among Competitors: It Requires Social Memory and an M-Form Society

That the Japanese computer industry has come from way behind to be a world-class competitor is undeniable. That the principal impetus for this success has come from the competitive drive of each individual company is equally clear. None of the joint research efforts was so important as to have singlehandedly raised the industry to a new level. Indeed, most were of modest significance. FONTAC was only a modest success, if a success at all. DIPS, PIPS, and the supercomputer projects each had some success, but none were so important as to transform the industry. The VLSI Research Association was perhaps the most important of these joint efforts, and it ranks in importance with the funding of leasing through JECC.

What stands out most clearly is the structure of associations, public-private institutions, and public discussion groups, such as the Dietmen's Federation for the Promotion of Information Industries, the Keidanren Committee on Data Processing, JEIDA, the Electronics Industries Association of Japan, JIPDEC, The Japan Industrial Technology Association, AIST, the MITI staff in the Electronic Policy Division, the MITI Discussion Council on Machinery and Information Industries, CDL, NTIS, and the welter of other institutions which, in the end, serve the sole purpose of creating a setting in which competitors can arrange nonadversarial relationships for the common good. It is these institutions that are the loci of the social memory. Each actor participates in many such institutions and thus knows that the future memory of his or her current behavior will be stored, remembered and justly rewarded or punished. Thus, five competitors can enter into joint research on a critical subject without even the protection of clear patent agreements, yet secure in the knowledge that no party will cheat the others, because cheating will surely be detected and punished in the future, over and over again. We have seen that self-interest has not been diminished in the least, not on the part of the individual scientist at the VLSI joint laboratory who worries about his career at his home company, and not on the part of Hitachi or Fujitsu, who cooperate only with the utmost difficulty. We see that a close dialogue with government will always present the strains of overzealous bureaucrats vying with profit-minded private firms, but we see also that a balance can be achieved in which neither side overpowers the other.

In Japan, the forces of the marketplace are clearly in working order. It is the fundamental drive for success in the marketplace that caused the Japanese makers to refuse the MITI attempt to reorganize the industry and that drove each company to its best efforts over a period of twenty years. On the other hand, we see also that bureaucracy exists with government imposition of rules and procedures, objectives and targets on the firms. Often, we see the companies turning to a trusted source of hierarchical power, such as JEIDA, to achieve an equitable solution to the problem of where to locate the VLSI joint lab when market forces were incapable of a solution. We see that the companies were willing to submit to the hierarchical authority of a bureaucrat, Mr. Nebashi, to arbitrate disputes between companies in the Operations and Technology Committees of the VLSI Research Association. Finally, we see in the network of institutions the fundamentals of a social memory capable of achieving serial equity, and making possible the exercise of social choice, focus, and successful economic development.

This cooperative form of competition in Japan is not limited to the computer industry. Other research associations currently in place include one to develop laser manufacturing technology between steel companies as users and scientific equipment companies as laser makers (1977–1983), another for ocean-bottom drilling technology combining oil drillers, shipbuilders, electronics companies and others for a total of eighteen companies (1978–present), another combining fifteen chemicals companies (1980–1987), one to develop ceramics for use in the semiconductor industry (1981–1988), another combining chemical companies and textile companies (1981–1990), and others in biotechnology, automated sewing, manganese nodule mining, medical treatment instruments, jet engines for aircraft, and others.

The superstitious ideology of competition in the West abhors all these projects. We believe that if we permit competitors to collaborate on basic research, in the long run we will give them the comfort of knowing that their competitors possess no knowledge superior to theirs. The result, we fear, will be a loss of competitive spirit, a slackening of competition, and a slowdown in economic growth. Perhaps, however, this idea rests on our observation that, in the technologically simpler past, our companies succeeded by competing singly, by remaining in every way adversaries. Certainly, it would seem to require a willful blindness to the vast research enterprise lodged in U.S. universities and paid for with mostly public funds. Might that observation be superstitious? Perhaps our companies succeeded alone simply because they had few competitors, perhaps they have in fact cooperated more than we like to remember, and perhaps our superstitious ideology is in need of major overhaul. Some of the joint research of our economy might take place in industry as well as in universities. It would be bold for me to declare an unambivalent conviction that more interfirm cooperation would be better for American industry; I cannot. IBM has succeeded nicely on its own, as has most of American industry. I wish only to raise the issue, to see that it receives serious thought and scrutiny. In Japan, it appears, aggressive competition can co-exist with occasional, if strained, cooperation.

There are presently before the U.S. Congress several bills that would permit the formation of joint research ventures similar to those in Japan. Such a bill would diminish the antitrust barriers to cooperative R & D in a measured way. The time is ripe for a public acknowledgment that this part of our economic ideology is in need of change. While we should welcome such a change, we should also ask ourselves why the Japanese passed such a law twenty years ago. Is it that our business-government system is so diffuse that it responds only to crisis? We can improve our ability to respond as a nation by putting in place some of the coordinative mechanisms of an M-Form society. Those mechanisms of social memory will permit at least enough cooperation among competitors to permit a coordinated attempt to address the needs of each industry and the needs of society at large.

A Postscript

From the *Japan Economic Journal* (*Nihon Keizai Shimbun*), January 8, 1984:

"Japan has begun to develop the Sixth Generation Computer, a more advanced intellectual machine than the Fifth Generation Computer. The Science and Technology Agency is organizing this project to develop a computer that operates like a human brain. It will be able to learn and communicate in human speech. The Fifth Generation can deduce from data that are put into it, but this will function like a human brain. For this project the Science and Technology Agency is seeking the participation of the finest psychologists, physiologists, and linguists."

6

DISAPPOINTMENT AND HOPE
technology development in the United States

It doesn't take a genius to know what the important needs of an industry are. It does take someone who is involved in the industry on a day-to-day basis, someone who knows what is possible and what is needed. In a large multidivisional company, there will typically be many research projects that might be undertaken and not enough money to fund all of them. Each division manager wants to see his or her project funded, and competition for the capital to fund projects is keen. Although the chief executive and the corporate staff may be well informed, they will never know as much about each potential research project as the line managers themselves know. As a result, proper decisions can be made only if the line managers communicate honestly, openly, and effectively with the top management. Often, there will be the possibility for two or more divisions to collaborate on one aspect of the research, which each division can then use separately in its own new products. That cooperation does not come easily, however, because each would rather have the money to do its own research in its own way. Only through an effective coordination by some legitimate superior can that cooperation occur.

In Japan, joint research projects have depended critically upon the trade associations, the MITI councils, and the MITI staff for their success. In the first place, those bodies guarantee that price-fixing will not occur under the cloak of joint research and that the public interest will not be abused in other ways. In the second place, those bodies assure each participating company that the other corporate venture partners will not be allowed to take advantage of them. In the third place, the public continues to support the allocation of tax funds to joint research because it gets a large return on the use of those tax funds. Without effective coordination and oversight, none of those benefits would be forthcoming.

In the United States, we have no framework in place that can oversee joint research, except in the Department of Defense. As a result, the public is reluctant to allow competitive companies to get together in joint research, fearing that unanticipated and illegal collusion will also take place. The companies themselves are reluctant to become involved in such efforts, fearing that other companies may seek to take advantage of them and that they will incur large legal expenses as a result. The public has become skeptical of the use of tax funds for these purposes because the returns in the past have often been too small to justify the investment.

Within the Department of Defense, we have seen as a nation a clear need to place scientific advancement ahead of these concerns. As a result, the Department of Defense has enjoyed a nearly unique charter in the public eye, a charter permitting it to engage in bringing competitors together for the purpose of developing new defense technology. On the one hand, this anomaly allows us to see how a Japanese-like R & D process works in the United States—it works very well. It gives us reason to believe that joint research and development where very large investment is required can and does succeed in a Western nation. Despite the individualistic tendencies of U.S. companies, despite our economic superstitions, the fact is that joint R & D on a large scale is succeeding in the United States now, under the guidance of the Department of Defense.

On the other hand, it should not escape our notice that we confine this benefit to very narrowly defined military procurement. The job of the Department of Defense in this area is to procure as much defense as possible for as few tax dollars as possible. The job is not to sponsor the creation of new jobs for the economy and not to advance technology in the United States. As a consequence, although some defense projects have spun off significant new commercial technology, the vast majority have not. Observers in Europe and in Japan often believe that the large electronics procurement of the U.S. military constitutes an enormous R & D subsidy to American industry. By and large, that conclusion is wrong.

Not only is the conclusion wrong, but our policy is wrong. Why should we not have in the United States the capacity to create those social endowments that can create jobs and future economic prosperity? We have no state government agencies and no federal agencies with the capacity to manage such a task. We have no associations in industry sufficiently influential to undertake such an effort.

We may not have the M-Form structure necessary to undertake major R & D projects except in the military; nonetheless, we make the attempt from time to time. What happens in such a case? Does U.S. industry somehow coalesce? Does government find a way to provide the necessary leadership, does the problem somehow get solved, the objective achieved? Consider what happened when we attempted, as a nation, to develop a solar photovoltaic industry in 1978.

The Photovoltaic Project: Disappointment

On November 4, 1978, the U.S. Congress enacted the Solar Photovoltaic Energy Research Development and Demonstration Act. The act provided funding of $1.5 billion over ten years to develop this technology to the point of its viability as a partial replacement for other forms of generating electricity. It seemed that the Congress was responding well to the threat of the OPEC cartel by acting to develop a new source of energy that, in the future, would make the United States less dependent on foreign oil. The program was divided into five major activities: Advanced Research and Development (no useful products for many years), Technology Development (technology for products in a few years), Systems Engineering and Standards (for products soon), Tests and Applications (of existing products), and Market Development (to find uses for products actually available). In 1979, $118 million was spent, in 1980 the figure rose to $151 million, but in 1981 the total dropped to $133 million, and for 1982 two of the activities, Systems Engineering and Standards and Market Development were dropped and total funding reduced to $74 million. For 1983 two more activities were eliminated, leaving only Advanced Research and Development, and the total budget request was for $27 million. The bold vision was over, the photovoltaic project was aborted, although some important research had indeed taken place, and the spending was stopped. What had happened?

The photovoltaic effect, which permits the direct conversion of sunlight into electricity, was discovered in 1839, and by the 1880s selenium PV cells had been built with efficiencies of 1 percent to 2 percent in converting sunlight to electricity. However, the cost of the cells was so high relative to the electricity produced that the technology was not feasible for commercial use.[1] Work continued, and by 1954, the Bell Labs had produced a silicon PV cell with 4 percent efficiency. During the 1950s and 1960s, PV cells were used for highly specialized purposes, mostly in the space program, such as powering the radio of the Vanguard satellite in 1958. A few companies with major technology abilities dominated the infant industry, while many smaller companies came and went, often existing only for the duration of a single federal contract. By 1978, total sales by U.S. photovoltaic makers were $10.6 million, and six companies (Solarex, Solar Power Corporation, ARCO Solar, Motorola, Sensor Technology, and Spectrolab) accounted for 95 percent of that.[2] Government purchases accounted for 50 to 60 percent of the total. The companies were clearly in the business for the long haul, with estimated R & D expenditures of a total of $180 million in 1978.[3] In the world market, U.S. companies represented 75 percent of the total, with the Japanese makers (Matsushita, NEC, Sharp, Toshiba, Kyo-Cera, and JSEC, a collaborative including U.S. and Japanese firms) accounting for 5 percent.[4]

Organization of the Project

In order to undertake this massive project, the Department of Energy enlisted the Solar Energy Research Institute in Golden, Colorado, to oversee projects in advanced research and development, and the Jet Propulsion Laboratory in Pasadena, California, to oversee technology development and applications. These two independent organizations coordinated with several other research centers designated as major contractors with additional oversight responsibilities: Sandia National Laboratories, MIT Lincoln Laboratory, Aerospace Corporation, MIT Energy Laboratory, Brookhaven National Laboratory, and NASA Lewis Research Center. Interested parties were invited to submit applications for research contracts, and these applications were evaluated by experts from SERI, JPL, and Sandia Labs.

At the time that the $1.5 billion R & D program was approved by Congress, there were approximately 15 U.S. companies engaged in small-scale manufacturing of PV cells, with another 46 companies engaged only in PV research (some examples: American Cyanamid, Dupont, Eastman Kodak, Exxon, IBM, Rockwell International, TRW, and Westinghouse). During the roughly three-year period of research funding, 502 research contracts were let to 250 different contractors, of which 57 were universities or university-related institutions.[5] The number is surprisingly high, as is the fact that there was no apparent attempt to form teams, to encourage joint work, or to seek the detailed guidance of the industry and of university scholars in the design of the $1.5 billion effort.

Over the period 1972–1981, federal expenditures on PV totalled $550 million. A 1978 survey by a private management consulting firm reported that only one-third of the companies felt that the program would have a positive effect, while half felt that the overall effect would be negative.[6]

It has become customary to denounce such an effort as another example of government waste or of the impossibility of government pushing research and development ahead, but that would be unfair and misleading. The peak expenditure of $151 million in 1980 on PV is small compared to the $1 billion in annual incentives provided for the oil industry, $296 million in annual incentives to the coal industry, and $1 billion per year for R & D in nuclear energy.[7] What is important here is that the researchers in academia and in industry had no preexisting organization through which they could engage in a dialogue with the Congress, the National Science Foundation, or the Department of Energy. The bureaucrats in charge of the program held several hearings, visited several companies, sponsored several conferences. But even a thousand conversations do not have the impact of two or three ongoing associations having a continuous existence and serving as a point of contact between public and private sectors. Faced with a highly atomized industry whose members could not get together to develop constructive guidelines, and faced with a nation jittery about the unreliability of foreign oil supplies, the Congress had to do something. What it was able to do was simply inappropriate.

In January of 1979, the American Physical Society published the report of its study group on solar photovoltaic energy conversion. The study group included eleven members drawn from business and academia, including Harvard, MIT, General Electric, the California Institute of Technology, and others. The study group had two conclusions of particular importance: 1) "Utilization of PV as a major source of electricity in the United States, with a market penetration exceeding 10 percent of the total consumption, will, in all probability, be a long-term venture requiring perhaps fifty to sixty years . . . It is unlikely that photovoltaics will contribute more than about 1 percent of the U.S. electrical energy produced near the end of the century." 2) "Until recently, the DOE funding formats have been too goal-oriented, overmanaged, and too restrictive in other respects. R & D management styles and funding formats should reflect the long-term nature of the problem . . ."[8]

Looking back, it appears that the members of the study group were right. In this kind of basic, long-term research, a steady and dependable stream of funding to individual scientists is what is called for. Instad, the program began with a semimanaged effort to oversee the efforts of 250 contractors, and Congress was given the expectation that results would come soon, with budget categories including sums for testing of the new devices, as well as for the development of commercial markets. These expectations were entirely unrealistic, the funding was cut off, and instead of providing a steady, long-term effort to develop this critical new technology, government has created doubt in the minds of researchers that they can safely plan major research efforts. The public has good reason to view skeptically any future government efforts to assist research and development in new, high-technology fields.

The PV project was organized according to normal competitive principles, yet it failed. Potential contractors were invited to compete for funds, and the long-run competition for a potentially huge new market should have caused each company to press ahead at full speed. But the companies were interested only in basic research, not in commercial development and the large-scale funding that implies. On the other hand, several of the companies were glad to have federal subsidies in any form, and were not about to complain.

It is highly unlikely that all 250 of the contractors were in fact capable of undertaking research in PV at a high level of technological expertise. There may not even have been 250 scientists in the entire United States capable of basic research in the field. But who was to decide? There was no reliable trade association in place that could team weak companies with strong or deny the requests of those obviously incapable of doing the research, so the decision was thrown to the managing private laboratories. They, however, were not trade associations or legitimate arbiters among member companies, but rather private firms with superior knowledge. Were they to deny a request from a company with good political connections, they would have invited future trouble they didn't need.

There was no government council in place with visibility and legitimacy in the public eye that could counsel Congress and the president against a major PV development effort, and thus take some of the pressure off them to solve the oil energy crisis. The consequence was a forcing of the issues into the Congress, which was ill-equipped to deal with the arcane technicalities of the field.

VHSIC—Hope for the Future

In 1937, a U.S. Navy destroyer carried aboard equipment that contained sixty vacuum tubes. By 1952, it required 3,200. Only 60 percent of the electronic equipment in the navy worked properly, and half of the failures were due to tube problems.[9] There clearly was a market for the transistor. Between 1950 and 1970, the federal government spent $900 million (in constant 1965 dollars) on semiconductor research and development.[10] The advances in technology were swift. The Bell Labs junction transistor was put into use by the telephone company in 1951, but the big spurt in transistor use came after Texas Instruments announced its silicon transistor in 1954. In addition to serving military and space uses, this silicon transistor became the foundation of the second generation of computers. Texas Instruments later invented the integrated circuit in 1958, which became the foundation of the third-generation computers. Meanwhile, the necessary reliability rose, as the failure rate of the T.I. integrated circuit dropped from 7 to 20 percent per 1,000 hours in 1962, to 0.0012 percent per 1,000 hours in 1979.[11]

Defense was the big customer. Defense purchases of semiconductor devices grew from 30 percent of the industry's total output in 1955 to 45 percent in 1959. In 1962, the National Aeronautics and Space Administration and the Air Force jointly decided to use integrated circuits in the Apollo program and in the guidance systems of the Minuteman ICBM.[12] The initial Apollo orders alone called for the delivery of 200,000 circuits.

Meanwhile, the application of semiconductors in the computer industry had taken off. In 1960, there were 9,000 computers in use around the world. That number rose to 110,000 by 1970, and to 450,000 by 1978.[13] As a result, although defense purchases of semiconductors rose in dollar amounts from $15 million in 1955 to $600 million in 1980, the defense share of the industry's output dropped from the 45 percent of 1959 to 21 percent in 1970, and to 5 percent by 1980.[14] Recall that the first commercial computer, ENIAC(1946), had used 18,000 vacuum tubes. By comparison, the IBM computer of 1955, which was many times more powerful, used 2,200 transistors, was far smaller, and consumed 95 percent less power.[15] The semiconductor had found a vast market.

By 1980, the market for integrated circuits was 23 percent in computers, 22 percent in consumer electronics, 15 percent in industrial instruments and controls and office equipment, 13 percent in telecommunications, and only 5 percent in government, including military use.[16] As a consequence, the U.S. military, like any small customer anywhere, had to take what it could get. On November 27, 1978, *Business Week* reported: ". . . few semiconductor makers are willing to support a military program consistently. One reason for this is that circuits for such applications must undergo special processing and testing procedures, driving up manufacturing costs and often requiring separate production facilities . . . As a result, military components now are usually special versions of circuits originally developed for commercial application, and that usually does not give the military customers what they want . . . and the high-speed devices, which the military prizes, have been too costly and power-hungry to command much attention."

The results of this off-the-shelf approach to military electronics were summarized by Dr. Edith Martin, Deputy Undersecretary of Defense for Research and Engineering and overseer of the VHSIC project, "The electronic components in the newest U.S. fighter aircraft are less sophisticated than those in the digital watch on your arm or in your kid's electronic game." Quoting her boss, Dr. Richard

DeLauer, she continued, "Electronics is the most critical of all technologies: for the next several decades, at least, it will remain the cornerstone of deterrence for the United States and its allies ... Military might consists of more than guns, tanks, planes, ships and missiles. Such munitions are just what the Russians have more of. U.S. defense must rest instead on those things which electronics does best: strategic and tactical information acquisition, control, communication, identification and tracking, guidance, and electronic suppression."[17]

The main fear was that the U.S. technology lead over the Soviets, once estimated at ten to fifteen years, had slipped to only three to five years. At that rate, the Soviets would soon lead not only in the number of weapons, but in the sophistication and accuracy of those weapons as well. To make matters worse, the military, which had formerly gotten the latest semiconductors three or four years before they were commercially available, currently gets them two or three years *after* they are commercially available.[18]

Organization of
the VHSIC Project

Beginning in 1977, Department of Defense planners carried out discussions on how to meet these urgent needs. In 1978, the intention to develop a major research and development effort was announced, Congress authorized funding in 1979, and in 1980, the six-year, $324 million program was begun. The military knew what it wanted: extreme high speed, reliability, and radiation-hardness in several new semiconductor devices specifically targeted for military uses, rather than designed for general use and later refined. As Botkin, Dimancescu and Stata (1982) summarized the VHSIC goal: "What is so special and valuable about VHSIC chips to warrant these expenditures? The primary answer is speed. Thumbnail in size, by 1990 these devices will perform at speeds unimaginable to the layman—from 2 to 12 billion additions or multiplications per second. This represents an increase anywhere from 10 to 100 times faster than today's fastest chips. The requirement for increased speed depends on the application: for radar, 50 times faster; for weapons targeting, 100 times faster; for electronic warfare, 50 to 200 times faster."[19]

In order to achieve these speeds, the devices had to be made incredibly compact, with geometries initially at 1.25 microns and eventually down to 0.5 micron, a considerable reduction from the 4 micron geometries then available. The technology was within reach, but no company was yet capable of achieving it. Not only that, but the Defense Department was not interested in theoretical designs nor even in experimental prototypes, but in "brassboards," actually working and producible chips that could guide a missile or control a radar device. No defense contractor possessed the semiconductor technology necessary to achieve this goal, and the computer and semiconductor firms that did have the technology were unable to insert such a technology into a defense system, or to navigate the maze of Pentagon bureaucracy. The DOD set out to convince the computer, defense, and semiconductor industries that first, they should team up with one another and not worry about losing valuable expertise to current or potential competitors; and second, they should actively pursue this small and specialized market.

There were few enthusiastic supporters in the beginning. Several critics felt that the move to chips specialized for just one use would not attract any industry support, since the markets would be so small. Others pointed out that the military should first make use of what was already available. *Business Week* (November 27, 1978, p. 140) quoted Andrew S. Grove, then executive vice-president of Intel: "What is the point of spending all this money to develop submicron geometries when they are not using the commercially available 4-micron geometries? What the government needs to do is light a fire under its procurement chain and make sure that high technology gets utilized." Intel, the inventor of the 1K RAM and of the microprocessor, and one of the most highly regarded of semiconductor firms, refused to join the project.

The Congress was concerned, as well. First, a program of this size was unprecedented. The typical R & D program in the DOD is less than $1 million, and VHSIC was originally budgeted at $224 million. Second, the Congress was skeptical that any government agency could aid corporate research successfully. Third, the industry objections had reached the ears of congressmen, as had the fears of smaller companies that they would be left behind as giant companies received government subsidies to push ahead in research.

In early May of 1979, the House Armed Services Committee

killed the VHSIC program, deleting the entire $30 million budgeted for fiscal year 1980. The committee feared that the project would end up leaving the military dependent entirely on one source for each of its key components, thus leaving U.S. defense in a precarious position as well as shutting out smaller competitors. The potential bidding companies, however, refused to take on "second source" partners—competitors to whom they would license their VHSIC designs and against whom they would then have to compete to sell products based on those designs. However, the DOD staff proved its mettle. Leonard Weisberg, the VHSIC director, and Larry Sumney, who was to be his successor, aided by a concerned congressional committee staff and the top executives of the Department of Defense and the services, calmed the fears of the congressmen, and the funds were soon restored.

Had there been an interservice rivalry along with the other difficulties, the whole program might have collapsed. However, there was no such rivalry on VHSIC because VHSIC was the first project of its kind in the history of the Department of Defense to be run not by any one service, but by the DOD itself as a joint activity. Economic necessity had overcome pride of service, and Dr. Martin summed it up nicely in her 1982 remarks: "DOD and the military services are still organized and operated as they were when U.S. technology was less advanced and thus more affordable. In times past, the United States could afford redundancy—and did. We did not duplicate everything—the army does not have aircraft carriers and the air force manages to survive without tanks . . . However, the escalating costs of technology, the inefficiencies inherent in triservice competition, and the convergence of technology requirements across the board has rendered redundancy obsolete. Norman Augustine, chairman of the Defense Science Board, noted the impact of the cost/complexity increases when he extrapolated the costs of tactical aircraft to the year 2054. In that year, if current trends are followed, it appears that the entire defense budget will buy one airplane, which would have to be shared by the air force with the army and navy."

Leonard Weisberg, now a vice-president at Honeywell, describes his role as VHSIC Director in coordinating the nearly 400 military "contact points" involved in VHSIC planning: "There were numerous briefings—I don't know how many I gave. Costs, benefits, structure—they wanted all the information on this. Getting the services to work together was a challenge. I briefed chiefly by service. I showed army people what the program could do for the army, such as electronic warfare, weaponry, precision guided missiles, artillery-firing accuracy, etc. I did the same thing for the air force—for satellites; for the navy for torpedoes, detecting submarines, and so on. You had to have numbers in there. What new capabilities it could provide. Savings in fuel, maintenance, reliability, and so on. I had to say, 'Instead of needing three vans you can carry this stuff around in half of a van'."

Reflecting on the aftermath, Weisberg continues, "Someone commented in the army that VHSIC happened because its time had come. Nothing could be farther from the truth. It's easy to say this now, but five years ago this program was under so much fire that I'd pick up a magazine with trepidation. We had so many objections and problems . . . Now that it's in place, people are enthusiastic. The Defense Science Board 1981 report singled out VHSIC as the single most important technology program in the DOD. I read this and said, 'Where were you three years ago when I needed you?' "[20]

The Four Phases of VHSIC

VHSIC was initiated as a six-year program of four phases, to be funded with $224 million (later increased to $324 million) of direct government contracts to private industry. Phase 0 was to be from March to December 1980, and was to be a planning period, at the end of which the competitors would submit their plans for the work to commence in Phase I. Phase I is from 1981 through 1984, the year in which Phase II will commence and run through the end of the program in 1986–1987. Phase 0 is intended to identify potential contractors for the actual work. Phase I is intended to move semiconductor technology ahead by an amount that is challenging but has a high likelihood of success (1.25 micron geometry). Phase II will involve more detailed development of these devices and will attempt to take an even larger technological leap, with a larger risk that the task will prove impossible (0.5 micron geometry). Phase III is not actually the last phase, but rather a separate small program funding approximately sixty research projects, many within universities, to work on scientific issues related to the central thrust of VHSIC. Phase III runs from 1980 through 1985.

In June of 1979, *Electronics* magazine reported that the Pentagon expected to receive VHSIC Phase 0 proposals from four teams of companies and from five individual companies. In January of 1980, the magazine reported that fourteen proposals had been received, representing in all nearly thirty companies. Nine winners were chosen, and a total of $10 million distributed among them for the nine months of work to specify the system architecture, chip architecture and design, circuit-processing technologies, and testing approaches to be used. Of the winners, IBM and Texas Instruments applied singly. The other winners comprised seven teams, each headed by a prime contractor: (1) TRW with Motorola, Sperry-Univac, GCA-Mann; (2) Hughes Aircraft with Signetics, Research Triangle Institute, and Burroughs; (3) Rockwell International with Sanders Associates; (4) Westinghouse with National Semiconductor, Control Data Corporation, and the Mellon Institute; (5) General Electric with Intersil and Analog Devices; (6) Honeywell with 3M; and (7) Raytheon with Fairchild Semiconductor and Varian Extrion.

Finally, on May 4, 1981, the Phase I winners were announced. Some changes in teams had been made, and six prime contractors were identified: (1) TRW with Sperry-Univac and Motorola; (2) Westinghouse with National Semiconductor, Control Data Corporation, Harris, and Carnegie-Mellon University; (3) Hughes Aircraft alone on one contract, and another with Perkin Elmer and ETEC; (4) Texas Instruments; (5) IBM; and (6) Honeywell. The army was assigned to oversee two teams, the air force, two, and the navy, two.

Why VHSIC Is Succeeding

On February 17, 1982, the Defense Science Board, a group of civilian experts who advise the Secretary of Defense on matters related to science, released their evaluation of the VHSIC program. They found that "In the context of its political, management, and technical environment, the VHSIC Program has exhibited exemplary progress."[21] Indeed, the chairman of the Defense Science Board was sufficiently impressed that his covering memorandum to the Secretary of Defense and the chairman of the Joint Chiefs of Staff recommended: "I would particularly call to your attention the recommendation that the VHSIC program be used as a model for the organization of other high-thrust areas of the defense technology base where the needs of the services are very similar and, for cost efficiency, a highly focused, coherent program is required."

Although it is too early to judge the success or failure of VHSIC, the early signs all seem favorable. In addition to the praise of the Defense Science Board, the program readily won an increase in the Phase I budget from the Congress, which has become an enthusiastic supporter. More importantly, the VHSIC program has involved, in one or another stage, fourteen of the twenty-four largest integrated-circuit makers in the United States, including the top three: IBM, Texas Instruments, and Motorola. Jack Robertson of *Electronics* magazine reported in October of 1982 that military systems makers were starting to line up to be the first to get the new devices: "'Everybody is rushing to the Defense Department VHSIC office to get in line for the first VHSIC chip sets. There's a big priority battle going on with everyone trying to get their hands on the first prototypes,' explained Richard Gillette, vice-president of Northrop's defense systems division."

More telling, perhaps, are the personal reactions of those directly involved in the program. Some comments from the VHSIC staff in the Department of Defense: "We have received strong support from the firms. I have heard from them: 'We put in $4 to your $1.' I've also heard $2 to our $1. I would say that all are outspending their DOD contracts. There is also a great deal of enthusiasm within the teams. The whole industry is talking to each other. They're sharing their yields, the strongest indicators of how well they're doing together. This is virtually unheard of—firms just don't reveal their yields. There is also a sense of excitement because VHSIC is the cutting edge. This work and program are highly visible. During Phase 0 the firms were very standoffish and reluctant to reveal information. There is still some of this, but very little is left. The feelings have been positive. VHSIC isn't regarded as a 'risky' program that is going to get cut or lose its funding from Congress. Industry knows it can depend on this program to continue to its end."[22]

Another VHSIC staff member adds the following, making it clear why cooperation has been as good as it has: "I've been on the road more than half the time. Twice a year we hold an executive review where we talk turkey about how things are going. The process is very open. In addition, the service directors have their own meetings. There is one rule of the game: no one service can decide a major policy without running it through the triservice arena. Prior to Phase 0, Len Weisberg would have meetings with the services, the industry groups, and everyone. There were both formal and informal meetings. They would meet in small groups and large groups, have VHSIC workshops and on-site visits similar to the ones we undertake now . . . We were all surprised that the teams worked out so well. We didn't think they would. In the army program, Rockwell, RCA, and Hughes have worked closely together. They've shared information; it's been very friendly. The firms got together on their own to form the teams. The DOD didn't engineer the teams and we don't really know how they arranged them."[23]

These positive sentiments come not only from the DOD staff, but from the industry contractors as well. Harley Cloud, the VHSIC project manager for IBM, comments: "The VHSIC program has involved a different management style on the part of the DOD and the services. It is different largely because of the high degree of cooperation . . . The technology developed by VHSIC would have been developed by industry. But VHSIC has accelerated its coming by a few years. We will find the applications. We're not worried about that . . . The state of U.S. technology is on everyone's mind. VHSIC insertion has heightened everyone's interest in how we manage technological advances in this country. You can't quantify the work of this project—either in technology, awareness, visibility, management—in terms of dollars."[24]

A Westinghouse manager involved in VHSIC offers similar evaluations: "The air force people we work with have the sophistication to understand the technical problems and design issues. Between the three services, not much slips by. No one is an expert on everything, but they're sharp. We meet with members of the executive committee every six months—they come here to Westinghouse. I would never have believed this five or ten years ago, and the firms are truly working together . . . I would agree that VHSIC has allowed the technology to be stepped up by two to three years by focusing the attention of firms in this area."

Perhaps the most important factor behind the successful launching of VHSIC, however, is the general consensus on its importance and, more critically, on how to run it, according to Jack Robertson of *Electronics:* "When it comes to the needs and problems of industry, the Japanese had just completed the VLSI project. It was known that money went into the project, but the outcomes weren't known, just a perceived threat. The capital needs of the industry were getting to be horrendous. The industry knew that the high costs of dense technology required joint financing. Congress was confronted with the consensus of both groups—industry and the military. And the Congress has been very supportive. The members of Congress saw that both the DOD and the firms were putting in dollars to make the program go."

The VHSIC program has not been without problems. Some critics still point out that 2-micron capabilities exist within the industry, so that the 1.25-micron goal was too modest, while others maintain that the eventual goal of 0.5-micron geometry is too bold.[25] At the end of 1982, for example, Hewlett-Packard was shipping 1-micron processors that exceeded the VHSIC goals, and had done the R & D entirely on their own. Since the underlying purpose of the program is to achieve superiority over the Soviets, the program has understandably adopted strict security controls, and these provoked a disagreement with the major universities, who argue in favor of academic freedom as a necessity for productive research, and who point out that in some major university departments of science, half the research assistants and doctoral candidates are foreign, so that research teams could not be assembled if U.S. citizenship were required. Nonetheless, the early signs are extremely promising.

Perhaps the enduring importance of the VHSIC project is its clear demonstration that competitors can collaborate, even in the United States, and even in the highly competitive defense, semiconductor, and computer industries. It is also instructive to note that VHSIC had in place something that the photovoltaic solar energy program did not, a coordinative mechanism in the form of a permanent DOD staff experienced at working with industry on research and development. A community of defense, semiconductor, and computer companies had been in business for some time and had, in many instances, worked for one another as subcontractors. Therefore, although markets alone were insufficient to produce the defense technology needed for national security, the VHSIC project was able to rely on both bureaucratic and clan mechanisms of governance. Customary procurement procedures went on, the normal audits of contractors and subcontractors were and are taking place, and the public bureaucracy is helping to govern the effort. However, the ambiguities of responsibility are so great and the interconnections between the parties so complex that a strict application of bureaucracy would have doomed the project from the start. Had there been no memory in the Department of Defense and no memory between firms, all relationships would have had to be strictly contractual. No company would have spent a penny more than the contracted amount if it felt that others would not remember. In fact, almost all of the contractors began work before their contracts had been officially approved, and most of the subcontractor team members were well into their first year of work before concluding legal agreements with the contractor who led the team.

The Lessons of the PV and VHSIC Projects

VHSIC is not a program intended to advance general research and development in the integrated circuit industry of the United States; it is an effort to procure specific hardware necessary for our national defense. Thus the VHSIC companies need not fear criminal antitrust suits from the Department of Justice nor civil suits from competitors who failed to win VHSIC contracts. There is no need to ask whether the companies should have received loans rather than contracts or whether the money should be repaid, because they are delivering a product for a price. All these issues and more will have to be addressed if there are to be joint business-government efforts in research and development.

More generally, VHSIC is important because it demonstrates that business and government can still work effectively together in the United States. It may be that in other cases, an effective dialogue between business and government would lead to an entirely different result involving no joint action. In the photovoltaic project, for example, it appears now that if the firms had been organized or if, alternatively, the Department of Energy had possessed an effective discussion council, the program would have developed quite differently. A close analysis would have convinced the industry participants that PV commercialization was many decades away, and pressure on the Congress to solve an unsolvable problem might have been reduced. Faced with a united industry, assisted by a well-informed bureaucracy, the Congress surely would not have allocated funds for the commercial testing and market development of PV. Instead, more realistic goals could have been set, perhaps resulting in a steady stream of more productive long-range research.

The organization of the PV project can best be described as laissez-faire. The competitive market was at work, with each of the 250 contractors having an incentive to achieve a major breakthrough, yet little progress was realized. In part, this occurred because the companies in the industry were not able to carry out an effective dialogue with the Congress and persuade legislators of the need for a slower, longer-term research strategy. It also occurred because the fruits of research were so many years away and the undertaking of major research so risky that no one company made an effort large enough for a breakthrough. Both errors of judgment are attributable to a failure of the competitive marketplace. The production of major research advances will inevitably constitute a public good, which the inventor will end up sharing with many competitors. If each company works alone on such research, it will do so only if public funds flow to each company in an amount large enough to pay for most of the costs of that research. There isn't enough money to allow 250 companies to undertake research on such a scale in a field as basic as the conversion of sunlight to electricity. Only through direct cooperation such as that in the VLSI Research Association can such an effort be mounted.

In the case of the VHSIC project, that kind of direct cooperation was brought about and appears to have created a major success. When the Congress grew skeptical, the companies were able to pool their arguments to win the day. When the companies and the services grew wary of one another, the DOD staff was able to bring them together to resolve their differences. In this effort, the DOD project staff has taken a role analogous to the role played by JEIDA in the VLSI Research Association.

It may be that by the year 2054 the entire budget of the Department of Defense will buy only one airplane. If so, it may also be that in that year the entire R & D budget of the United States will fund only one research and development project, which will have to be shared by electronics with the energy, transportation, and chemical industries. We all would like to believe that each U.S. company can exist entirely on its own and be self-sufficient. We would like to ignore the fact that our companies have prospered only by dint of the many social endowments that we as a nation have created: the endowments of universal education, a system of laws, public safety, and university-based research. Having created those endowments, we would like to feel that our job is done, that each company can be an island. But the job is not done. Social change is essential to keep up with technical change. As the demands of an economy change, so must the social and political institutions of the society change.

We would be foolish to abandon our basic economic and political beliefs without a struggle, however. Our belief in the free enterprise system has served us well. We do not wish to throw those beliefs over wholesale, but rather to examine them closely to see what to keep and what to discard. In so doing, we must once again study and understand the organization of our economy in order to discover its strengths and its weaknesses. Having satisfied ourselves that there is a substantial and reasonable basis for change, we will be able to undertake the task.

PART 3

THE M-FORM IN
THE UNITED STATES
an action agenda

7

THE POLITICS OF BUSINESS IN THE UNITED STATES

The current debate on industrial policy in the United States is confusing on several counts. We have observed that the confusion is based in part on an incorrect understanding of industrial policy in Japan. A second major source of confusion arises because those who ought to be for a U.S. industrial policy are largely against it. The objective of industrial policy is to assist American industry in becoming more productive, more profitable, and more successful. It would seem that the leaders of U.S. industry should be unanimously in favor of such a goal, yet most of them are against industrial policy. Why is that?

The answer seems to be that industrial policy in any form implies a closer relationship between business and government than we have now. Most business executives find their current dealings with government to be sufficiently burdensome and unproductive that they reject out of hand any policy that calls for more of the same. That is, American business already has extensive dealings with government at the local, state, and federal levels, but that contact has been fractious and unproductive rather than reasoned and fruitful. Indeed, one might even argue that the actual contact between business and government in the United States is greater than it is in Japan. Perhaps it is the quality rather than the quantity of business-government dialogue in the United States that needs to be altered. Consider some broad facts about that relationship.

In 1976, sociologist Michael Useem counted a total of 1,159 councils, commissions, and advisory boards through which 23,000 U.S. citizens gave advice to the many arms of the federal government.[1] As Useem studied the world of corporate boards of directors among the 800 largest U.S. companies, he focused on an elite group of top directors, each of whom serves on four or more of these top boards. Of those active directors, 30 percent also serve on one or more federal advisory boards. Indeed, Useem found so many interconnections between the business and government worlds that he raised the question of whether the relationship was too close. He worried that a cohesive network of top business executives may be wielding far too much power over the affairs of government. If that is so, why do those same executives reject the idea of industrial policy? Why do they argue that government intrudes too deeply into business affairs, and why have they been unable to prevail on government to solve the problems of our steel and automobile industries?

The problem is not that our government is understaffed or remiss in its efforts. We have a year-round Congress with a staff of 30,000, federal and state payrolls employing 20 percent of the labor force, and a business community that claims to be overrun by government. In Japan, by comparison, the Diet has a staff one-tenth the size of our congressional staffs which meets for only two-thirds of the year, only on alternate days. Japanese government agencies employ 9 percent of the labor force, and the business community says that it has a good relationship with government. Is it possible that the Japanese engage in government-directed central planning, while the United States has an unbridled system of free enterprise? The evidence is to the contrary.

A Garbage Can Model
of Political Choice

The United States has in place the essential business and government bodies that are necessary to an M-Form society; however, they do not now work as a team but as adversaries. What we need to do is to reorganize some of these groups, add some elements of social memory, and then over time permit the teamwork to develop. It doesn't seem an insurmountable task. Before we can begin to design these changes, though, we must develop a common understanding of the business and governmental bodies in the United States, and creating that understanding is the task to which we now turn.

At present, the decision-making process in our government can best be described as a garbage can into which we throw people looking for opportunities, problems looking for solutions, solutions (often unrelated to the problems at hand) looking for problems, and a few windows of opportunity or choice points. Every now and then, a problem, a solution, a person, and a window of opportunity come together, and we take another step in our progress as a nation. The process is similar to the process of decision making in American universities.[2] A 1974 report of the Carnegie Commission on Higher Education described that decision process as a "garbage can" and noted, "It is clear that the garbage can process does not do a particularly good job of resolving problems."[3] It is not a flattering metaphor, but it is apt. All of the ingredients necessary for economic development are present in our business and government communities, but they are currently thrown together like so much garbage, rather than being organized in a more effective manner.

As we learn about these institutions of the United States, we will again want to keep clearly in mind our goal of seeing the whole picture rather than simply the pieces. If there is to be a dialogue between business and government over questions of economic development, who shall speak on behalf of government, and who shall speak on behalf of business? At present, each company speaks for itself, with the result that even the most development-minded government will find that it cannot sustain a dialogue with the business community because there is no community of business. Certainly, we do not wish to confine such a dialogue to only one representative of government or to one elite business association. Instead, we can imagine structuring a dialogue in which there are several parties, all of whom are in constant communication with one another, and all of whom together compose an effective network of social memory. Once we understand what we have now, we should be better able to see what we would like to create for our future.

The Structure of Politics:
Japan and the United States

The Japanese Diet is a bicameral legislature with 511 members in the House of Representatives for four-year terms and 252 members in the House of Councillors, with half up for reelection every three years for terms of six years. There is a rough correspondence between these and the U.S. House of Representatives with its 435 members and the U.S. Senate with its 100 members, but the differences are more telling than the similarities. First, the Japanese Diet is completely dominated by the house, which can pass a bill over the opposition of the House of Councillors upon a second vote of two-thirds of those present. Second, the Diet selects the prime minister from among its members and virtually all postwar ministers have been drawn from the Diet, so that the legislative-executive branch conflict of the U.S. government is ameliorated.[4]

As noted earlier, the Diet has a limited legislative role. Over the period 1975–1980, the ministries sponsored a total of 104 bills per Diet session with 80 percent passing, while Diet members in all sponsored an average of 51 bills per session with 18 percent passing.[5] By comparison, an average two-year session of the U.S. Congress sees the introduction of 22,000 bills, of which 5 percent ultimately pass.[6] In Japan, the Diet tends to approve bills with broad language, permitting the bureaus wide latitude in applying them with discretion to changing situations and trusting them to do so wisely, in part because they know that the ministry is headed by a Diet member, and in part because the bureaucracy is so open to and in tune with the public that it cannot stray far from a reasonable course of action. By comparison, in the United States, the Congress has no power over what the president or his bureaucracy does to a bill once passed, with the consequence that bills are written tightly in the attempt to limit their use to that intended by the Congress, but with the further consequence that a new bill may be needed for each variation on a problem. In the 1977–1978 Congress, of 22,314 bills introduced, 625 were originated by the bureaucracy, and of these, 44 eventually passed—a rate higher than for member-sponsored bills.[7]

Of some interest also is the internal organization of politics in each country. In Japan, the 511 representatives are elected from 130 districts, with each district electing not one, but 3, 4, or 5 repre-

sentatives. In the House of Councillors, the 252 members are selected in two ways: 152 are elected from the 47 prefectures, with
each prefecture electing from 2 to 8 councillors depending on its
population, and the remaining 100 are elected at-large in a national
election.[8] Except for a brief period in 1947, the conservatives have
continually been in power in Japan, and ever since the Liberal Democratic Party (LDP) was formed by merger in 1955, it has held a
wide majority in both houses, almost two-to-one.[9] This means that
LDP candidates are running against other LDP candidates in most
prefectural and district elections. The LDP, in fact, consists of a
collection of contending factions, each putting its own candidates
forward in every race.

Despite this party factionalism, the Japanese political parties
are highly disciplined; discord is allowed within party caucuses, but
all votes are strictly by party line.[10] To some extent, this discipline
is enforced by members' dependence upon the party faction for election funds, election support, and nomination. In the United States,
such strict party discipline would be unthinkable, although it is still
true that party affiliation is the single best predictor of voting behavior among members. The Japanese Diet and the U.S. Congress
have nearly identical numbers of standing committees in both upper
and lower houses and similar patterns of committee assignment,
but recent reforms in the U.S. Congress have created independent
subcommittee chairmen, with the result that virtually every newly
elected U.S. senator immediately takes on one subcommittee chair
or ranking committee post, and nearly one-third of house members
enjoy that power.[11] In the U.S. Congress, one consequence of this
diffusion of power has been that as many as five subcommittees
will lay claim to the right to settle a politically beneficial issue such
as the recent Environmental Protection Agency fracas, and witnesses may be called to testify before several such subcommittees
on the same issue. Needless to say, this situation does not promote
the thoughtful development of long-range plans for economic development in which one party must stand aside so that another may
progress.

On a more mundane but interesting level, a Diet member in
1980 received a salary of $60,444 (of which 25 percent is paid in the
form of lump-sum bonuses, as in industry), a transportation and
communication allowance of $34,667, plus $32,000 for legislative
costs (which goes to the party office), two secretaries, and no other

staff.[12] It is just as well. There is no place to put additional staff, because the entire office space allocated to a typical Diet member is just slightly larger than the waiting room of a typical U.S. senator. The Diet operates on an annual ordinary session of 150 days, and an extraordinary session is convened two or three times in addition. A special session will follow an election of the House of Representatives. As the political scientist Koichi Kishimoto notes: "During a regular session the House of Representatives convenes at two in the afternoon on Tuesdays, Thursdays, and Fridays and the House of Councillors at ten in the morning on Mondays, Wednesday, and Fridays . . . Quite often a meeting will be called toward evening when an important bill is to be considered. There have been cases when such a meeting lasted the entire night and into the following day."[13]

In 1980 a U.S. representative received pay of $60,662, plus an allowance of $308,328 with which to hire up to 18 full-time and 4 part-time aides. Another $80,000 was allotted, on average, for travel, communications, and the maintenance of an office in the home district. A U.S. senator received the same pay, but a larger office with office and other expenses based on state population and ranging from $711,646 for senators from the least populous states up to $1,259,874 for the senators from California. The average U.S. senator had a personal staff of 35, the average house member 16.5. In addition to these personal staffs, committee and subcommittee chairmen in the house had additional staff members numbering 2,784, with Senate committee staff numbering 1,700. In addition, all members of Congress have access to the large staffs of the Library of Congress, the Congressional Budget Office, the Office of Technology Assessment, and the General Accounting Office. The total number of congressional staffpeople today is approximately 37,000.[14] These employees serve a flood of requests from constituents and prepare for the approximately 6,000 committee hearings held in each session of two years.[15]

Members of the U.S. House of Representatives are elected for two-year terms, and only one representative comes from each district of roughly 450,000 population. Senators have overlapping six-year terms as do councillors in Japan, but two senators are elected from each state regardless of its population and none are elected at-large. Anyone who has visited the U.S. Congress knows that the typical senator or congressman starts work before eight in the morning, sees literally dozens of visitors, confers with staff, and attends subcommittee meetings, hearings, party caucuses, and floor votes until eight or so on a typical night. It is a full-time, year-round job.

But no matter how hard a U.S. legislator works, no matter how dedicated his staff, they cannot possibly understand the hundreds of important technicalities underlying each of the 22,000 bills they must face in each session of Congress. They might turn to industry associations or lobbying groups for advice on technicalities, but these special-interest groups tend to be so narrowly self-interested that their advice can be accepted only at some risk. Instead, the Congress either does nothing or drafts its own solutions without the benefit of advice from those who stand to be regulated, helped, or changed by their legislation.

In Japan, it is the executive branch in the form of MITI and the Ministry of Finance that helps to organize private industry into a coherent voice. There is no good reason that the executive branch of the U.S. government, represented by the Department of Commerce, cannot do the same. In order to play this role, however, the department will have to be reorganized. It is not an insurmountable task, but it is not a simple one, either.

The Department of Commerce

The U.S. Department of Commerce is charged with prime responsibility for the business affairs of our nation. Commerce is organized fundamentally into three major business groupings, each headed by an undersecretary (See Appendix VI–B). The three are Economic Affairs, International Trade, and Travel and Tourism. Whereas MITI consists of roughly 14,000 employees, including approximately 4,000 doing research (such as in the Electro Technology Lab) and 2,300 in the patent office, thus leaving 7,700 staff and secretaries in the seven bureaus dealing with the business community, the U.S. Department of Commerce in 1983 counted nearly 35,000 employees. Most of these were in a collection of specialized activities having nothing at all to do with the governance of business, such as the National Oceanic and Atmospheric Administration (Aeronomy Laboratory, National Severe Storms Laboratory, National Weather Service, National Marine Fisheries Service, satellite operations, and a dozen other activities), the Bureau of the Census, and the Patent Office. Commerce probably has a much smaller business liaison staff than does MITI.

The Undersecretary for Economic Affairs has four major units, which are (1) the Bureau of the Census, (2) the Bureau of Economic Analysis, (3) the Bureau of Industrial Economics, and (4) the Office of Productivity, Technology, and Innovation. The Office of Productivity, Technology, and Innovation might seem a promising place in which to look for the start of a JECC, a VLSI Research Association, or a Fifth Generation computer project for the United States. Instead, it contains the U.S. Patent and Trademark Office, the National Bureau of Standards, the Product Standards Policy Office, the National Engineering Laboratory, the National Measurement Laboratory, the Institute for Computer Sciences and Technology, the National Technical Information Service, the Strategic Resources Office, and a small Office of Productivity, Technology, and Innovation. Some of these might readily become active centers for a dialogue with the AEA, the EIA, the Iron and Steel Institute, and the Business Roundtable, but as of today they are not.

Elsewhere within the domain of the Undersecretary for Economic Affairs, one might consider the Bureau of Economic Analysis or the Bureau of Industrial Economics. The Bureau of Economic Analysis itself is divided into four divisions: National Economic Accounts, National Analysis and Projections, International Economics, and Regional Economics, all sounding much more like the groupings within a university department of economics than like sectors of American industry. Within the Bureau of Industrial Economics there are more familiar divisions into Basic Industries, Producer Goods, and Consumer Goods and Industry Services, but the bureaucratic occupants of these offices have no discussion councils or business groups attached to them, no one with whom to begin a dialogue.

Such discussion groups do exist at the commerce level, and they are attached to the Undersecretary for International Trade. Since 1974 the Undersecretary for International Trade has had the advice of nearly 500 business executives serving on 26 Industry Sector Advisory Committees (some examples: Aerospace Equipment, Automotive Equipment, Consumer Electronic Products and Household Appliances, Food and Kindred Products). These ISACs represent, by all accounts, an effective blending of business and government, and have been helpful in producing a more successful export and import policy for U.S. industry.

For the U.S. company or trade association that wants to have a dialogue with government, there may be help in the Department of Commerce, but it will be difficult to locate. With few exceptions, the department is not organized in a way that permits easy discussion with or expert knowledge of specific industries and their problems. It is not organized in a manner that invites dialogue with business, and in fact provides no discussion mechanism at all except on the issues of international trade. Moreover, the attentions of the Secretary of Commerce must of necessity be devoted in some part to those activities, such as the Bureau of the Census and the National Oceanic and Atmospheric Administration, having nothing at all to do with the governance of American business. Finally, even those companies or associations with a primary interest in trade issues are in trouble. It is true that the Undersecretary for International Trade maintains twenty-six advisory councils and has specialists in key industries as well as in key trading nations, but he or she is not in charge of international trade. If the issue is an important one, such as automobile imports from Japan, textiles from China, or U.S. machinery in Europe, the responsibility is probably held by the U.S. Trade Representative, an entirely independent body with its own office and staff and located closer to the White House.

The Government Advisory Councils

The Department of Commerce is not the only place to go. There are in addition those 23,000 citizens who serve on the 1,159 councils, commissions, and advisory boards to our federal government. These include the Citizens Advisory Board on Youth Opportunity, the Medical Libraries Advisory Board, the Cape Cod National Seashore Advisory Commission, the Atomic Energy Commission, the Federal Hospital Council, the Tuna Fish Commission, and the National Advisory Heart Council. Each of these is advisory to some bureaucratic office and all are composed of private citizens, many of whom are business executives. However, there is no mechanism for dialogue among the several bodies concerned with business, no means of maintaining among them a memory of who has yielded to whom in the past, and thus no hope of cooperation between them and us.

These councils may not be quite what we need, but they provide an adequate foundation on which to build. Consider, for example, the High-Speed Transportation Advisory Committee of the Department of Transportation. The committee consists of seven leading experts in the field of high-speed transportation. The rules set down by the Department of Transportation specify that if a meeting of an industry advisory committee is held, then the meeting must be called and chaired by a full-time, salaried government employee, a verbatim transcript of the proceedings must be kept unless it would interfere with the discussion, and that in any event, all activities of the committee are subject to antitrust laws and the committee members can be prosecuted by the Department of Justice should they engage in illegal activity during such a meeting. These protections seem to be at once sufficiently strict as to protect the public interest and sufficiently flexible as to make candid discussion possible. Thus a legal structure is already in place to enable such councils to operate, and they do. The only problem is that the members will not be able to seek the necessary cooperation from the several other advisory councils with whom they will have to work if they are to accomplish a major policy objective.

There is in the Department of Commerce no office of small and medium-size business, no bureau of computer makers or auto makers, no specialized department of industrial policy. There is not even a structure capable of coordinating trade policy with domestic policy and informing these through an ongoing dialogue with business. But the fault does not lie solely in the organization of the bureaucracy. In the world of industries and of trade associations, there is no one body or stable confederation of bodies able to speak for U.S. industry, and therefore no private arena in which the conflicts between industries can be resolved by those most knowledgable in the technical details. Instead, the raw conflicts are thrust upon the U.S. Congress, which itself is not organized to know about industries, technologies, or special problems.

How much better it would be if the different interests could settle their differences directly and then approach the Congress with a consensus, thus providing the balance of an M-Form. The members of Congress are well equipped to protect the public interest. They are not elected by companies but by citizens. The members of Congress are not equipped to deal with the narrow technical issues of an industry, however, and if they are forced to become overnight experts on technology by a warring industry, the result cannot be good public policy.

The Private Associations

It falls to the private associations to provide common ground on which more narrowly focused interest groups can directly thrash out differences with one another. The private associations may be roughly divided into three types. At the grass-roots level lie the specialized associations that serve the interests of a single industry, civic, ethnic, religious, or other group. Often these specialized associations themselves become members of more general federations of associations much like the AFL-CIO, the United Council of Churches, or the National Association of Manufacturers. Finally there are the peak associations, the largest and most important federations which, like the Keidanren of Japan, bring together not only the like-minded but the unlike-minded as well, so that big business and small business can fight it out in private, or the energy-using aluminum makers can attempt to find a political solution acceptable to the energy producers before either side approaches government people. It is these peak business associations we lack.

Some recent estimates place the number of lobbyists in Washington, D.C. and their support and clerical staffs at 40,000 people, representing the special interests of some 500 corporations, 1,600 trade associations, and perhaps 5,000 other special interests groups.[16] The groups with representation range from the U.S. Chamber of Commerce and the American Bankers Association to the National Association for the Advancement of Colored People, the National Council of Churches, the National Parking Association, and the Web Sling Association (which is represented through the Small Business Legislative Council, composed of 70 small business associations and operating as a separate arm of the National Small Business Association). Among the general, or peak associations are the AFL-CIO (a confederation of labor unions) and the National Association of Manufacturers.[17] Among the more specialized associations are the Pharmaceutical Manufacturers Association, the Young Farmers of America, and the American Textile Manufacturers Institute.

Within the arena of business, the major associations are the U.S. Chamber of Commerce, the National Association of Manufacturers, the Business Roundtable, and the American Business Conference, with the Conference Board serving as an issues and research organization similar to the Keizai Doyukai. Within the electronics industry, the most general associations are the American Electronics Association and the Electronics Industry Association. Let us consider these major organizations briefly.

The Major Business Associations

The U.S. Chamber of Commerce, founded in 1912, is massive. Its membership includes 2,800 state and local chambers of commerce, 44 American chambers of commerce in other nations, 1,350 trade associations, and 234,000 individual companies, of which 86 percent have fewer than 50 employees.[18] The headquarters staff numbers over 400 people, who coordinate the work of dozens of standing committees and hundreds of task forces each year. The chamber provides to its members a wide range of educational programs, consulting services, and government representation. However, just six years ago the chamber had 50,000 corporate members, not much more than the Tokyo Chamber of Commerce, which is but one of the 478 local chambers of commerce in Japan. By comparison, the Los Angeles Area Chamber of Commerce, which serves a population roughly equal to that of Tokyo, was founded in 1888 and has today 3,800 member firms.

The U.S. chamber has often found itself rent by internal dissention on major issues on which the big companies and the small companies have taken opposing positions, or on which companies in one industry have lined up against those in another. In such cases, the chamber has learned simply to avoid speaking out, rather than serve as the common ground on which to seek a consensus.

Alexander Trowbridge, president of the National Association of Manufacturers (12,000 manufacturing companies), describes the problem: "There is no question that we would be better off if we could get agreement among industries on major issues, such as trade policy with China. It is entirely plausible for us to get a group of people together within our organization to iron out the cross-industry positions. Our organization would also have the legitimacy to call in representatives from various other associations to deal with issues at that level. We do have the capability of doing this: the question is, do we want to? Such an effort is very time-intensive, and the people who would need to be involved in such policy decisions already have severe constraints on their time."[19]

Do the heads of the U.S. auto companies, the machine-tool companies, and the major labor unions have something better to do with their time than to work out their differences so that their industries can move ahead? Of course not—not if that time spent together might produce some positive results. What Trowbridge sees perhaps more clearly than most of us is that there is no social memory in Washington, at least not in the major associations representing business. Without a social memory, there cannot be social choice. Without choice, there can be no focused development.

In recent years a new association, the American Business Conference (ABC) has come to some prominence as the spokesman not only for its approximately 150 medium-sized and fast-growing member firms, but for a broad range of American business. The key? According to Jack Albertine, president of ABC, "Our effectiveness as a trade association results from two factors. First, we are issue-oriented. We fly into a city, have a discussion on a specific issue, and then fly out. We have no social events, we have no spouse programs. Our meetings are solely work. Second, our members don't listen to speeches, they engage in dialogue with key public policy makers . . . Our meetings are small and designed for maximum exchange and mutual impact."[20]

The model for the ABC, which was founded in 1981, was the not-very-much-older Business Roundtable, founded in 1973. Today, the Roundtable is near its self-imposed membership limit of 200. The organization is led by a chairman and three vice-chairmen who together compose the executive committee. Their policy initiatives are discussed by the 45-member policy committee, which meets for a full day once every other month.[21] Other members are appointed to one or two of the roughly 16 task forces that consider specific issues. The Business Roundtable is widely considered to be the most influential spokesman for big business in Washington, but it suffers from its reputation as being anti-small-business. The Roundtable members do not publish any information about their organization or its members, and many outsiders view the organization as narrowly representing the selfish interests of only the largest companies in America.

These criticisms notwithstanding, the Roundtable has sometimes been an effective force, largely because it engages in grass-roots lobbying. Rather than maintaining a large professional staff of lobbyists, Roundtable executives arrange for members to prepare positions and to personally present those positions to top-level politicians and bureaucrats. This strategy succeeds in part because these employers have access to top-level officials and in part because each member has a large staff that can do his research; but it succeeds mostly because the members themselves are willing to take the time to pursue their self-interest in Washington. On the other hand, it succeeds also because it does not attempt to develop positions on issues that might divide the member companies. The member companies do not meet often enough nor are they sufficiently committed to allow the Roundtable to become a common ground for settling interindustry disputes.

Perhaps it is shocking to realize that the leaders of the 200 largest American companies are actively pursuing their self-interest through the Business Roundtable, or that the yet-more-elite 150 members of the Business Council (which meets twice yearly) are doing the same.[22] Yet even among such an apparently homogeneous group, there are major differences in goals. For example, if the president and the Congress show a willingness to reduce business taxes in order to spur growth, then some members of the Roundtable will want to press for lower corporate income taxes, while other companies that pay no income tax anyway will prefer a different form of tax reduction. If they cannot resolve their differences, they will take no position at all as a group. More commonly, when they see the likelihood of such an impasse, they will avoid the issue entirely. They will not attempt to settle their differences directly, preferring instead to lobby the Congress individually. The result, of course, is 22,000 bills introduced but no action taken and no problems solved.

Perhaps the most distinctive characteristic of the Business Council and the Business Roundtable is that they make no claim to represent small business. By comparison, nearly every other trade association in Washington claims to be the voice of small business. Franklin Roosevelt asked the Department of Commerce to convene the Small Business Conference in 1938, in the hopes of building political support for the New Deal. He was instead criticized by the attendees, who wanted no part of government intervention, but the discovery of small business as a major political constituency has endured. In the year following that conference, nearly fifty new organizations appeared, each trying to sign up small-business members and claiming to represent them in Washington. Many of these associations (most now defunct) were themselves small businesses run by an entrepreneur whose primary goal was to collect dues from members. Today, three major representatives of small business remain: the Small Business Center of the U.S. Chamber of Commerce (which represents the 86 percent of chamber members with less than 50 employees), the National Federation of Independent Businesses (600,000 members), and the National Small Business Association (100,000 members). The small-business associations represent both the promise and the paralysis of the government-business relationship in the United States. Everyone claims small business as his or her natural constituency: the Republicans claim to stand for the free-enterprise system, which is the backbone of small business, while the Democrats claim to fight for the common man of small business against the powerful and rich major firms. Both sides agree, however, that small business has only a weak voice in Washington, because there is no framework through which the large membership of the associations can develop a common point of view and press it home.

The General Associations of the Electronics Industry

In Japan, the essential projects such as JECC, VLSI, DIPS, PIPS, and the Fifth Generation computer did not originate in the Japan Chamber of Commerce or in the Keidanren, but in the more specialized industry associations, such as the EIAJ, JEIDA, and JEMIMA. What of their counterpart organizations in the United States?

Electronics trade associations in the United States can be divided, as in Japan, into general and specialized. The major general associations are the Electronics Industry Association and the American Electronics Association. They are not terribly different from the Electronics Industry Association of Japan, except that we have two of them rather than one.

The Electronics Industry Association (EIA) was founded in 1924 as the Radio Manufacturers Association and today serves more than 1,000 member companies. Its primary activities consist of getting member companies together to agree on standards so that equipment produced by one company is compatible with that produced by another, collecting and disseminating statistics, organizing trade shows at which the smaller companies can display their wares, and conducting laboratory tests. As with most trade associations, the EIA carries out some lobbying and other political activity, which constitutes a small portion of its total work but which is the most challenging and glamorous assignment for the staff. The EIA welcomes foreign members and in fact has several Japanese company members that are quite active.

The American Electronics Association was founded in 1943 as the Western Electronic Manufacturers Association and today serves nearly 3,000 corporate members. During the past few years, the AEA has become perhaps the most celebrated of all trade associations in America, having almost singlehandedly reduced the tax on capital gains from 49 percent to 28 percent in 1978, a change which produced a flood of new venture capital without which the U.S. semiconductor and computer industries could not possibly have continued to grow. Along with the EIA and the SIA, it followed that success with another in 1981, a tax credit for new research and development that has resulted both in more industrial research and in large gifts of computers and other equipment to American universities, to ensure a future flow of engineers.[23] We will return later in more detail to this success story.

The Specialized Associations of the Electronics Industry

Below these large, general associations are several specialized ones. Because the industry is young and rapidly growing, several of these are relatively new. Among the most politically active is the Semiconductor Industry Association (SIA), founded in 1977 and today representing fifty-five companies in the semiconductor and computer industries. The SIA is an example of a common U.S. response to disagreement among the sectors within an industry. The SIA members were active within the AEA, where they pressed for a strong protectionist position against the Japanese semiconductor makers, who were making large advances in the U.S. market. The AEA, which has long supported free trade, refused to go along, with the result that a subset of members formed their own association. Initially, the SIA's sole purpose was to undertake political activity in Washington in order to bring to the attention of policy makers the Japanese threat to U.S. semiconductor firms. Early on, however, the SIA shifted its emphasis from protectionism to support for the U.S. semiconductor industry and targeted the high cost of capital and the shortage of engineers as its primary areas of emphasis. Today, the SIA also stands for free trade and against protectionism. In order to achieve this end, the SIA has sponsored several costly and detailed studies in order to provide data to policy makers, and its members have engaged in extensive grass-roots lobbying.

More typical of specialized associations is the National Electrical Manufacturers Association (NEMA). In 1982, NEMA served 550 U.S. electrical manufacturers with a staff of 90 and a budget of $5 million. The association consists of 70 product committees in which member companies work together to develop standards so that customers can put together components from several companies into a system. Like other associations that deal with the specifics of product design, NEMA has developed a rather elaborate set of precautions against the possibility of antitrust violations. In part, this is their description: "Because a trade association is by definition a combination of competitors, NEMA has always been careful to ensure that all its activities are conducted under strict legal scrutiny. All matters pertaining to antitrust, including reviews of minutes and monitoring subdivision activities, are handled by outside counsel that is expert in antitrust law."[24]

The Scientific Apparatus Makers Association (SAMA) was founded in 1918 and today serves 200 member companies. Annual dues range from $1,150 per year for the smallest companies to $14,200 for the largest. SAMA is active in government representation, often combining forces with the AEA, EIA, and SIA to press for changes such as the 1981 research and development tax credit. In addition, SAMA undertakes several product standardization activities for its members through 35 committees and task forces. Much of this work is not very glamorous but is quite necessary. For example, "Standards for fume hoods and metal hospital casework were revised to reflect technological changes in the products and to insure more rigorous test procedures.[25] Like NEMA, SAMA has a carefully articulated set of procedures to avoid antitrust violation. (SAMA's "Policy Statement on Meetings" is attached as Appendix VII.)

The Association of Data Processing Service Organizations (ADAPSO) was founded in 1960 and today serves 218 member companies that provide data processing services to their customers. ADAPSO's staff researches upcoming legislative issues which will affect the industry and takes them to one of the 28 committees. If the membership reaches a consensus, then ADAPSO represents it informally to politicians and bureaucrats and officially in committee and subcommittee hearings. Much of ADAPSO's interest is in telecommunications, in which 217 of the member companies will often oppose member number 218, AT&T. In such instances, the two sides will typically not attempt to reach a compromise, preferring to have the "big business versus small business" issue resolved in the committees of the U.S. Congress, and thus presenting the Congress with a sharp intraindustry division, rather than consensus. If the 217 non-AT&T companies are unanimous, then ADAPSO may take an official position on an issue against AT&T.

Tom Carter, the Dallas businessman who won the right to plug his mobile radio into the national AT&T network, established the North American Telephone Association (NATA) in 1970. Today, NATA represents 350 businesses in the communications industry, with a majority of members employing fewer than 20 people. NATA has a professional staff of 12, which assists members in dealing with the FCC, keeps them informed of the many developments affecting their industry in the Congress, and focuses on opposing AT&T on most issues.

These small and highly specialized associations represent an effective way for small and medium-sized companies to be represented on an issue that would otherwise be controlled by a very large competitor who could dominate the Congressional proceedings by providing data and research that no one small company could offset on its own. On the other hand, the very fact that such associations exist gives expression to the inability of big and small businesses to reach a compromise, and it is this failure that has by and large accounted for the continual growth of regulation and of government intervention in the United States.

There are several other specialized associations in the electronics industry. The National Cable Television Association (NCTA) represents the 1,808 companies that install cable television equipment in your home. The Semiconductor Equipment and Materials Institute (SEMI) produces trade shows and industry standardization task forces for its 400 corporate members. The Computer and Business Equipment Manufacturers Association (CBEMA) each year publishes nearly 40 reports with statistics such as total sales of business machines and supplies broken down into 300 metropolitan county areas for its 40 members, which include 3M, Bell & Howell, NCR, and Xerox. Even in the United States, competitors are both permitted and capable of some limited forms of cooperation.

If the associations tend to react to government policy rather than initiate policy, it is because the companies making up an association are unwilling to get together and engage in the long process of discussion that is the necessary prologue to effective action. If the associations have failed to initiate significant research and development activities that would move the industry ahead, it is because their members fear antitrust retaliation either from competitors or from the U.S. Department of Justice. If the associations are largely ineffectual before the Congress and the bureaucracy, it is because those bodies cannot make policy without a public consensus, and the associations themselves rarely even attempt to reach consensus between big companies and small or between one industry and another. Instead, all rail against the encumbrance of government intervention, apparently having failed to notice that each regulation was called for by one industry group seeking protection from another industry group.

Breaking our Political-Economic Gridlock

We have no need for more associations of the specialized, narrowly focused type. We do need those peak associations that can bring the private contenders together, sustain a dialogue between them, and do it in an atmosphere conducive to creating the kind of balance that characterizes an M-Form society. But is that possible? Is it the case that the Japanese are unique in their ability to forge a consensus within the private sector?

It is not that the Japanese are unique, but rather that the United States is unique, according to several business historians, including Alfred Chandler of the Harvard Business School.[26] In Europe as in

Japan, big business developed after a large public bureaucracy was already in place, and this large bureaucracy both regulated big business through administrative influence rather than law, and assisted the growth of big business. Thus, the small business sector, always a potent political force, was not threatened by the rise of big business. In the United States, however, big business appeared before the government bureaucracy was in place. The result was that big business ran roughshod over small business and that small business, having more political clout, responded by achieving regulation through law at the national level.[27] Thus it was the small shippers rather than consumers who pressed successfully for the creation of the Hepburn Act of 1906, which gave the Interstate Commerce Commission the power to set railroad rates to protect them, and it was the small retailers and distributors who were threatened by the mass merchandisers and marketers who pressed for the Sherman Act, the Clayton Act, and the Federal Trade Commission.[28]

By 1880, when the railroads came to the United States and thus permitted the growth of large-scale industries that could ship goods cheaply and mass retailers who could supply branch stores reliably, all of which threatened small business, the Japanese government was already well established. At that point, it owned three shipyards, five munitions plants, ten mines, fifty-two factories, and seventy-five miles of railroad.[29] When these were later made private, they established a basis for close business-government relations.

More important, in Japan as in France and Britain, the government was well organized to look after its small business constituency, so that big business grew up in a manner that often replaced some small business but did not create a panic. In the United States, by comparison, the total government employment in Washington totaled 1,014 civilians (in 1880), and by 1929, the U.S. government still had fewer nonmilitary employees than either Standard Oil, General Motors, or U.S. Steel.[30] Ever since the beginning of industrialization in the United States, therefore, small business has been fighting for its life by winning legislation that would protect it from the new giants. Some might say that by 1984, they had succeeded too well, for in addition to regulating the growth of big business, small business had thoroughly implanted an anti-big-business sentiment into Washington. The current anti-big-business atmosphere of our nation is not simply an eternal extension of a generalized desire for individual freedom, a desire which also characterizes the people of every nation in the world. It is more specifically the consequence of a peculiar historical pattern of development. There is no reason to believe that we cannot change it, given the will to do so.

We have in place most of the ingredients necessary for an M-Form society, one that can produce social endowments in amounts sufficient to sustain economic development at a high level. We have a hardworking and reasonably well organized congress, a Department of Commerce that can be reorganized to work more effectively with business, and a welter of trade associations. What we need is to make a few changes here and there, to create a few peak associations, and then to meld the whole into a loosely coupled but not atomized democracy.

The system does work sometimes. In fact, when all of the pieces fall into place, we are capable of sending a man to the moon, of building a national system of highways and dams, of sustaining an agricultural industry that is the world leader. When an emergency arises, the president can work with the Congress and bring together a special commission that can reorganize our politically sensitive social security system or mount a war against drug abuse. How much better off we would be if we had in place the institutional system that could attend to these issues before they become emergencies, and that could attend to the thousands of smaller issues that will never arouse the public but which are essential to the vitality of each industry. In the next chapter, we shall see how one such success story developed, a success depending upon the kind of active trade association that is commonplace in Japan but rare in the United States and a success requiring a huge commitment of time and energy from one private citizen. It is the kind of success that we will be able to repeat time and again if we can pull the pieces together into an M-Form society.

8

M-FORM SUCCESS, AMERICAN-STYLE

We may not have in place all of the elements of an M-Form society, but we do have in place the skeleton. We all know that we can bring that skeleton to life and infuse it with the wholeness of a body politic when an emergency arises. In some cases, however, we can animate the body with something less than a crisis. What it takes is the grass-roots willingness of many people to put in the time and the energy to argue through their differences with others who have legitimately opposing views. If the will is present, the dialogue can be sustained. If the dialogue continues long enough and draws in enough of key constituencies, a solution will ultimately be found. Washington loves consensus on solutions. Washington has too many problems without solutions and too many solutions without problems, but very rarely does it encounter the two in correspondence. That happens only when the people who have the problem talk to one another until they arrive at a solution. At that moment, the Washington establishment springs to action.

It is probably the case that more than half of all U.S. citizens are each represented in Washington by three or four interest groups. Each of us works for a company that probably belongs to at least one trade association; we may belong to a labor union that is represented in Washington; and we may have a religious group and an ethnic group that also represent us. Most of us probably don't even know it. We think of political access as something only professional lobbyists have, but we are wrong. They may walk the halls of the Congress and send out position papers, but they do not have access to the ears of legislators or presidents, mayors or governors. True access is had only when citizens take an active interest in an issue; at those times the lobbyist can effectively represent them. But if the citizens do not care, then lobbyists are engaged in a charade in which we pretend to be looking after our government by employing lobbyists and lobbyists pretend to be earning their keep by visiting with Congressmen and bureaucrats.

Our democracy depends upon participation. It is the most elemental lesson in civics, but one that we have forgotten. We have forgotten because we know that we cannot individually talk to the president or the Speaker of the House, nor do we participate in associations that give us the direct opportunity to engage in debate on the issues about which we care. But we can revive those associations and make them into something more than narrow instruments of personal gain. We can take control of them and build through them the peak associations that can break our political-economic gridlock. How do I know that all this is possible? Because Ed Zschau did it. Ed Zschau, who was just another guy running a 200-person company, did it with the assistance of a grass-roots association made up of other guys who worked for 25-person and 50-person companies. In the end, they were exhilarated and overwhelmed with the immense achievement of their success. It was just the kind of exhilaration in which we all can share by participating in the institutions of an M-Form society.

The Problem Was Urgent

In 1975, the U.S. electronics industries were in desperate financial straits. The new industries related to the computer business had just gotten off the ground, and they needed additional capital with which to finance their continued research, development, and growth. But the supply of capital had slowed to barely a trickle. In 1969, there had been a total of $171 million of private venture capital invested in new businesses of all kinds, and the smaller companies (net worth less than $5 million) had raised $1.4 billion in 698 separate public offerings. In that same year, the federal tax on capital gains was raised from 25 percent to 49 percent in the Tax Reform Act of 1969. The result was a shutting off of venture capital. By 1975, new private capital was down to a barely noticeable $10 million, and the smaller companies raised only $16 million through four separate public offerings.[1] Meanwhile, in Japan, the financial needs of the competitive industry were being met in part through the lease-financing of JECC, financed through loans from the government bank, and research and development efforts were being subsidized through projects such as DIPS, PIPS, and the supercomputer. It looked as though the United States government might have finished off its economic future.

The urgency of finding new capital was not just stimulated by greed. Every company in the high-technology centers of Boston, Silicon Valley, Denver, Dallas, Seattle, Portland, Phoenix, and the Research Triangle saw massive investments ahead. The 16K RAM and the 100-gate logic device were the state of the art, and the third generation of semiconductors had arrived. There were rumors in Silicon Valley, California, however, of a new Japanese project, soon to begin, that would usher in the fourth generation with a 1,000K RAM and a 1,000-gate logic device. (This was the VLSI Research Association, which in fact achieved the 1,000-gate logic device by its conclusion but reached the technology only for the 256K RAM— nonetheless a major achievement.) It was clear that the 64K RAM would be the next major event, with or without the Japanese. However, none of these possibilities could be realized without massive new infusions of capital. An SIA report described the problem: "The 64K MOS RAM, unlike the 16K MOS RAM, is not simply an extension of prior production techniques. It requires such fine geometries that in-place production equipment and techniques cannot be used. A new generation of production equipment is needed."[2] The money with which to buy this new equipment was nowhere in sight.

In 1976, Jimmy Carter was elected president on a campaign that promised in part to close tax loopholes favoring business and eliminate the celebrated if mythical "three-martini lunch." The Democratic party, still in the wake of Watergate reform, held a two-thirds majority in both the House and the Senate. Business was in for it, at least as far as taxes were concerned. Swimming against the tide was the National Venture Capital Association (NVCA), whose seventy member firms made their money only by arranging new financing through venture capital. They raised the alarm, but their protestations were widely discounted as motivated by the narrowest of self-interest.[3]

The AEA Enters

Robert Johnson (who was then a Harvard Business School doctoral candidate) described the events that followed in a detailed history.[4] The NVCA companies assisted many Silicon Valley companies in raising venture capital, and many of these companies were members of the American Electronics Association (AEA), which at the time had 900 corporate members and an annual association budget of $1.5 million. David T. Morgenthaler, president of the NVCA, approached the AEA in 1976 and again in 1977 to suggest a lobbying effort, but the most that the politically inexperienced AEA could do was take the matter under consideration. The manner in which the AEA dealt with the issue was conditioned by its underlying grass-roots approach to the organization of the association. As Johnson describes the AEA at that time, "Unlike many trade associations, it preferred not to act as a spokesman for the interests of its members before governmental bodies. Instead, its aim was to catalyze and coordinate the members' own voluntary lobbying efforts. In accordance with this point of view, the AEA maintained a lean organization.

"Most of the AEA's members were small (over two-thirds had under two hundred employees), relatively high-technology manufacturing companies. The AEA did, however, have some large and a few very large members, e.g., Hewlett-Packard and IBM. The AEA's fees were quite modest. They ranged from $200 per year to a maximum of $7,000 for those with revenues over $2 billion. The maximum contribution was deliberately kept low to ensure that the association would remain sensitive to the needs of its smaller members."[5]

In May of 1977, the AEA was planning to hold its annual AEA Capitol Caucus at which the member companies would both hear from key legislators and bureaucrats and offer their key positions to those officials. As the meeting approached, according to Johnson's history of the events, word came that the Carter administration was planning to target capital gains preferences as the key thrust of its tax reform bill. The AEA determined to take a position against this proposed reform and selected as its spokesman a member who was president of a small, high-technology company, Dr. Edwin W. V. Zschau. At the Capitol Caucus breakfast that May, the AEA entertained Al Ullman (D., Oregon), who was chairman of the House Ways and Means Committee and had many AEA members in his state. Ullman told the AEA members of his plan to push for the end of the double taxation of corporate dividends (taxed once as a corporate profit and a second time as income to the individual recipient of a dividend), and was surprised at their lack of enthusiasm. Most of his audience consisted of the presidents of small, fast-growing companies that paid no dividends, instead reinvesting all profits back into their businesses. If dividend-paying shares became more attractive, they told him, the net effect would be to make it even harder for companies like theirs to raise capital. Ullman, who must have been a true believer in the efficacy of democracy, gave them some important advice. As Johnson relates it: "Ullman's closing remarks were to the effect that, if this were really the way the audience felt, they should not be complacent. He indicated that a democracy only functions properly when interested citizens actively participate. They should therefore make an effort to organize and document their thoughts for their representatives, and to see what sort of impact they might have on federal tax policies."[6]

Ed Zschau Comes to the Fore— But Not Entirely by his Choice

That evening, in response to Ullman's challenge, the chairman of the AEA announced, without having checked with Zschau or anyone else, that the AEA would be forming a task force on capital formation and that Ed Zschau would chair it. Fortunately, Zschau is a man who is fast on his feet. During a previous career on the faculty of the Stanford University Graduate School of Business, Zschau had been famous among the M.B.A. students for his song-and-dance rendition of "Doing the L.P.," his attempt to bring some humor to the often drab task of teaching the applied mathematics of linear programming to his students.

Zschau quickly put together an eleven-person task force which included six heads of small or medium-size companies, two public affairs directors of medium-size companies, two venture capitalists, and one investment banker. At least one of these, according to Johnson, initially asked not to serve on the committee, feeling that it was pursuing a hopeless cause, but he "came along as a personal favor."[7] At its first meeting in July, the task force members discussed the contents of a briefing book that had been prepared by Zschau (who was still running his company of 200 people full-time) and Ken Hagerty, the newly hired Washington representative of the AEA. At this meeting, Johnson reports, the task force members adopted two policy positions, which were to differentiate it from more experienced associations and which, ultimately, were to prove to be decisive: "1) The task force should put forth its own proposals rather than simply react to the programs of the administration or other groups. Furthermore, whatever suggestions the task force ultimately were to make should be very specific. The extensive 'laundry list' approach adopted by the Roundtable, which set forth numerous objectives but failed to establish priorities, was held up as a perfect example of what it did not want to do. . . . 2) The task force should seek some new, hard data to buttress its position and also to differentiate itself from the masses of individuals and organizations that routinely argued their cases using only overgeneralized assertions and unsubstantiated 'sob' stories."[8]

The ability of the task force to take these positions stemmed entirely from the participative nature of the AEA itself. Only if the members of an association engage in the process of dialogue and choice can they adopt a focused initiative. If no member is willing to give way to another, then they will be left with a laundry list of items they would like, and with such an unfocused approach it is most likely that they will achieve none of their objectives. The new data the task force meant to gather was the kind of information on profitability these young entrepreneurs were embarrassed to reveal to one another, mostly because their companies were, by and large, marginally profitable. No trade association executive could suggest that members reveal such information, but one member could indeed make such a suggestion to his fellow members. Without extensive member control of the association, this kind of information-gathering would not have come to pass.

Progress in Washington, D.C.

Meanwhile, the issue of capital gains taxation began to attract national attention. President Carter let it be known that his goal was to increase capital gains taxes still more, and an op-ed piece in the Sunday *New York Times* of August 14, 1977 by a law professor of the University of Pittsburgh referred to the existing capital gains preference as welfare for the rich. The *Wall Street Journal* came out in favor of a capital gains reduction five days later, and *Business Week* reviewed the pros and cons of the issue for its readers.[9]

Meanwhile, the AEA task force was trying to find someone in Washington who would listen to them. It wasn't easy. The AEA wrote to the chief counsel of the Ways and Means Committee to ask for permission to testify at the upcoming hearings. The request never even received a reply. Meanwhile, however, Senator Gaylord Nelson (D., Wisconsin) was looking for people to testify at hearings of his Senate Select Committee on Small Business on the danger of foreign takeover of small American companies. He approached the AEA, which was not interested in his committee but saw the opportunity to gain a friend in the Congress. The AEA had collected data that they felt would attract a good deal of public attention, and Nelson wanted those results to be first announced in the hearings of his committee. The AEA bargained hard for position, and as Johnson describes it: "It was even given the leadoff slot—an advantage in getting publicity, since the first few witnesses heard were usually considered the most important."[10] Zschau and his task force did well—so well that the committee's chief counsel remarked ". . . that it was, perhaps, the most significant testimony that had ever been given before his committee, and although Senate and House functions were traditionally quite separate, he promised to see what he could do about contacting people on the other side of the Hill to find out whether a hearing could be arranged before the Ways and Means Committee."[11]

Meanwhile, Hagerty continued to supply information to newspapers and magazines in the hope that they would write stories on the need for cuts in capital gains taxes, asked AEA members to do the same, sent another letter to the chief counsel of Ways and Means, and relied upon the success before the Senate select committee. Success, in this case, refers to giving testimony that attracts the attention of the press and of the Congress. In a sense, the Congress is a year-round theater which produces perhaps three thousand committee and subcommittee hearings each year. Each hearing, of course, needs some speakers, and so speakers who can attract press coverage are in demand. Press coverage is absolutely crucial both for promoting programs (which leads to reelection) and for public recognition (which leads to reelection).

A Hearing Before Ways and Means

Finally, the task force succeeded in winning an early and therefore desirable place in the scheduled hearings of the Ways and Means Committee. However, as Johnson relates it, the more experienced hands still regarded the AEA proposal to cut capital gains taxes as something that "any seasoned observer would have to regard as a quaint but unlikely proposal to roll the clock back ten years on capital gains taxes."[12] President Carter had asked Ways and Means to take up the issue of capital gains taxes for the purpose of finding ways to close loopholes and, in the end, raise those taxes on business. He faced a Democratic House and Senate that had found great success since 1969 in raising taxes on business, in particular the capital gains tax. The public was in favor of taxing business, the mood was against business, and Ed Zschau and the AEA, a former professor now running a tiny company and an unknown trade association, sought to swim against this tide. Their testimony was allotted the standard time of five minutes, after which the committee members might ask questions that would permit further responses.

In order to provide for more detailed appreciation of its data and arguments, the AEA's part-time lobbyists put a copy of the report in advance in the hands of two junior members of Ways and Means, William A. Steiger (R., Wisconsin) and Ed Jenkins (D., Georgia). The two junior members of Congress agreed to meet privately with Zschau on March 7, the day he was to testify. Zschau met with Steiger at 8:30 A.M., before the hearings for the day began, and presented his case, concluding that the AEA felt that capital gains taxes should be zero, but that they would settle for the pre-1969 level of 25 percent. As Johnson tells it, "Zschau asked Steiger whether he would be willing to introduce legislation to accomplish what they were discussing. Steiger replied, 'I'd be very interested.' Zschau asked,

'What would it take to get you to do it?' Steiger replied, 'Get me a bill.'

"It was actually fairly uncommon for congressmen to ask lobbyists or their constituents to provide bills in legislative language. All members of Congress have free access to the House Legislative Counsel, whose job is to assist the member in drafting legislation. But on an occasion such as this, when the member knew that those petitioning him had access to good legal talent, that the matter was potentially quite complex and thus easily confused when communicated to third parties, and that the member himself was feeling pressed for time and did not want to bother with following up on such a chore, such tactics were sometimes used."[13]

Zschau was one of seven panelists who represented small business before the committee and who were supposed to air their views on the whole tax bill, not just its capital gains features. At the conclusion of the testimony, Ullman, the chairman, asked the panelists "whether they, as a group, had any sort of consensus as to where the first priorities of small businesses lay."[14] Of the seven groups represented on the panel, five said that they wanted a lower corporate income tax rate. Only Zschau and one other group called instead for a capital gains tax reduction.

The AEA Was Not Like Other Associations

The AEA had maintained relations with several like-minded groups, of which the most important to the effort was the American Council on Capital Formation (ACCF). The ACCF was not at all like the AEA, but was in reality a means to employ the services of three or four highly respected and skilled lobbyists on behalf of a wide array of corporations, partnerships, and individuals who had an interest in protecting the capital base of the economy.[15] During the period surrounding the Ways and Means hearings, the ACCF took moderate positions, seeking to shape legislation so that it would be less harmful to their constituents, while the AEA struck out with its own proposals, rather than trying to find out what President Carter was thinking, what the Secretary of the Treasury or the Council of Economic Advisors might favor, and then responding. This difference is one that perhaps necessarily arises between those associations that have the active and direct participation of their members as opposed to those that simply hire a lobbyist and leave the work to him or her. Johnson emphasizes the importance of the incentives facing the citizen-lobbyist as compared to the professional Washington representative whose members come to town only for White House tours: "The AEA task force was an ad hoc group comprised primarily of operating executives. It was less political and less inclined to look for a compromise than those more familiar with Washington. Its members did not earn their living as lobbyists, and they did not have to produce quick legislative results to survive. They could afford to be stubborn, to behave in a manner others saw as 'unrealistic,' and to pursue without compromise the solutions that they felt were right.

"The ACCF, on the other hand, was permanent and professionally staffed . . . Hence, the ACCF inclined toward seemingly attainable goals, and was reluctant to be as adventuresome as the AEA.

"The result was that, while both groups were about equally interested in reducing capital gains taxes, the AEA plodded doggedly ahead on its own, without first having surveyed its prospects, whereas the ACCF stood back and waited for an opportunity to make itself felt. In consequence, although the ACCF was, in many respects, better connected and more powerful in Washington, on this particular issue it took the singleminded effort of the more independent AEA task force to actually formulate specific proposals and lay the groundwork for the future campaign."[16]

March 1978: The AEA had its hearing before Ways and Means, Congressmen Steiger and Jenkins offered to sponsor the AEA bill in the committee, and the ACCF had begun to take an interest. It may sound as though important support for the AEA bill was building, but recall that a typical two-year Congress sees the introduction of some 22,000 bills, of which 5 percent will ultimately pass. Not only that, but the AEA had to choose between the two potential sponsors of the bill and run the risk of alienating the one not chosen, and both were junior members of the committee, without much influence. In this case, the AEA would have to gain the support of at least nineteen members of the committee in order to have them attach an amendment to the omnibus tax bill that would be reported out. Their claim would have to compete against dozens of others.

Both Steiger and Jenkins were respected members of the Congress, and both had shown a serious interest in the AEA bill. Steiger, however, was a Republican and therefore more familiar to the AEA, and he had already won the support of two other committee members, including Jim Jones of Oklahoma, a highly respected Democrat. With the immense number of bills introduced in each Congress, it is clear that no member of Congress can hope to read even a summary of all possible bills. Thus, members rely heavily on the reputations of those of their colleagues who are expert on a bill and who show their support for a bill by becoming a sponsor or co-sponsor of it. The AEA task force finally settled on Steiger as well as on a name for their bill, calling it the Investment Incentive Act of 1978. The bill was introduced by Steiger, with co-sponsorship of Jenkins, Jones, and Frenzel on March 22, 1978. H.R. 11773, as it was known, started its life with two Democratic and two Republican sponsors, and with a chief sponsor in Steiger, who although young was widely known and respected within the Congress.

The Veteran Lobbyists Take a Serious Look

At this point, the ACCF began to take H.R. 11773 very seriously and threw its very considerable expertise, weight, and good reputation in the Capitol behind the bill, according to Johnson's history. As the expert lobbyists of the ACCF began to move in, control over the AEA bill began slowly but inexorably to slip away from Zschau and his task force and into the hands of the political process, which of necessity makes its own creation out of those few issues that emerge from the mass as deserving of a serious look. Had the AEA bill come in with the support of the U.S. Chamber of Commerce, the American Bankers Association, the Business Roundtable, the AFL-CIO, the National Association of Manufacturers, and the National Federation of Independent Businesses, no further political manuvering would have been necessary. Instead, with the groups most interested in the bill in agreement, the committee members could have focused on the appropriate questions of public interest, asking whether the rich should be allowed to get richer, no matter how positive the consequences for the workingman in the form of new jobs, wondering whether the rights of every citizen were in any way compromised, and attending to the local needs of constituents. Because such a coalition almost never forms in advance; because the associations had not talked about the balance between pushing for lower corporate income taxes versus lower capital gains taxes; because each special interest group was instead pushing for its narrow self-interest in attempting to shape the omnibus tax bill, it was instead the politicians and the experienced lobbyists who now took center stage.

The story of the moving of H.R. 11773 through the House Ways and Means Committee is a tale of various congressmen competing to introduce a variation on the bill in order to end up as its final sponsor. It is a story of the senior members of the Congress using their power over the junior members to assume that sponsorship privilege so as to take credit for the bill's passage. The bill itself nearly failed as these would-be proponents fought over parental rights to a bill that would warm the hearts of potential campaign contributors, thus opening the way for opponents of the bill to come very close to defeating it. However, the story has a happy ending.

By April 5, 1978, as Johnson reports it, success was visible but still perhaps too far away: ". . . the ACCF's list showed seven Republicans and five Democrats willing to co-sponsor the Steiger bill, and at least three more Republicans and one more Democrat firmly in support of it without co-sponsorship. This brought the total to sixteen votes. Nineteen were needed to carry the committee."[17]

The bill was reintroduced with its new co-sponsors and was assigned a new number as H.R. 12111. It had picked up some additional association support from the National Venture Capital Association (NVCA), the National Association of Small Business Investment Companies (NASBIC), the Securities Industry Association (SIA), and one corporation, TRW Systems. But the major associations were still on the sidelines. The new task force consisting of both the ACCF and AEA, with Zschau very much in the center of things, looked for more support. They thought that large insurance companies, which hold their policyowners' funds in investments that are subject to capital gains taxes, might be a natural ally. "However, it turned out that these companies, as heavily regulated businesses, were already deeply involved with the federal government regarding other matters. As a result, they either found it difficult to get worked up about this specific matter, or they thought they had better not push their goodwill too far by adding yet another item to their list of contentions."[18] Had the insurance industry and the electronics industry shared membership in a large organization like the Keidanren, they would have been far more capable of discussing this issue, and their joint support for the Steiger Amendment would not have worn out their goodwill with the Congress, since it would have been only part of a general business consensus.

On April 17, the committee began its "markup session," considering each of the suggestions for tax reform made by President Carter as well as those bills proposed by members of Congress. As the early sessions began, it became clear that the president's program of closing tax loopholes did not have much support, in part because he had failed, in the eyes of his Democratic committee members, to approach them in a flexible manner. By April 20, the president's tax reforms were clearly in trouble, and it appeared that the committee might end up cutting taxes instead. At this point, the professional lobbying organizations began to join the fray, sensing a possible success. The Securities Industry Association began to lobby actively for the Steiger Amendment, as did the firm of Merrill Lynch, and on April 20, the U.S. Chamber of Commerce swung into action, asking its members to contact members of the committee representing them, with special attention paid to those who had not yet decided whether to vote for or against the capital gains tax cut. By April 24, the ACCF had managed to draw in the biggest companies, which had their own lobbying staffs in Washington, and which were for the first time considering active support of the Steiger Amendment. Included at the ACCF meeting were Lockheed, U.S. Steel, Mead, Smith Kline, Merrill Lynch, Kennecott Copper, Weyerhaeuser, and others.[19]

The Wall Street Journal Legitimates the Effort— Everyone Jumps on the Bandwagon

On April 26, Jude Wanniski published an editorial in the *Wall Street Journal* entitled "Stupendous Steiger." Wanniski gave the credit to Steiger rather than to Zschau and the AEA, but certainly Steiger deserved a good deal of praise. In part, the editorial read, "The Carter tax package, already reeling from other setbacks, has been stopped in its tracks by the Steiger Amendment. Mr. Carter wants to raise, not lower, the capital gains rate . . . The key to Mr. Steiger's sudden success is one argument: A lower tax on capital

gains will raise more money, not less, for the government . . . Meanwhile, the Business Roundtable and the National Association of Manufacturers stand silent . . ."[20] Two days after the
article appeared, the NAM called Steiger to offer its assistance, and
other companies contacted the ACCF. The capital gains tax cut
looked like a winner, and everyone wanted to be part of it. Also on
April 28, Senator Hansen offered to introduce a Senate version of
the bill, in order to speed passage once the House had passed its
initiative. (Although the House must initiate all legislation dealing
with taxes, the Senate must agree.)

On Wednesday, May 3, Zschau came to Washington to meet
with Hansen and with Senator Bentsen, and on May 4 he met with
other senators, including Long, chairman of the Senate Finance
Committee, which would have control over the bill in that chamber.
Johnson tells the Senate story well: "By Friday, Senator Hansen had
all of the Republicans and four of the Democrats of the Finance
Committee signed on, a total of eleven out of a possible eighteen
votes. Monday, he had fifty-one Senate co-sponsors—an incredible
accomplishment in so short a time for such a controversial
bill . . . Hansen's bill was scheduled to go in Thursday afternoon . . . by the time he finally entered it, S.3065 had sixty senators."[21] On May 18, the AEA again held its annual Capitol Caucus.
This time, Congressman Al Ullman, seeing what his admonition of
the previous year had wrought, said to the AEA members, "Last
year I suggested that you go do your homework and think about the
issue. I did not intend that you nail the barn door open and shoo
out the livestock." By this time, the lobbyists were preparing for
votes of the full House and Senate, and were attempting to build
public opinion to the point that President Carter would not dare to
veto the bill. As Johnson continues, "In late May, Merrill Lynch
alone arranged to send out 1.6 million flyers asking for support of
the bill, and hundreds of thousands of others were being distributed
by E. F. Hutton, Smith Barney, and other securities companies. Ultimately, over 6 million pieces of mail were sent out by at least 84
firms."[22]

The Final Steps

Meanwhile, the AEA and Ed Zschau continued their program
of grass-roots lobbying by asking AEA members to contact their

congressmen and senators to express support for the bill. In July, the task force sent to each member of the U.S. Congress a tape recording of a new song that Zschau had recorded, "The Old Risk Capital Blues."[23]

> We've got those old risk capital blues,
> Folks don't invest, consumes what they choose,
> The gains are what attracts 'em
> But not when we high tax 'em
> And there's high risk they could lose.

Who could resist that kind of lobbying? As the press paid more attention to the Steiger-Hansen bill, the public became more aware of the issue. And as it became more aware, to the surprise of many, the public supported the capital gains tax reduction. According to Johnson, a Roper pole released on July 26 "supported the continuation of the preferential treatment for capital gains and did not consider it a 'loophole.' A Harris survey released on August 14 had the public supporting a reduction in capital gains taxes ... by a majority of 66 percent in favor to 28 percent opposed."[24]

On August 9, Zschau visited the White House to talk with the senior staff, in the hopes of avoiding a presidential veto of the bill. On the strength of overwhelming floor votes in the House and the Senate, the Investment Incentive Act of 1978 reached the White House. President Carter had been resoundingly defeated by his own party in his attempt to raise the capital gains tax. Rather than having a conciliatory public signing of the bill, as Johnson concludes the story, "On the night of Monday, November 6, President Carter signed the Revenue Act of 1978 privately, with no warning—and no photographers."[25]

Robert Johnson's finely detailed history of this event gives us the rare opportunity to see how the tide of public opinion can be turned. It gives us a feeling for the impact one person can have in bringing about a massive change few had thought possible. It gives us some insight to Ed Zschau, who entered the U.S. Congress in 1983 not as a private citizen but as a member, representing a district in northern California that includes Silicon Valley, a new congressman who was dubbed the star of the freshman class of Congress by the *New York Times*. More importantly, however, it provides us with the raw material from which we can consider the pattern of influence that created this change.

Not everyone would consider the passage of the Steiger-Hansen bill a great success. There is no doubt that it produced the desired effect: new private capital committed to venture investment, which had declined to a total of only $10 million in 1975, was back up to $900 million by 1980. Equity capital raised by small and medium-size companies, which was down to 4 offerings totalling $16 million in 1975 had risen to 135 offerings totalling $821 million by 1980. The new high-technology companies were faced with a flood of new investors offering the cash needed for new equipment and willing to take the high risk of failure associated with these ventures. New jobs were created and the new electronics industries were supported. However, it is true that the rich got richer. In the whole story related by Johnson, the United Auto Workers were never brought into the dialogue. Common Cause did not have a voice, and the United Council of Churches never had a hand in the decision. Certainly, no one thought to ask the Web Sling Association what its members thought.

Rather, the decision very much came out of the garbage can of Washington politics. A problem came together with a solution and a man who created the opportunity for change. The other bystanders waited until they saw the coming of a decision, and then supported it—some for the simple reason of being able to report to their clients or constituents that they, too, had been responsible for the tax cut. The public interest was probably in no danger of being abused in a major way—each member of the Ways and Means Committee had in mind a broad constituency which went far beyond venture capitalists and high-technology company presidents. Had the proposed change in fact been against the public interest, its weakness would have been found out, and the bill could not have succeeded.

The Importance of Participation—The AEA as a Grass-Roots Association

Today, the American Electronics Association is approaching a membership of 3,000 companies. Its staff has grown from 22 professionals in 1977 to 90 in 1983 and its budget to over $8 million per year.[26] Its basic philosophy has not changed. Ken Hagerty, vice-president for government relations, comments: "We are able to get constituents excited because we are achieving the self-interest of their companies. But what makes the constituents especially excited is that they're achieving their own self-interests while at the same time they're working for the best interests of the country.

"AEA does experience disagreement at both the committee level and at the association level. At the committee level, motions are often made which are not supported. Such motions experience a slow, subtle, and tactful death. At the association level, there was recently a strong disagreement between large constituents and small constituents. This issue was never resolved, and AEA decided not to take a specific position."[27] Rather than simply add up each company's requests and end up with a meaningless laundry list of issues, the AEA will not take a position unless consensus exists. However, rather than permit that policy to degenerate into an equally ineffective cloud of probusiness or antigovernment rhetoric, the AEA members debate with one another until they can arrive at a consensus on key issues.

Ed Ferrey, president of the AEA, explains why the association can develop a consensus supporting a task force like Ed Zschau's where other associations fail: "First, when the electronics industry first began during World War II, survival of all the companies depended on their cooperating. The goal of this cooperation was to develop sufficient leverage so as to divert some of the defense contracts to the California defense industry. Second, during World War II, many of the engineers who were starting their companies were young and felt a need to share technological information. While they shared information on basic engineering, they remained competitive on production and product technology. Third, the informal interaction style, which characterizes the high technology industry in California, is simply a reflection of the informal style of California society as whole . . . In Silicon Valley, we have developed the kind of corporate memory that you have suggested."[28]

The AEA is led by a fifty-person board of directors, which meets four times per year. Because the AEA is a grass-roots association, active participation rather than symbolic membership is expected. As Ferrey says, "If a member of the board misses two meetings, I meet with the member to discuss whether or not it would be appropriate for the person to resign. When a new board member is selected, that person is expected to make a two-year commitment."[29] Under the board are seven steering committees, each charged with the goal of advancing one of the seven basic objectives formulated by the board. Announced in March 1983, the seven steering committees were: National Competitive Strategy, Government Relations, Capital Formation, Innovation and Small Business, Technical Education, Management Programs, and Health and Safety.[30] Each steering committee is headed by an AEA member who is typically the chief executive officer of his or her company. Below these are the standing committees and task forces, which typically include specialists from each company on the issue at hand. In the field, the AEA consists of thirteen area chapters, called AEA Councils, each of which has meetings of its members at least once a month.

In 1981, AEA once again called upon its grass-roots organization to lobby hard—and successfully— for further capital gains tax reductions as well as for tax reductions for new expenditures on research and development. On June 11, 1981, 160 chief executives of AEA member companies descended on Washington, D.C. and conducted 83 separate lobbying sessions with key congressmen, senators, and members of the administration. In that effort, the AEA was joined by the related electronics associations: CBEMA, EIA, SAMA, and SIA. In Massachusetts, the Massachusetts High Technology Council (founded in 1977) worked closely with Representative James Shannon, who authored some key provisions of the 1981 tax bill. These recent successes have given the electronics associations greater visibility within the federal government as well as greater enthusiasm and support among their member companies.

In part, the AEA succeeded because the electronics industry currently enjoys public appeal: it represented newness, growth, entrepreneurship, and the future of American inventiveness. In part, it succeeded because it engaged in the most effective forms of lobbying: giving well-organized and credible information, and personal appearances by working executives from the industry. A 1980 study of lobbying techniques asked 159 chief legislative assistants of congressmen to rate the various forms of lobbying in terms of effectiveness. The two most effective were those used principally by the AEA: direct contact with congressmen by constituents, and the giving of information through expert witnesses, personal visits, and technical reports. The two least effective techniques are those typically used by the traditional trade associations: letter campaigns, media campaigns, and the publishing of voting records; and direct pressure through threats of political harm or control of financial support.[31]

Most importantly, however, the AEA was able to put forth a coordinated effort because it had first created a framework through which to achieve consensus among its members, large and small. Without that consensus, the AEA could not have mobilized its resources, and nothing would have been achieved. The success of the AEA is all the more important because its primary membership is from companies with 50 to 200 employees, not the giants. Other research has suggested that industries composed of a few very large firms tend to have more political influence as measured by their success at winning special tax reductions, whereas industries with many smaller firms are typically unable to form a consensus and thus are unable to wield political power.[32] It is above all the lack of industry consensus that stymies the political process in the committees of the House and the Senate. A busy congressman cannot waste time refereeing a war between factions within an industry, and instead will ignore their possibly serious needs. If the intraindustry or interindustry conflict is very great, then the member of Congress runs the risk of alienating one or another constituency if he or she takes sides. On rare occasions, the power groups may maneuver congressmen into the role of brokers, in which case each side will barrage its target with conflicting "facts" on the same issue. Good policy cannot possibly emerge from such a garbage can of choice.

The Political-Economic Gridlock

David Price, a political scientist, has reviewed the proceedings of the Senate and House Commerce Committees over the period 1969–1974.[33] What he finds is that legislation proceeded only when consensus existed among the industry groups concerned. However, because consensus was rare, action rarely occurred, and many serious problems went unresolved. For example, cable television is still not as widely available nor as highly developed as the public would like, because the cable operators, networks, public television stations, and other parties have been unable to reach agreement. Rather than deal with an obvious need to create a statutory base on which cable TV could develop, the committees over that five-year period passed the following twelve bills: six dealing with matters such as COMSAT board election procedures and the conditions under which amateur radio licenses may be granted to aliens; one regulating campaign broadcasting; one ending local blackouts of sold-out professional sports events; and four public broadcasting authorizations.[34] In the area of surface transportation, Price reports that, "The prospect of conflict does not always discourage initiatives—in fact, surface transportation ranks high in the number of bills reported and the days of hearings held—but it often dooms what initiatives are taken to failure. During the 91st–93rd Congresses the landscape was littered with bills that had enough industry and congressional support to be reported by a committee or passed by one house, but ran afoul of crosscurrents of opposition short of final enactment—a proposal permitting railroads to charge freight forwarders lower rates than other shippers, a requirement that states spend 5 percent of their federal highway funds on rail-highway crossing improvements . . ."[35]

On another issue, the truckers and the railroads finally came to terms with one another in order to support a package of $5 billion in subsidies to their industries, and their willingness to cooperate, according to Price, prompted this assessment from Vance Hartke, chairman of the Senate Surface Transportation Subcommittee: "The transportation industry is its own worst enemy. There are so many differences among the railroads, the truckers, and the water carriers that we cannot make a start on solving the industry's problems."[36] Although the federal honey had brought the bees together in this case, in the end they were opposed by some shippers, farm organizations, and local communities, and the legislation did not pass.

In the fishing industry, Price quotes a Senate staff member: "Fishing is basically a dying industry, but it's very sad, because the industry will shoot down any proposal that would bring meaningful change . . . they have all kinds of conflict among themselves—anybody who puts something forward is sure to offend somebody, so most politicians simply shy away."[37]

It is currently very much the fashion for American executives to complain that our government is so disorganized as to be incapable of solving our problems. Even I have sounded such a note in my perhaps overly critical appraisal of the organization of the U.S. Department of Commerce. The view is expressed succinctly by political scientists Lester Salamon and John Siegfried: "Despite the deceptive symbolism of a single chief executive giving direction to the executive establishment, the federal bureaucracy is really a bewildering smorgasbord of institutional types with varying degrees of autonomy. Rather than unified administrative structures, Cabinet-level departments frequently resemble loose collections of warring fiefdoms, only nominally subservient to a common sovereign. Add the numerous government corporations, the quasi-independent regulatory agencies, the special commissions, the advisory committees, the singleheaded and multiheaded agencies, the institutions and institutes, and the interagency committees, and the impression of unity and consistency disappears like fog under the morning sun."[38]

In the offices of bureaucrats, one often hears similar criticism leveled at the House and the Senate. It is often said, especially recently, that each of the nearly two hundred subcommittees of the Congress constitutes a separate domain that is largely unresponsive either to party leadership or to congressional leadership, with the result that policy cannot be produced across these competitive bodies. In the end, the question must be: whom do we want to be in control of our nation's business, and where should the power reside? Do we want initiatives to emanate from the bureaucracy or from the congress? If so, then we should properly look to them for cohesion, consensus, and leadership. If, however, we expect those initiatives to stem from the private sector, then the cohesion and the consensus must originate there, and we can place more limited and perhaps more realistic demands on the role of government.

The Best Industrial Policy Is a Participative Democracy

Nolan Bushnell, the founder of Atari, is not confused about who should be in charge of American business: "I guarantee you that no government agency can target the right industry; in fact, I'll almost guarantee they'll target the wrong one. The targeting role belongs to the entrepreneurs. The problem is that these Atari Democrats would never have targeted Atari."[39] But in America, business and government are inexorably intertwined, and thus business, if it is to supply the initiatives, must be capable of forming consensus positions and presenting them. Consider the appraisal of a member of the White House staff in 1983: "The decisions that come out of this place are often not informed. Only four or five electronics associations have significant contact with this office: AEA, CBEMA, SIA, and EIA. The other associations are interested in having the vice-president speak at their annual meetings, having pictures taken of him with the chairman of the board of a member of the association, arranging tours of the White House, and so on. Most trade association contact deals with trivia 90 percent of the time."[40]

9

MINNEAPOLIS
the M-Form
in action

Collaboration is possible between competitors, even in the United States of America—Ed Zschau and the American Electronics Association demonstrated that. The test, however, was not a fully satisfying one. True, the various elements of the business community preferred tax cuts in forms other than capital gains and ultimately arrived at a consensus on a capital gains cut. But a tax cut is a tax cut, and no business sector is fundamentally opposed to lower taxes. Furthermore, the success of the task force required a red-hot level of energy and of commitment for only a few months. True, the AEA has sustained its grass-roots style ever since its inception, and it was the internal participation of the AEA that made the success possible, but the other elements of the business community came together for only an instant. On the next major issue they will have to be brought together all over again. Maybe we can do it from time to time, but the Japanese seem to keep it up forever. Perhaps it is a cultural difference at bottom, one that simply must stand.

Those are the doubts that we all harbor, the doubts that hold us back from committing ourselves, that prevent us from taking control of our political and economic future. Remember those doubts as you read about Minneapolis.

Minneapolis, Inc.

Minneapolis works. The twin cities of Minneapolis and St. Paul, Minnesota, with a combined population of slightly more than one million people, are by any measure successful cities. An August 5, 1980 story by Lawrence Ingrassia of the *Wall Street Journal* summed it up: "Now that Chicago doesn't work, Minneapolis is being viewed as the city that does—at least as well as any aging Northern city can. With a bit of good government, Minneapolis has managed to avoid the big-city blues. A diversified economy, civic-minded businessmen and forward-looking public officials share the credit with a strong tax base and generous state handouts. Downtown Minneapolis is thriving. Fancy new office buildings complement a stylish shopping mall and 'skyway' network of second-story walkways that connect major buildings. Growing agribusiness and high-technology companies make Minneapolis a white-collar town. And though a few neighborhoods are tattered, most are flourishing. Compared with other big Northern cities, Minneapolis has no ghetto. In studies by urbanologists, Minneapolis comes up again and again as a fiscally and physically healthy city. It scored third-best (after Dallas and Seattle) in a 1978 report by the Congressional Budget office that ranked 39 cities by social need. (Newark, New Jersey, Cleveland and St. Louis were judged worst off. New York was nineteenth.) Minneapolis finished 1979 with a $17.2 million budget surplus. It has a AAA bond rating from both Standard & Poor's and Moody's."

Minneapolis has some built-in advantages. It ranks thirty-eighth in population among U.S. cities, with 375,000 people, is geographically isolated, thus perhaps promoting a sense of community, and has a largely homogeneous ethnic community, with Chicano, black and Native American populations comprising ten percent of the total. More importantly, Minneapolis is comprised largely of a locally run economy. Most of the companies in Minneapolis are headquartered or were founded there. Roughly half of the manufacturing workers are employed by locally based firms, the highest ratio in the country. Of those who work for companies headquartered or owned by the "outside," ninety percent are in companies that had originally been founded in Minneapolis and were subsequently sold to outsiders.[1]

Minnesota's Economic History

Minneapolis has done what many other American cities now hope to duplicate: it has succeeded at developing one new major industry after another, thus continuing to provide jobs, growth, and prosperity for its citizens. In the 1830s, Minnesota industry began with the lumbering of the 70 percent of the state covered with trees. Soon thereafter, grain and flour milling developed, so that by 1860, farmers in the state were growing 2 million bushels of wheat, and there were 85 mills in Minnesota. By 1890, production was up to 50 million bushels of wheat, processed in more than 500 flour mills in the state.[2] From this industry grew five major corporations which, by 1980, had combined sales of $20 billion: Cargill, Inc., Pillsbury Co., Peavey Co., General Mills, and International Multifoods.

Minneapolis has not always benefitted from its economic resources, however, as Don W. Larson notes in his history of Minnesota business: "It's a surprising fact to many, even today, that for five decades starting in the 1890s, Minnesota produced more than half of all the iron used in the entire country . . . Approximately two-and-a-half billion tons of iron ore have been taken just from the Mesabi range, an area about 100 miles long and not much more than a mile wide . . . the unbelievable wealth created by the rich iron ore in northeastern Minnesota could have had more long-lasting benefits for the state . . . Instead, the bulk of the treasure created by the iron ore flowed back East to shrewd capitalists who simply outfoxed the industrious Minnesotans who were long on hard work and dreams but woefully short of the investment dollars it took to develop the mining, and even more lacking in the cunning that business matters required in those days."[3]

It is interesting to note that the St. Paul-based Minnesota Mining and Manufacturing Company (3M), the makers of Scotch Tape as well as of many high-technology products, was never in the mining business: "The company was formed by five men, who had no experience in mining, to mine a product, which, as it turned out, didn't even exist. It took a St. Paul financier and two green farm boys to correct this mistake and eventually to make the company one of the world's largest diversified industrial corporations."[4]

Having had its forests denuded and its mineral resources pillaged by outsiders, depending still on agriculture and milling, Minneapolis was delicately balanced to face the Great Depression. Following the Panic of 1893, the St. Paul-based Northern Pacific railway fell into receivership, a dozen Twin Cities banks closed, and many meat packers went out of business. Yet out of that period, the Geo. A. Hormel meat packing company emerged ready to grow, Investors Diversified Services was founded, to become the largest financial company of its type, and the Dayton Hudson Company, among the nation's largest retailers today, began. The Gamble-Skogmo Company was formed (by 1977, it had grown to 3,144 retail and financial services outlets), the Minneapolis-Honeywell Company was founded, and eleven farmer-owned creameries joined together to form the Land O'Lakes cooperative, which today represents more than 150,000 farmers organized into 900 local cooperatives to market their butter. Entrepreneurship and the free enterprise system were creating jobs and prosperity, and then came the great Crash of October 1929.

As Larson relates the history, Minneapolis survived the Great Depression in much better condition than did the rest of the nation. This was due in large part to cooperation among the local bankers who reorganized themselves in order to be able to continue to provide credit to their customers and to avoid bank failures that would lead inevitably to foreclosures on farmers and small and medium-size businesses, thus worsening the effects of the Depression. "Banking leaders in Minneapolis and St. Paul . . . were worried about economic conditions a full year before the 1929 crash, and, fortunately, were taking some drastic action . . . The concept that was settled upon was a form of group banking. Based on the idea that in union there is strength, group banking seemed to offer advantages to the large city banks, as well as to the hard-pressed rural institutions. Above all, it promised to bring stability to what was rapidly becoming a chaotic situation. . . . The stability of the banking system, especially in the Twin Cities, reflected on many other businesses throughout the Depression, and although there was a large number of failures among the marginal companies, nearly all of the major firms survived."[5]

World War II saw more than 300,000 Minnesotans leave their jobs to join the military, while Munsingwear converted from civilian to military clothing, Minneapolis-Honeywell converted to military production, Cargill built tankers for the navy, the Andersen Corporation constructed wood huts for the army air corps to use around the world, and dozens of defense plants sprang up around the state. The workers of Minneapolis worked three shifts a day, seven days a week, to help the national cause. When the war ended, however, so did the orders.

High Technology Comes to Town

On January 8, 1946, William C. Norris and a group of associates founded Engineering Research Associates, a new computer company. The new company successfully developed Atlas II, a supercomputer that it continued to market after the company was acquired by Remington Rand. In 1955, however, Remington Rand was merged with Sperry Gyroscope, forming the Sperry Rand Corporation. Its computer division, the Univac division, was headed by Bill Norris, still has its main manufacturing facilities in Minnesota, and today employs 12,000 people in its Twin Cities plants. But Norris moved on, founding the Control Data Corporation in Minneapolis in 1957. By 1970, Control Data had more than 40,000 employees throughout the world, with sales over $1 billion. But more importantly, Minneapolis had entered the age of high technology.

Some of the companies that have sprung up in the field of microelectronics have names that might have come from the home ground of the field, Silicon Valley, California, or Route 128, outside of Boston: Fabritek, Midwest Circuits, Transistor Electronics, Data Display, General Magnetics, Comserv, Telex, Whitehall Electronics, Electro Med, Comten, Flo-Tronics, Theratron, Tronchemics Research, United Software, and Community Electronics are some of them. Relating this history of new growth, Larson summarizes: "Of the world's top five computer manufacturers, four of them—IBM, Honeywell, Sperry Univac and Control Data—are either headquartered in Minnesota or have huge facilities here. There are more than 100 electronics-related firms based in Minnesota, with about 80 devoting most of their efforts to computers ... As one industry executive says, 'The computer industry has done more for Minnesota's self-image, in the quality of life area, than the Guthrie Theater and the Mayo Clinic put together.' "[6]

Corporate Giving in Minneapolis

In this age of self-centeredness and in our system of free enterprise profit-maximizers, Minneapolis is anomalous. In 1981, 62 local companies gave 5 percent of their pretax profits to charity, creating social endowments. Another 21 were members of the Two Percent Club, giving that level of pretax earnings. For the United States as a whole, corporate giving has remained steady at 0.66 percent to 0.75 percent of pretax earnings. For all of the state of Minnesota, corporate giving averages 50 percent above the national rate. For example, in 1977, the 3M Company gave $5 million (1.5 percent of pretax profits), General Mills gave $3.3 million (2.5 percent), and Pillsbury $1 million (1.25 percent). H. B. Fuller gave $425,000 (5 percent), and in 1973 started a Community Affairs Council, consisting of employees, shareholders, and a customer, to screen requests for donations. In 1979–1980, Minnesota businesses and foundations gave $112 million back to the communities in which they operate: 58 percent in the Twin Cities, 14 percent throughout the rest of the state, and the remainder in other states in which they operate.[7]

The giving is not restricted to big business. A 1982 study shows that among companies with fewer than 25 employees, 38 percent gave more than 1 percent of pretax earnings, at 26–200 employees 27 percent gave at that level, at 201–1500 employees 43 percent gave more than 1 percent, and of firms with more than 1500 employees, 61 percent gave at least 1 percent.[8] In 1976, the Greater Minneapolis Chamber of Commerce formed the Minnesota 5 Percent Investment Program, more commonly known as the Five Percent Club. The Five Percent Club has grown from 23 charter members to 62 members in 1981. Its members include the large and the small. Some of them are: Anderson's China Shop; Bolger Publications Creative Printing; Dayton Hudson Corporation; First National Bank of Minneapolis; Graco Inc.; Harold Chevrolet, Inc.; Kidder, Peabody, Inc.; Minneapolis Star and Tribune Company; and Plywood Minnesota, Inc.

Where does the money go? Each corporate donor makes its own decision, sometimes aided by civic consultation. Overall, approximately 44 percent goes to health and welfare (Afton Lakeland Preschool Center, American Indian Health Care Association, Big Brothers, Childbirth Education Association of Minneapolis, Children's Home Society of Minnesota, Dakotas Adults Inc., Loring Nicollet Meals on Wheels, Minneapolis Hearing Society, Sabathani Community Center, Sholom Home Inc. Auxiliary, and Youthcraft Industries are a few of them); 24 percent to education (Augsburg College, Flight Unlimited, Minnesota Alumni Association of the University of Minnesota, Plymouth Montessori, and United Ministries in Higher Education, for example); 14 percent to culture and art (African American Cultural Center, Bloomington Historical Society, Metro Boys Choir, Minnetonka Orchestra Association, Twin Cities Catholic Chorale, and Weavers Guild of Minnesota); 13 percent to civic activities (YMCA, Council of Community Councils, Midway Club, Powderhorn Residents Group); and the remainder to assorted groups such as the Armstrong Hockey Boosters, the Twin City Yoga Society, Minnesota Public Radio, Legal Assistance of Ramsey County, Old Town Restorations Inc., the Twin Cities Center for Urban Policy, the Twin Cities Tree Trust, Good News for Israel, and the White Bear Lake Babe Ruth League.[9] Every city has similar civic, educational, and other groups, but the typical city funds these groups at two-thirds the level of Minneapolis. Why? Is it simply "a bit of good government," as the *Wall Street Journal* noted, that enables Minneapolis to avoid the "big-city blues"? That interpretation echoes the descriptions of "Japan, Inc." as having succeeded through better bureaucrats.

Some might argue that publicly owned businesses should not give to charity at all, that instead they should return dividends to shareholders, each of whom can choose the charity he or she prefers. In essence, the logic of free choice underlying such an argument is unassailable. The fact, however, is that each of us benefits through a healthy community and in Minneapolis, that community is sustained largely through corporate giving. The pattern of corporate giving in Minneapolis makes it clear that the corporate decision-makers are small enough in number and tied closely enough together to comprise a community with a memory.

The Social Memory
Produces Social Endowments

Why did Anderson's China Shop donate $1,000 in 1976? "My grandfather founded the company in 1879 and I came into the business thirty years ago. It's a natural thing to give at least five percent. We're part of the community", said President Alan Anderson in an AP story.[10] That is precisely the motivation of Dayton-Hudson to give 5 percent of its earnings each year for more than thirty years, a sum that currently amounts to more than $5 million per year. The reason is cited by Brandl and Brooks in a study of Minneapolis: "The civic involvement of business leaders is by no means entirely a matter of individual choice. There is conscious and explicit peer pressure to participate in public affairs; the area sees itself as a community."[11]

What is most striking about Minneapolis is not its level of corporate giving, nor its consistent ability to develop new industries, nor its ability to reorganize its banking industry in order to survive the Great Depression. What is remarkable is that Minneapolis is a community. It is a community of people who are connected to one another, who place peer pressure on one another, who remember for fifty or one hundred years who has been helpful in the past and who has not. Like any community it can at times be forceful, perhaps even heavy-handed in insisting on local values, but on the whole, it succeeds not by diminishing individualism, but by creating a balanced environment in which entrepreneurs like the maverick Bill Norris can build companies and create visions, in which a Luigino Francesco Paulucci can create visions like the Chun King Corporation and then Jeno's. Their individual energies are balanced by a network of concerned peers, with an interest for the long-run health of the community. These individualists, rather than being narrow-minded profit seekers at odds with their environment and adversaries of their city, become part of the community. The Business-Higher Education Forum concluded that we can overcome our adversarial relationships only with a new spirit of cooperation, but added that "very few institutions are capable of facilitating such cooperation. This major gap must be overcome." This major gap does not exist in Minneapolis.

The Units of Social Memory

The community exists in a web of relationships that brings together the business, civic, political, and other sectors in close contact. These contacts take place within dozens of committees, councils, and other private groups organized by concerned citizens. Among these, the most important are the Downtown Council, the Minnesota Association of Commerce and Industry (MACI), the Minnesota Business Partnership, the Citizens League, the Minneapolis

Project on Corporate Responsibility, and the Greater Minneapolis Chamber of Commerce. Many people are simultaneously active members of three or four of these groups, siding with one interest group in one setting and against them in another, but knowing always that they will be remembered for their deeds throughout the community.

The Downtown Council

In the 1950s, Minneapolis, like other cities, was worried that major employers were beginning to move to the suburbs and to look at the Sunbelt cities, that the inner city would decay, that the area would lose its vitality. The major retailers, banks, and other businesses in the downtown area formed the Downtown Council in 1955, for the purpose of reversing that trend. Today, the downtown area boasts the Nicollet Mall, a $400 million construction and development project that houses shops, offices, and residences. The principal office and shopping buildings downtown are connected by the Minneapolis Skyway, a system of pedestrian bridges linking thirty-five city blocks with thirty-four bridges. The bridges are lined with shopping arcades, restaurants, and service shops. It allows pedestrians to avoid the cold winters and the street traffic, and encourages them to come downtown.

Today, the Downtown Council has more than 700 citizens working on 16 different committees, such as the Committee on the Future, the Governmental Relations Committee, the Pedestrian Circulation Committee, and the Riverfront Committee. The Council is headed by a group of 36 officers and directors, of whom 31 represent businesses, 4 the press, and 1 a downtown church. In 1981, the council president was a banker. His predecessors were the head of Charlie's Cafe, a representative of the Lutheran Brotherhood, and a newspaperman. Although big business is clearly in evidence, it would be difficult to describe the Downtown Council as the tool of business interests.

The council operated in 1983 with a budget of $265,000 and a paid staff of four. Clearly, its power derives from its members. O.D. Day, the director of the Downtown Council, sees the objective as that of creating and sustaining a dialogue: "If you ask me who is in the partnership, it depends on the project. Business, city government, and organized labor are all involved. By talking together and working together we stop a lot of misconceptions . . . Most failures comes from poor planning, no financing, and poor communications . . . In the first round of the Dome Stadium, the newspapers killed us. John Cowles, president of the *Star-Tribune*, was chairman of the Metro Dome Committee. Yet, the *Star-Tribune* wrote very critical articles about the project. You have to keep the press informed." Again, the key is peer pressure: "The peer pressure is great. The best way if you're out raising money, is to say that X, Y, and Z are already in. However, there are a couple of corporations downtown who are not really involved. This is because of bottom line pressure and because they are 'professional managers.' We are getting more professional managers in place of the old families. This raises some concerns."

Despite these concerns, the Downtown Council has developed a vibrant, growing core. In large part, it has succeeded by developing a constructive relationship with government. John Berg of the City Planning Office notes: "Public-private cooperation goes back twenty-three to twenty-four years in Minneapolis. In the late fifties, General Mills decided to move into the suburbs. This caused alarm among local businesses, which caused the formation of the Downtown Council. The Downtown Council did a lot of planning. They didn't go out and hire consultants like other cities. The Downtown Council decided they needed a close relationship with City Hall . . . Planning between City Hall and the Downtown Council was really done jointly. We meet every two weeks on large projects. We have joint broad-breadth plans every ten years. There have been conflicts, but they have not turned into public conflicts." Clearly, however, the planning office of the city does not attempt to direct centrally the future of Minneapolis. For example, the Loring Park project involves creating new downtown housing in a nine-block area. A combination of public and private financing has led to a successful development, but "We do not get out in front of these developments. We react more to initiatives from the private sector."

A strong Downtown Council might turn simply into a contest between narrow interest groups, one calling for more parking and another for better electrical power access, for example. But it appears that such attempts to gain selfish advantage are rare here: "I think it might be tried. But there is a strong tradition of that not happening. The council does not let that happen . . . The peer pressure phenomenon is really true. Zoning is really loose. The former planning director used peer pressure to solve problems. The Skyway and the other private developments are the result of peer pressure . . . The leaders of business and the community were smart in doing a joint government thing . . . A city needs a political situation where there is enough trust that what's good for downtown is good for anyone. All of the big companies have stayed. Pillsbury and Green Giant merged and decided to stay downtown. Downtown has become the place to be. Companies have to pay a premium for office space downtown, there are no financial breaks for firms that stay downtown, taxes are a little higher than in the suburbs; the reason they come downtown is that of peer pressure."

When a company operates outside the network, outside the influence of peer pressure, the difference becomes clear. "We are working with Company X [a foreign company], but it's not the same. They are less committed. Company X has been stung by the press and by their peers, however. An interesting example is a store sign in the Hennepin entertainment district. The firms there had agreed to put up signs in a particular way. Company X's president came through town and saw the sign up on his property. He hated it and ordered that the sign be taken down immediately. But after much criticism from both press and peers, he is now anxious to put that sign back up there."

The Minnesota Association of Commerce and Industry

With all this talk of peer pressure, with the ethnic homogeneity and the geographical isolation, Minneapolis may seem to be a uniquely united city, a place where few disagreements arise—indeed, another Japan, Inc. Yet consider the views of an official of another central group, the Minnesota Association of Commerce and Industry (MACI): "Generally in Minnesota you will find an enormous confidence gap between the public and private arenas. In the history of Minnesota you will find that there was a strong populism . . . Today, government has a suspicion of business, and vice versa . . . This mistrust exists at all levels of government." The task of MACI is to articulate the interests of the business community: "A lot of things businesses once said but now don't want to say—that's my job . . . We and the lobbyists of the other business groups try to see that we are working on the same things. For example, the lobbyists from MACI, the Minneapolis Chamber of Commerce, the Saint Paul Chamber of Commerce, and the suburban chambers of commerce will meet together and establish what five things we agree on."

The task is to discover where the consensus lies among these groups, and the process is indistinguishable from that of the Keidanren: "We develop the consensus. We try to find it. We try to present what is a consensus. It's very dangerous for a nonprofit organization to take action without having a consensus of its members." MACI has 42,000 members, and thus takes positions only on very broad issues: "Our view of the future is what Minnesota does in agriculture, manufacturing, timber, tourism, and as a large service center for the Federal Reserve Center." The positions often require debate over an extended period of time before a consensus emerges: "In the 1960s, a campaign developed to rebuild the personal property tax. The campaign took eleven years. The primary beneficiaries were the farmers and the future computer industry. Another example was the indexing of the income tax. This took five years. Another example was the repeal of a very onerous death and estate tax. This helped keep the wealthy here. It is quite a trick to educate a populist legislature on the benefits of having wealthy people in the population."

Again, however, it is difficult to think of even MACI, the self-described lobbyist for business, as a powerful cabal of selfish schemers: "Minnesota politics are seen as very clean. In Minnesota, the location of the State Capitol is that of the major business center as well. This makes a big difference to the separate groups. The mayors of Minneapolis and St. Paul have prided themselves on their ability to work with business and to rebuild their cities . . . We open the minutes of our meetings to the scrutiny of anyone who wants to look at them. Anyone who thinks we're out to do something devious must be nuts. We are not very self-interested. We have a strong investment in the future of Minnesota and we want to see that it works."

The Minnesota
Business Partnership

Compared to MACI, the Minnesota Business Partnership is an elite group of leaders of the biggest companies. Founded in 1977, the Partnership includes the top officers of 61 Minnesota companies, such as the First National Bank of St. Paul, the Bemis Company, General Mills, Burlington Northern, Dayton-Hudson, Land O'Lakes, Northwest Airlines, the 3M Company, Control Data, IDS, Honeywell, Pillsbury, and Republic Airlines. The Partnership grew out of a seminar held in 1976 at the Minneapolis Chamber of Commerce on the topic of corporate social responsibility.[12] Some of the executives at that meeting came away with the disappointed feeling that their colleagues were largely uninterested in and uninformed about the topic. They set out to create an organization patterned after the Business Roundtable, a national association of top executives of the 160 biggest companies in the United States. The purpose of the partnership was not to lobby on specific issues, but, "to involve Minnesota corporate chief executives and their senior managers in public matters affecting not only their own business interests but also the interests of Minnesota and its citizens." Members meet regularly with the governor, mayors, labor leaders, and others by going to see them, rather than waiting to be called upon. One task force ultimately grew to 75 volunteers from 20 companies, who prepared a complete report on Minnesota's economic competitiveness and presented it personally, with each of several members holding simultaneous press conferences across the state. In October of 1979, the Partnership gathered 150 energy specialists from member companies for a one-day conference on conservation steps that others could take. On a more personal level, in one month alone, 18 members held 16 meetings with 35 legislative leaders of both parties, one or two at a time. This personal involvement by CEOs came about partially as a result of advice from Martin Sabo, a member of the Democratic-Farmer-Labor party who had served as speaker of the state house of representatives for several years: "Legislators tend to discount the viewpoints of hired hands lobbying on behalf of the business community." Presumably, what Sabo had in mind was that corporate leaders and legislators would both attempt to influence each other. The result could be a better mutual understanding of what is possible and what best serves the interests of the broader public.

Members of the Partnership have learned also that government itself recognizes its inability to solve the complex problems of our society in a centralized manner and seeks the involvement of well-informed private groups. Similar organizations have been formed or are underway in Ohio, Massachusetts, Pennsylvania, Delaware, New York, New Jersey, Virginia, and other states, and a more established California Roundtable has existed for several years.

The Minneapolis Project on Corporate Responsibility

The small circle of executives who founded the Partnership also gave birth to a second group, the Minnesota Project for Corporate Responsibility, whose charter is to give rise to a better integration between corporate and civic objectives. The project currently numbers fifty-seven companies and annually holds five seminars of one or two days' duration each; it targets chief executive officers and includes many of the same companies active in the Partnership, MACI, the Downtown Council, and the Chamber of Commerce. When the Project was started, many corporate leaders felt that "corporate social responsibility" was nothing more than a public relations problem activated by Ralph Nader and fueled by the press. Today, however, their views are quite different, owing to the leadership of a few among them. A *Star-Tribune* story of May 26, 1982 describes an annual meeting of the group: "The all-day meeting was strictly business: no long breaks, no cocktails before lunch, no joke-laden speeches. And the meeting was strictly blue-chip: more than fifty chief executives and other high officials of Minnesota companies. It was the annual meeting of the Minnesota Project on Corporate Responsibility, a four-year-old organization of top executives.

"The reports and workshops were wide-ranging: from corporate philanthropy to volunteerism; from the hard-to-employ to summer jobs for youth; from inner-city schools to delivery of social services. Mayor Don Fraser, School Superintendent Richard Green, Ramsey County Chairman Bob Orth and St. Paul Mayor Lattimer's chief aide, Dick Broeker, participated . . . As the day closed, MPCR members looked to its future: expand, stay the same, or call it quits. 'The last alternative should not even be discussed,' responded Edson Spencer, head of Honeywell. It wasn't."

Don Imsland, executive director of MPCR, echoes the themes that others have raised in describing the essence of Minneapolis: "Partnership is a very accurate characterization of what takes place here . . . It goes back to the community commitment, maybe the religious traditions, of the founding fathers. There has been a formation of a regional culture. When executives come here from other places, it is assumed by everyone that they will become involved. They get called. They get tapped. They are told that they ought to join the Citizens League. [Note: the Citizens League, another active group, is a collection of 3,000 individual members and 600 corporate members. Anyone may join upon payment of an annual membership fee of $20. Subgroups of the league will study a major issue for several months and often issue a position paper.] If you're a top executive, you are going to be asked to serve on an arts board . . . In my work with MPCR, I have seen again and again how willing the CEOs are to get involved. They are very, very busy, but they will find the time. Seven o'clock breakfasts are quite common. The Normandy has a large, free parking lot. The network meets there for breakfast."

What are they discussing at breakfast? "There are new challenges to the quality of life here. There is a potential brain drain if our college graduates cannot find good jobs. They will go south and west to find jobs. We have to supply the significant high-tech industrial base. Also, Minnesota is very heavy on the social service side and has been very generous in social spending. Thus, high taxes have resulted and may discourage businesses from coming in. The extreme temperatures also raise energy costs. Nonetheless, there is an attitude of can-do here. Every problem has a solution."

It begins to sound as though deals are being made, perhaps not in back rooms, but over breakfast at the Normandy. Imsland notes: "Some say that there are an incredible number of backroom deals. For example, two CEOs mounted an enormous capital campaign for the orchestra. They got a lot of money committed. In fact, it was all aboveboard, but it was seen as a power play. Once, a task force recommended a one-time postponement of all 'favorite projects.' No one took it seriously. However, there is a feeling that not a lot of backroom deals go on. It would be very risky to get involved in one. There is a lot of interchange and information passed among CEOs at the Minneapolis Club." It should be added that the press plays an important role in keeping things aboveboard. The tradition seems to have been clearly expressed in the policies of the late John Cowles, who ran the Minneapolis *Star-Tribune*. His son, John Cowles, Jr., headed the project to build a Metro Dome downtown, but he was opposed by suburban and rural groups. MACI, for example, found its 42,000 members, many of whom were rural, split nearly fifty-fifty on the issue and thus took no part in the debate. The Cowles newspapers wrote several articles critical of the project. According to several people, the reporters would often write articles critical of things Cowles or his company endorsed. His reporters became so widely respected for their knowledge and independence that they had a great effect on the legislature as well as on private groups. Without such an active and respected press, it is doubtful that the public would have felt comfortable with so many committees and associations dominated by large business interests in Minneapolis.

Constrained Self-Interest
Is an M-Form Society

The Minneapolis Chamber of Commerce was the originator of the Five Percent Club. When the club was started, approximately eighty companies across the United States gave at the level of 5 percent or more of pretax earnings; Minneapolis accounted for half of this. One might expect to find in the chamber at least a public commitment to altruism, if not a deeper private belief in it. Why do they give? These are the words of an official of the chamber: "Self-interest. A broader definition of doing business. Self-interest. There is a different social climate here. There is a critical mass of consciousness among CEOs. There is no stockholder uprising against the diversion of corporate profits into social giving."

Self-interest is universal. Yet, how is it that self-interest is converted into a successful community rather than into a babel of competing interest groups stalled in a political-economic gridlock? Why is it that these powerful combines of business in Minneapolis have not abandoned the city center, beaten down the tax base, left the schools to decay, ignored the old, the infirm, and the poor? If it is self-interest at work, then how do we explain the anomaly of this community?

Over the years, I have often visited Minneapolis, and members of my research team conducted the interviews reported here. We had expected the movers and shakers of Minneapolis to describe clearly the means through which cooperation is achieved, the design that has been wrought. Instead, we found that most people were aware that Minneapolis was unique, but that very few could articulate the reasons for that uniqueness. When pressed, some surmised that the ethnic homogeneity held the community together, others attributed the cohesiveness to the geographical isolation and the harsh winters. In short, most people active in civic and business affairs are just like you and me, people attempting to do a job, achieve a modest goal, earn a pay raise and put their children through college. Yet, while each can be said to be in pursuit of his or her self-interest, all end up by working within a network of constrained self-interest having the appearance of a partnership.

The mechanism that transforms narrow self-interest into a balanced state of cooperation among independent individuals is the network of associations, study groups, committees, and other small groups of private citizens. Each small group will typically consist of like-minded individuals, perhaps physicians who oppose regulation of health care, farmers who oppose estate taxes, or bankers who favor tax deductions on savings. At this stage, the classic form of interest-group politics is set. If the interest groups each pursue narrow self-interest, then the city will be paralyzed, with a multitude of voices expressing opposing claims. In Minneapolis, however, many of the same individuals and groups belong to the Citizens League, the Chamber of Commerce, MACI, and may be serving on one or two small task forces working on specific issues. Thus the owners of dry cleaning shops and ice cream stores may find themselves opposed to the bankers on one issue but with them on another. More importantly, a group that yields its position in favor of a competitive one in the Downtown Council will find that other members will remember their sacrifice and will repay that debt, perhaps by yielding their self-interest on another issue that comes up in MACI. It is the connection among self-interest groups and the mutual understanding that the citizenry together can progress while separate interest groups cannot, that produces the partnership in Minneapolis.

Minneapolis is not simply another middle-size city like all others; it is different. According to an experienced urban planner,

"I used to go to Syracuse, Boston, and Benton Harbor working on a project, and there is no question that there is much more dialogue and cooperation in Minneapolis. People in other places have more adversarial relationships. The environment and the problems in other places are so much worse." The reason for the difference has everything to do with the existence of a social memory. The point was made clearly by Ronnie Brooks, manager of community development for the Dayton-Hudson Corporation: "There is an expected long-term longevity here, which has created a very long-term view, which in turn helped build the structure for a partnership. I used to do negotiations, and you can take advantage of people if you are not going to see them again. What matters is that there are lots of ways to interact and that there is mutual respect. Both understand that there is a role for the other. There is a sense of equality and a basis for negotiation. This basis for negotiation stems from an expectation of long-term involvement. CEOs know that their children and grandchildren will go to school here. The industries that are here are not portable industries (for example, lumber, flour milling, and railroads). However, things are changing. There is an influx of professional managers."

Brooks also has a clear view of just how the social memory operates to create a cooperative atmosphere among self-interested individuals: "You will have an easier time if you participate. For example, if you are an executive, you will be able to have lunch with people who later on may be able to help you in your business . . . Other incentives are that you have access to more things. When I go places I have clout. People do not ask, 'What have you done for me lately?' " The process thus converts narrow self-interest into a constrained form of self-interest, but it never has to rely upon the development of altruism or selflessness, qualities which, given the imperfections of human beings, are to be viewed with skepticism.

That is not to say that Minneapolis is perfect nor that the network always succeeds. Again, Brooks comments: "Public debate gets in the way in terms of efficiency but not effectiveness. For some [real estate] projects, the discussion went on so long that interest rates went up and the project was no longer feasible. On the other hand, when consensus emerges, the project goes through."

That this process of dialogue depends upon the institutional network and not upon cold weather or ethnic homogeneity is evidenced by the weaker links and less successful dialogue at the state level: "It is more adversarial. There is no community. There is less ability for dialogue. There is no continuity in the actors. Partnerships do not exist between the city councils. I think that may change. We need to translate the partnership technology to human services and state government."

This opinion is expressed also by a state representative: "It is true that at the state level there is not the kind of dialogue that takes place in the Twin Cities. I do not know why that dialogue has not occurred at the state level . . . State representatives are up for election every two years. State senators are up for election every four years. Most of the people I respected in the legislature when I came here are now gone. I think that's an important reason why the same kind of dialogue that takes place in the Twin Cities is not happening at the state level." Again, the process of dialogue is not always one of smooth and friendly relations, but rather is one of self-interested parties engaging in a constrained but nonetheless self-interested process: "I have a lot of contact with people at the Minnesota Business Partnership. They have been burned a little lately. They said they were going to come up with ways to solve the state's problems. But their report said to cut taxes and be more efficient. It was a joke. MBP is valuable because a number of their members are learning that government is not that easy . . . MACI has to criticize us to please some of its constituents, which really upsets us. I believe there are great differences between business and government in Minnesota. There are more ex-government people in business than ex-business people in government." Yet even with this skeptical view, the representative notes: "We have more people here thinking about public policy in nonself-serving ways than in other places. I am sure you will find the structures here. We are trying to institutionalize them."

To a great extent, these structures have been institutionalized. In a sense, the old traditions of community responsibility have been sustained as Minneapolis has grown, as outsiders have come in to take top positions as professional managers in leading companies. Corporate memory exists in the form of dozens of committees and discussion groups, and it is that memory that provides a balanced constraint of self-interest, without snuffing out individualism. Minneapolis is not a monolith. It can accomodate a maverick like Bill Norris, founder of Control Data, who draws the following kinds of remarks: "Bill Norris is just a fireball . . . He bulls his way through until he gets to the legislature." "Norris is a maverick. When he formed City Venture it was a new experience for Norris to go to other CEOs and ask for help. The others were dissatisfied because it had to be done Norris's way." "People develop their own style. For example, Bill Norris is not a team player. He does not deal through existing organizations." It should not be a surprise to learn that a community can accomodate mavericks, at least not if we understand a community as a loosely coupled confederation of individuals operating within a constrained arena of self-interest. Indeed, the more complete the interconnections between segments of the society, the greater the ability of any one party to reach all of the others. Dialogue, connectedness, and memory do not foster centralization of power, but rather a dispersion of power. John Cairns, executive director of the Minnesota Business Partnership, notes: "Unlike in other urban centers, here everyone knows one another. Thus, there is not a real center of power. No one party can make a large decision."

One central element of our ideology of competition has long been the belief that leaders of business should not get too close to one another, that they should not develop overly friendly relationships with government officials. Certainly, dishonesty occurs and self-dealing is more common than we desire. However, we should reexamine the belief that the knitting together of community leaders will typically produce an elite, decision-making class, or a military-industrial complex that we should fear. In considering this proposition, however, it is necessary for us to sustain the sometimes intrusive but nonetheless required role of an inquisitive and independent press that has ready access to these discussions.

In Minneapolis, the role of the governmental or civic affairs officer in the large company has also become important. In many other cities, large companies ask a veteran executive to take on this role in order to defend and explain the company to its community. In Minneapolis, by contrast, the typical community relations executive comes from government and has the principal task of explaining to other managers in the company how the city works, why their role is important, and how they can be more effective citizen-businesspeople. The boundaries between company and community seem to be quite flexible in Minneapolis, so that instead of an adversarial relationship, they have developed a partnership in cooperation.

Advice from Minneapolis
to Other Cities

We asked several people in Minneapolis how other cities might begin the development of a similar atmosphere of partnership. The answers were quite consistent. First, the advice is to identify those key business leaders, the chief executive officers of the largest companies in town, who have a sense of commitment to the community and to its future in a broad sense. It may be that only two or three such people can be found, but two or three are enough. The second step is for these leaders to structure an educational process, bring in outside experts and thoughtful observers, in order to stimulate interest. This must be a continuing commitment to self-education by the leaders, not a once-only seminar or meeting. The third step recommended is to create a small staff of one or two people and then to launch several small projects for the purpose of identifying new people for leadership roles. Next, the business group should take the initiative in learning about government and learning how to effectively present their views in government. Ultimately, the objective should be to create a network linking together the many special interest groups which make up a community, and to have them together commit to paper their shared vision of what that community can become.

Civic leaders in Minneapolis are not swept away with a sense of uniqueness or special skill at governing. Instead, they see their failures, their mistakes, and their commonness. As Brooks observed, "We've had tons of failures. I'm not sure that we are all that much better than other cities. However, people see the myth." Imsland adds, "We get all this praise and we say to ourselves, 'We're not that great.' It's not that complicated."

Minneapolis, Inc.: what might that mean? It is not a monolith or a centrally directed hierarchy, nor is it a completely atomized amalgam of disconnected actors. Business in Minneapolis appears to violate the central ideology of U.S. commerce, that the business of business is business. Yet Minneapolis has successfully developed from smokestack industries to high technology, thus maintaining its economic and social energy. It is a city with a strong tradition of populism, the home of many socialist movements. It is not a place of do-gooders or altruists, but of realistic, self-interested individuals who operate within an institutional network that constrains each person slightly, so that no one can achieve his or her selfish goals by interfering with others. No one person, group, or bureaucrat is wise enough to direct the whole city; indeed, no one does. There is, rather, a stable pattern of repeated exchanges over many years that make social choice and collective action possible, only because each person knows that if he or she yields narrow self-interest to a broader interest this time, the corporate memory will see that sacrificial support today will be repaid, somehow, in the future. Minneapolis does not exhibit the central planning of the Soviet Union nor the opposite form, the disconnectedness of Los Angeles. It is an intermediate form, an M-Form society.

10
AN ACTION AGENDA

Voting is not enough. In a small nation or a homogeneous nation, it is enough for citizens to keep their democracy healthy by expressing their will at the ballot box. In a large and heterogeneous nation, however, the legitimate disagreements are so large in number that laws and elected officials alone cannot cope. In that case, the nation will be able to resolve its differences and move ahead only if the interest groups confront one another directly and frequently and settle their disputes. If they do not, then the process of political and social choice will of necessity be carried out in a centralized fashion by remote governments that are influenced and informed only by those few special interests that have organized sufficiently to gain access to political influence. Such a political process cannot succeed. It will be cumbersome, unfair, and unresponsive in the extreme.

We tend to define the role of government as that of settling disputes, making laws, and arriving at choices. Where the grand conflicts are concerned, that role will remain with government. In addition, however, it must be the task of government to see to it that we create and maintain a political dialogue among interest groups within the polity so that the hundreds and thousands of lesser but still important disputes can be settled among those who will gain or lose by the settlement. Those are the institutional arrangements that form the basis of an M-Form society. Without them, we have only the choice between laissez-faire markets and their inevitable exploitation of social endowments, or centralized bureaucratic regulation with its inflexibility and stupidity.

Our lessons come from the field of management. Paul Lawrence and Jay Lorsch of the Harvard Business School published a landmark study in corporate organization in 1967.[1] In that book, they demonstrated through a series of empirical studies that the most effective and profitable companies are those that are able to differentiate internally enough to match the complexity of their environments while also being able to integrate their differentiated pieces into a whole. Differentiation and integration—that is the problem of our society. It is not that our nation is overly differentiated, but that it is insufficiently integrated. Our social gridlock stems not from the proliferation of interest groups, but from the lack of integration among them. We attempt to achieve that integration only at the level of government, which is a centralized solution and one that cannot work. We need instead an intermediate form of integration between the differentiated groups in direct confrontation with one another.

Perhaps, in fact, we actually need more rather than fewer interest groups. The problem may be that our society is insufficiently differentiated, that we do not have enough special interest groups. Most citizens do not participate directly in debate on political issues and rarely even vote because there is no group sufficiently small and specialized to catch their interest, because there is no hope that their views will be influential. It is inevitable that differentiation will be stunted if integration cannot be achieved. Without integration between interest groups, a small and specialized group will have no politial access and thus no voice. No one wants to participate in a debating society that will never be heard in the circles of power. Thus, the formation of special-interest groups that can effectively draw more citizens into the democratic process will stop short. Without integration, there cannot be full differentiation. Without full differentiation, there is no means through which we can express the full range of individual desires across the nation. We become instead a mass of undifferentiated voters or grossly defined and crudely understood constituencies such as "women voters," "small-business voters," or "organized labor." Those generalized labels do violence to the full range and coloration of individual difference in our polity.

The task of government must be to govern, not to make decisions for us, not to regulate us directly, or to pretend that it can see into our personal goals. To govern is to see to the creation and the maintenance of a process of dialogue among the elements of society, to oversee a national dialogue, to encourage, assist, and foster debate and confrontation among contending parties. Only then we will be able to work out our differences and move ahead. That is our national agenda.

Changes at the Federal Level

At the level of national government, changes are in order both in the public and in the private sectors. The public sector is less in need of change. Businesspeople are often heard to complain long and loudly about the inefficiency and disorganization of our government. I cannot count the number of times I have been told that while one federal agency directed our auto companies to make cars heavier so as to be safer, yet another directed them to make those same cars lighter so as to be more fuel-efficient, while yet a third agency told them not to share inventions with one another in solving these problems. More than once I have heard the criticism that the U.S. Department of Commerce consists largely of bureaucratic leftovers of staff, rather than the bright, dedicated people attached to the senior legislators and the U.S. Department of Justice. If those complaints are true, it is because those agencies and staffs reflect the business constituency they serve. If the executive agencies are in disarray, it is because they have not received thoughtful and consistent pressure from business to get organized. If the best staffpeople are not attracted to the Department of Commerce, it is because there is no action there. In short, there is nothing for commerce to do and no reason for the agencies to get organized, because there is no one in business to whom they can talk, no one with whom they can carry out a dialogue, no one with whom they can cut a deal that will be honored by all.

What we need, of course, is a resource that everyone wants and that they can get only by submitting to the constraint of their self-interest within the boundaries of an association of firms; that resource is effective access to government.

Our federal government can produce that resource by expanding the total effective influence of private parties in government. The creation of an effective network of advisory councils to replace the hundreds of purely symbolic councils now in place would expand the total effective influence of the private sector on government and thus would produce an inducement to many without having to take away access from anyone who currently possesses it. The need is not for more information or more position papers or more discussion groups, but more mutual influence. All the professional lobbyists and other actors in Washington can tell the difference between real influence and political decoration, and few would refuse the opportunity to have more of the former and less of the latter.

Forming Advisory Councils

In the first place, no one in government should unilaterally appoint a council. Several proposals are now in circulation which do just that, and all of them smack of central planning, in no small part because the very composition of the council has not been subjected to public debate but has been decided by a small group of politicians and their staffs. Instead, the Congress and the White House should jointly engage in a debate that includes the leaders of the major business trade associations, citizens groups, labor groups, and others who seek to represent broad sectors of the polity.

It is certain that there should be a large number of councils, and that each should include some form of liaison to similar councils in the states. One large economic policy council will find it impossible to address any but the most general and most meaningless issues, such as nonspecific commitments to economic health, low unemployment, and more exports. Instead, there must be specialized councils addressing the problems of specific industry groups, so that each industry group can reach consensus on its special problems. Then, each such specialized council can take its preliminary positions to the other relevant councils and to the one coordinating council for their views. Because we have legislatures and governors in each of our states, whereas the Japanese have only one national legislature, there must be effective liaison between the federal and state levels in our network.

Both the legislative and executive branches must be directly engaged in the council framework. In Japan, the government is parliamentary; the prime minister is chosen from among the legislators, so that a natural tie exists between the executive and the legislative. In our presidential system, that natural tie does not exist, and so we must provide for liaison. On the one hand, several legislators have argued that our political system is dominated by the president, so that to be effective, any such system must report to the president. On the other hand, to be effective, these councils must concern themselves with issues that will extend far beyond one presidency and must therefore be capable of sustaining a social memory that will also live far beyond the tenure of any president. The presidency may be powerful, but compared to the members of the Congress, the occupant of the White House is a temporary member of the government. For all these reasons, a system of councils must be connected to both the president and the Congress. Perhaps two sets of councils will be necessary (thus forming a matrix organization); perhaps one set could report officially to both masters. Whatever the solution, it must not belong to one or the other branch of government alone. Similar organizational forms are well known in industry, and there is no reason to think that they cannot succeed in this setting.

The powers of the councils must be purely advisory. We already have a system of government, and it works basically well. We don't need another government, and we certainly don't want to design one on short notice. Highly visible discussion councils that enjoy the confidence of the public do not need powers beyond that of free speech to be effective. If a council of business, labor, educational, and public-interest leaders were to reach consensus on a major issue, the government would of necessity pay heed to their recommendations.

The composition of the councils must be broad and representative of all those citizens who hold a stake in the industry. The point of the councils is to arrange an arena in which parties with opposing interests can work out their differences. In order to do so, it is first of all necessary that all of the participants be present. A council consisting only of business leaders would be pointless. Membership ought probably to be for a short term, perhaps two or three years, but there should be the expectation that most members will serve several terms, so that the councils will sustain a social memory of who has in the past been helpful and who has been selfish. The councils will not have the power to coerce any member into an act that he or she truly opposes, but acts of simple exploitation will easily be discovered and remembered. Of necessity, the time commitment to these councils will be considerable, and thus it should be expected that many of the members will be people who have recently retired from active leadership of their organizations. These will be the ones who can devote the time necessary to carry the bulk of the workload, and the younger members who are still actively pursuing other careers can take a different role.

How the Councils Function

The councils must be adequately staffed by the federal agencies. Both legislative and executive branch staff will be necessary to support the work of these councils, to do the background research, manage the agendas, and arrange the appointments. There should be no difficulty in attracting the best young people to these assignments. In addition to serving as staff, these people will become another element of memory. The MITI staff, for example, attend the full council meetings and the committee and ad hoc task force meetings of the discussion councils, and many of the staff keep extensive diaries of who asked for what, who relinquished what, and what transpired at each meeting. These personal logs are passed on to the next bureaucrat who inherits the job, thus preserving the social memory in another form.

The councils must be fully in charge of their own agenda, direction, and opinions. If the composition of the councils is of the most respected leaders of the private sector, this will not be a problem. Such people will not sit still for anyone telling them what they should talk about or what their opinions should be. However, the charter of these councils should make it clear that they are not tools of the government to be used for enforcing government policy on the private sector or for selling new initiatives to the citizenry, but are instead meant to be channels through which the private voice can be organized and expressed to the government in a coherent manner. Certainly, politicians and bureaucrats will attempt to influence council members informally, and that is both normal and acceptable. However, the dominant direction of initiative must be from the private sector to the public sector, and not the other way around.

Consider some of the results we might expect from such a system of advisory councils. First, each council would be limited to including in its membership only a few leaders of associations. This limitation would confer greater access upon those few and would cause them, in time, to become peak associations that the more specialized associations would join, thus creating a federation of associations. Second, the councils would become such an influential voice that they could effectively block the direct attempts of one company or labor union to gain special advantage by lobbying a key congressman or senator. Third, legislators, governors, and presidents would have an easy escape from clamorous constituents, directing them and their requests to the appropriate council for debate. In unusual circumstances, however, a single company, labor union, or other group could press a private issue in the government alone, thus leaving open the possibility of individual action when called for. Fourth, and most importantly, we would have created a setting in which social choice is possible, supported by an obvious, permanent, and enforceable social memory. We would be able to focus our national resources, accelerate first one industry and then another, and so engage serially in the process of economic development.

Antitrust and Disclosure

It would seem reasonable that one peak council be established and operate for two or three years before its members decide just how the other, more specialized councils should be composed. That first council should address two key issues of which not much has been said here, but both of which are critical to the conduct of this process of debate. First is the issue of antitrust enforcement and legislation. It is important that we maintain the essential strength of our antitrust laws, because they preserve the competitive drives that keep our economy healthy but which each company, acting in self-interest, will have reason to oppose from time to time. On the other hand, there seems to be ample evidence that our antitrust laws have become harmful rather than helpful to that very competitiveness they were intended to protect.

Businesspeople today are reluctant to join in any substantive discussions in trade associations for fear of provoking a private antitrust suit from a competitor who has been encouraged by the treble-damage award he will collect if he wins the case. Certainly, it seems reasonable to maintain a powerful incentive for one company to sue another if it has been dishonestly damaged, and the treble-damage provision should not be entirely scrapped. However, it seems equally clear that any discussion that takes place openly within a trade association on a previously announced agenda provides sufficient protection in most cases. Thus, it may be reasonable to eliminate the treble-damage provision for any cause that is begun in the open and to retain the treble-damage provision for any cause that is clandestine. The determination of what is open and what is clandestine will be difficult in many cases, but it is the sort of determination that our courts are good at making. In essence, we would be choosing to run a slightly greater risk of some antitrust activity occuring without punishment, but with the return of encouraging a far greater level of dialogue between private parties. It is time to move the pendulum slightly back in the direction of encouraging dialogue.

The second key issue for discussion by the first council is that of public disclosure. In general, more disclosure is better, but some privacy is necessary if labor leaders and business leaders are to openly express opinions to one another. In my view, the best guarantee of public disclosure is through the direct participation of the press, as in the Japanese discussion councils. I expect that most responsible U.S. journalists would initially oppose such an idea, feeling that they might be compromised by agreeing to withhold from their readers information to which they had direct access. Perhaps those claims are justifiable, and perhaps journalists should be excluded from membership on discussion councils. I, for one, however, would feel better if a senior editor from the *New York Times* and from *Time* magazine were included in the membership of the principal discussion council, with senior editors from more specialized publications serving on other councils. It would certainly be possible for each council to develop an informal but enforceable norm that a journalist may not disclose the proceedings of meetings in detail and should not write about a sensitive issue at all until deliberations are completed. University professors may fulfill a similar role, as they do in Japan. As one professor who is a member of a MITI discussion council observed: "When I was in disagreement, I wrote about my opinions of the council's position in the newspapers. It is acceptable for a scholar to do this." The more elite journalists of the United States regularly have access to private discussions with government leaders and regularly exercise judgement in knowing what to report and what to keep private. Journalists must walk a thin line between obligation to their readers and access to their sources, and that same balance could be struck by the journalist-members of discussion councils.

The Private Associations

If national and local governments show some inclination to bring trade associations directly into the dialogue where business is concerned, then companies will have sufficient incentive to begin to grant greater influence and resources to their trade associations. Once the trade associations begin to strengthen and learn how to work together seriously on their problems of product standardization, export, taxation, training, and education, they will be better able to participate in that dialogue. In time, an effective network will develop. As the network grows, it will inevitably be the case that mergers will occur among some competitive associations and that the more specialized associations will become subordinate members of a few peak associations. This development can be expected to occur at the level of states, municipalities, and at the national level. Each company can expect to ultimately support perhaps fifty or more such associations, some specialized by industry, other specialized by city or state, and yet others specialized by function (training, export assistance, safety). Rather than a monolithic hierarchy of associations, we can look forward to the development of a network of specialized associations linked together by a few peak associations. The formation of major peak associations will make the business community more readily accountable to politicians and to the public at large while simultaneously making the business community more influential. In short, the role of trade associations can be greatly improved in our society by the granting to them of political access, thus yielding a net increase in the mutual influence among parties in the society.

In order to accomplish this change, trade associations will have to build their internal strength. Their members will have to insist upon active participation by the executives of member companies in the association, and over time each company will have to learn that in exchange for having a voice in the political process, they must accept some constrainst on the narrow self-interest they pursue. Each association must see itself as a unit of social memory and construct its internal committees and governing boards in a manner that will give rise to both social memory and to the possibility of serial equity.

It is important that there be an effective confederation of the specialized associations in each city and state, and at the national level. If there are not such confederations, then one association will be able to impose social costs on other segments of business. For example, one association that succeeds at organizing its members will be able to run roughshod over other less well-organized industry groups in the state legislatures or in the U.S. Congress. If that occurs, then that narrow self-interest will become evident to others, there will be a general criticism of that narrow special-interest group, and the result will be a loss of legitimacy of the whole process, with a lessening of mutual influence in the system and a less effective society.

The associations must also have an effective channel of communication to the executive and the legislative branches. In the executive branch, the obvious primary channel of communication is through the Department of Commerce. If Commerce is to carry out this task, it will have to be reorganized in a manner that permits ready contact with the advisory councils and with the business community. The current form of internal organization of the department defies access by any but the most dedicated and persistent Washington insiders. The precise form of reorganization that makes sense should come about through the efforts of the senior career bureaucrats of the department, those who will remain to deal with the business community long after the political appointees of any era have departed. They could be assisted and guided in this task by a special task force appointed by the first advisory council. The Department of Commerce will also need to arrange an effective form of liaison with the other branches of government dealing with business, including the regulatory agencies, the other Cabinet departments, and the Council of Economic Advisors. This kind of interdepartmental cooperation does not come about as a matter of course because bureaucrats, if left to themselves, like the rest of us, will arrange things so as to advance their own careers rather than our well-being. Like other organizations, the bureaucracy does not work well unless it is subjected to the scrutiny of its owners. If we, the owners of that bureaucracy, concentrate our ownership power in the hands of a smaller representative group such as the advisory councils, however, that group can effectively mobilize the trade associations, citizens groups, and others who will bring close scrutiny and consistent public pressure to bear until a reasonable form of organization is attained. It would be a mistake for the Department of Commerce to reorganize before having received the advice of a well-organized advisory council.

If the business community is to communicate with the executive branch through the already existing but reorganized Department of Commerce, then the Congress will have to create a new avenue of access to ensure communication with the legislative branch of government. Precedents for such a congressional organization are in existence in the Congressional Budget Office and the General Accounting Office. The impact of an effective set of advisory councils on the operation of the Congress should be subtle but deep. In the first place, any major request from a business firm for legislative action can be routed through the appropriate discussion council, where the most obviously ill-considered requests will die a quick death without consuming the time and energy of a legislator who cannot easily say no to a constituent. Thus, the number of bills introduced into the Congress should decline steadily from its current level of 22,000 per two-year Congress to perhaps one-tenth that number within ten or fifteen years. More importantly, the existence of a social memory will make possible the kind of serial equity without which the legislative process does not work well. As Senator Daniel Inouye (D., Hawaii) noted in an interview: "We need to be more active in making our own system more cooperative, compared to world markets. For example, several small nations spend three times more total dollars to promote tourism than we do. Every developed country has people at the highest level in government involved in encouraging tourism, but not here. It is because of the way that Washington works: on any given issue relative to tourism, no consensus can be reached. Hotels are on the left, motels are on the right. The buses don't talk to the airlines and everyone is out to kill the other guy. There is no getting together, to the detriment of everyone concerned."[2]

Organized Labor

One implication of this analysis is that, just as firms should be forced to confront one another directly to settle their political differences, so separate labor unions within one company should be forced to confront one another in developing a single bargaining position in facing the management of that firm. Many U.S. companies will have five or six separate unions in one plant, and a railroad may have more than a dozen unions in a railyard. If each union bargains separately with the company, and if an employee cares only about the health of his or her own union, the result will be an attempt of each union to impose unreasonably upon the company, which is equivalent to imposing upon the other unions. The result will be bloated wages, unreasonable work rules, and an industry in ruin. We cannot allow the present structure of unionism to continue.

On the other hand, as a nation we cannot afford to allow the disappearance of labor unions. Given the imperfections of markets, there will always be some companies that will abuse their employees, take advantage of older workers who cannot change jobs or of the captive employees in a company town. Although such actions will harm the company in the long run, if the management is oriented towards the short run, such unacceptable acts will occur. Without the existence of labor unions, there will be the possibility that in times of economic distress such abuses may become as widespread and as excessive as they have been in times past. If the gap between management and labor were to become truly great, we would be in danger of revolution. It is therefore necessary that the labor union be preserved as a form of social organization in our nation, but in its current form it is in danger of extinction. The impetus for change is not likely to come from the union leaders. Instead, the pressure will have to come from the business community and from the union members themselves. The initial pressure must come from business because it is management rather than labor that holds most of the power in business, and management rather than labor that is entrusted by shareholders with the key responsibility for properly conducting the affairs of the firm. It is also true that within many labor unions, the primary beneficiaries of a more effective union organization would be those who are laid off and thus have no voice within the union. Many unions have arranged an internal system in which a drop in available work is handled by laying off the most junior of union members, rather than by lowering wages for all. If the senior members of the union hold power, they can be expected to have younger workers laid off rather than having everyone share a cut in wages so that none will be out of work. Thus, the impetus for change is not likely to come primarily from within the labor union.

It is another superstition that "enterprise" or "company" unions do not effectively represent the interests of workers. It is a fiction that in Japan, company unions are weak, workers are docile, and management is in full control of those unions. If the labor union is to survive in the United States, it cannot remain in its current form. Again, I cannot prescribe here the correct transformation of that form. Because unions are such a potent political force, there are few politicians or even academics who are willing to initiate a dialogue that labor leaders may oppose. If that situation continues, we can expect that future economic growth will occur only in those industries and those states that are union-free. If that occurs, then we will have created as a society a state of affairs that may lead in fifty or one hundred years to a situation in which management may take advantage of workers, industrial strife may reappear, and social upheaval may be the ultimate consequence.

The Proper Role of Banks

Consider the children in a divorce. One parent will have primary custody of the child and will carry out the functions of a parent. The other parent continues to love the child as before and may wish to continue to assist in the proper guidance, discipline, and support of the child, but will have difficulty doing so. The second parent will of necessity have to expend greater energy in order to know what the child needs and to effectively provide discipline or support to the child. The strain may be bearable if the two parents cooperate with one another, but consider how much more difficult the problem would be if the child had not two but twenty or one hundred parents. With one hundred parents, it is unlikely that any parent would have a sufficient stake in the child to be willing to bring the other ninety-nine together in order to make wise decisions for the well-being of the child. Our companies have not one hundred but ten thousand parents, and it is no surprise that they are improperly tended.

I am no expert in finance, but it seems to me that every company needs to have an informed and caring owner. The Civil War is long since ended, the U.S. Treasury has been replenished, and we do have a single currency in national use. The restrictions of the National Banking Act of 1864 should be reexamined. It is apparent that banks see a reason to hold equities in nonbanking businesses, since they continually go around the law by establishing bank holding companies that own such equities. Perhaps we should bring that practice out into the open where it can develop naturally and where it can be properly guided and regulated. If the analysis presented here is correct, then natural competitive pressures will over time bring about a concentration of ownership in the hands of banks and other institutions. Each major company will have a small group of parents, the short-run pressures on management will be ameliorated, and the necessary discipline will be brought to bear as well. The issue deserves a major share of our study and debate.

Change at the State and Local Level

Minneapolis works, and so can Buffalo, Greensboro, Los Angeles, and Kansas City. Within each state and each municipality, there are currently underway several attempts to improve the relationship between business and government so that the two can work together to produce more jobs and a healthier economy.

In the state of Michigan, business, government, and labor have joined together to create the Industrial Technology Institute, an independent, nonprofit Michigan corporation. The institute will serve as an experimental center and a training ground to assist medium and small businesses in developing the future robotic and computer technologies that will be necessary for the automobile and other industries to compete in the future. The Institute came about through a recommendation of the Governor's High Technology Task Force in 1982, and it plans to maintain a staff of 200 and an annual budget of $20 million. Twenty-five percent of the funding comes from the state budget, with the remaining seventy-five percent from the private sector, including major business foundations.

As one example, the Institute is constructing a prototype "factory of the future," which will integrate computer-aided design with robotic machine tools and an automatic transport system. Although such a factory will employ few workers, other companies will create new jobs to manufacture the robots and computers, and to supply a continual stream of new software to run these systems. The experimental plant will enable businesses large and small to see first-hand what kinds of skills, products, and jobs will be needed.

In the state of Hawaii, several developments involving business-government cooperation are underway. The governor's office conducted a study into the economic development needs of the state and found that one barrier to new business development was the lack of suitably zoned land. One response to that need has been the development of county economic development boards.

For example, the Maui Economic Development Board consists of roughly seventy-five citizens who serve on eight to ten panels, each of which is considering possibilities to create new business and new jobs on the island of Maui. One of these panels wrote to landowners holding parcels of five hundred or more acres, asking whether they would be interested in developing a research and development park. Eighteen responded in the affirmative, and four or five of these possibilities are now being considered in detail. The board works very closely with the State Department of Planning and Economic Development, which will be able to remove bureaucratic hurdles when a plan nears completion and zoning or land-use permits are required.

In 1983, the state of Hawaii created the High Technology Development Corporation, which is empowered to issue revenue bonds, the proceeds of which will be used to provide funding for the development of new industrial parks and other major economic developments. Also in 1983, the state created the Pacific International Center for High Technology Research, which is now in the early planning stage, to seek out those niches in which the people of Hawaii can develop something short of Silicon Valley's technical clout but nonetheless realistic for the State of Hawaii to benefit its economy.

Similar efforts are underway in Massachusetts, North Carolina, Colorado, Texas, and elsewhere. However, these efforts are likely to be short-lived unless they are undergirded by the development of a permanent network of advisory business councils similar to those described for the federal level. In each municipality and state, there must be encouragement by the government for the creation of a vital set of business associations that serve as the locus of social memory and through which the voice of the private sector can be expressed in a coherent manner. Minneapolis has done this in a purely private manner through the establishment of the Citizens League, the Minnesota Associations of Commerce and Industry, the Minneapolis Business Partnership, the Downtown Council, the Minneapolis Project on Corporate Responsibility, and other groups. In other places, the effort may require some assistance from the mayor or governor, but that assistance must not become domination of what is essentially a privately organized and sustained form of cooperation.

In each case, the objective is for the businesses of the state to produce as many social endowments as they can, and to limit the production of social costs. Social endowments are those public goods that no one company can produce on its own, such as better trained craftspeople and better use of land. Social costs are those results such as closed beach access, poor transit, dirty air, or polluted water, which each business will impose upon the public because no company pays the full cost of using that public resource. The endowments such as military might and the management of foreign affairs must be resolved at the national level, but many other endowments are more effectively captured at the level of states or municipalities.

Thus, proper land use is a social endowment that will benefit not only the landowners and the company owners on Maui, but will benefit all citizens through the generation of more jobs and more taxes, including those citizens of the future who have not yet been born. In a federal-level discussion council, the issue of land use on Maui would never make the agenda. Similarly, if that issue is to be resolved at the state level, it will receive less attention from both the private and public parties than it will at the county level. If the issue of land use on Maui were taken up at too low a level, such as in the town council of Kahului or of Lahaina, no resolution would be possible, because the appropriate stakeholders would not all be represented.

The Essence of
an M-Form Society

The essence of an M-Form society is social integration. An M-Form society represents balance, a balance between the need for government regulation and the need for independent laissez-faire action. A balance between one special interest and another. The role of government in an M-Form society is similar to the role of top management in an M-Form company. The role is to govern rather than to manage. To manage is to make the day-to-day decisions, while to govern is to set the conditions in which others will make those decisions in a balanced fashion. If the middle management of a company cannot work together as a team, top management will have to adjudicate disputes and make decisions for them. At that point, the company becomes overly centralized and it falters. The same is true of the conduct of national affairs.

If the middle managers of a company do not work together as a team but instead look to the top managers for resolution of disputes, the result will be a more and more powerful top management and a more thoroughly centralized company. In the end, the top management will be telling each middle manager what to do. Much the same is true of our business-government relationship. The conflict between business and government is real, but it is the product of unresolved conflict between one industry and another. The only way to modify the adversarial relationship between business and government is to improve the ability of business to resolve its own disputes internally and then to resolve its differences with other special-interest groups. If we continue to push our disagreements up to the government, we will force a centralization of power there.

The Japanese solution is not our solution. We study the Japanese because their business-government relationship is different from ours and is successful. It thus provokes our creativity and forces us to reexamine our superstitious beliefs about what works and what does not. Japan is a more homogeneous nation. It has greater ethnic homogeneity, greater religious, linguistic, and economic homogeneity. Japan is more compact and thus more readily brings national decision makers into regular contact with one another. It is possible for the Japanese to achieve what the French sociologist Emile Durkheim referred to as "mechanical solidarity."[3] By that term Durkheim meant the cohesion that binds a nation together through a commonality of history, belief, and social similarity. It is the solidarity of like people who readily develop common goals.

Durkheim's analysis of Western society is that our heterogeneity makes it impossible to achieve mechanical solidarity. On the other hand, he observed that without solidarity a nation cannot function. His solution was to argue that Western nations must achieve instead "organic solidarity," which is that form of social integration that ties unlike pieces into one whole. The body politic is in that respect like the human body, capable of survival only as an organic whole. The liver is distinctly different in form and function from the lungs, the heart, and the brain, but without all of the pieces working together the body cannot survive.

There must be a central nervous system coordinating the organs of the body politic. That nervous system is the network of social institutions that bring together the special interest groups. Without use, that central coordinative mechanism will atrophy. With the proper exercise, it will become vital and strong.

Many Western people might fear that the national agenda I have described may, in some unforeseen way, diminish their individual freedoms. It is a profound question and one to which Durkheim devoted a great deal of his thought. Let us examine it.

Durkheim argues that the expression of individual freedom lies in the ability of each person to discover that unique purpose to which his or her life is best suited. The greater the range of unique occupations available, the more complete the expression of individual freedom will be. That kind of individual differentiation is only possible through social life, however. If each person lives as an island apart, then each will have to undertake the identical chores of gathering food, preparing shelter, and fighting off enemies. Only if many individuals gather together into a society can there be specialization of labor and thus an array of choices for each person. Individual life thus stems from collective life, rather than the other way around.

As a society becomes more complex and more differentiated, it must develop routine mechanisms for social integration. Without these routine mechanisms to settle disputes between interest groups, Durkheim argued (in 1893), the society will become burdened by the need to strike a new bargain each time a conflict develops. That process will be so slow and so cumbersome that it will paralyze the nation. In Durkheim's view, government is incapable of providing the necessary adjustments: "Neither political society in its entirety nor the State can take over this function; economic life, because it is specialized and grows more specialized every day, escapes their competence and their action. An occupational activity can be efficaciously regulated only by a group intimate enough with it to know its functioning, feel all its needs, and able to follow all their variations."[4]

We like to think that each of us possesses freedom individually. We are thus reluctant to give up a part of that freedom in order to create an integrated society. Durkheim offers the opposite view. He argues that freedom is the social creation of the body politic and that each of us draws his or her individual liberty from that social body. It is of course among the oldest and the most important of political debates. It is also among the most contemporary of issues, one in which each of us must participate.

Each of us must be for a moment Locke, Hobbes, Rousseau, and Durkheim. We must contemplate the essence of democracy and liberty. Without the confidence that we understand the roots of our polity, we will not have the courage to discard that which no longer serves us well. Without that capacity for change, we cannot meet the challenge of our future. Given that understanding and that courage, however, we can easily meet the challenges ahead.

During the spring of 1983, I went to Washington, D.C. with several members of the research team. We spoke with leaders of the Senate, the House, top-level presidential appointees, the leaders of the Chamber of Commerce, the National Association of Manufacturers, lobbyists, and lawyers. At each stop, I related our analysis of the M-Form society. To each official I put the question, "Is it realistic to think that we could make such changes? Do we really need to make these changes? Or am I imagining our problems, dreaming them up?" People in Washington, D.C. tend not to be long on political philosophy; they tend to focus instead on the practical. The response that I remember best, the response that captures the essence of what we all should feel about our society, came from Tim McNemar, undersecretary of the Treasury: "Is there a better way to do it? The answer obviously is yes."

APPENDIX
NOTES
INDEX

THE THIRTY-EIGHT ADVISORY COUNCILS OF MITI—1982

Industrial Structure Council
(21 standing committees)

Industrial Technology Council
(8 standing committees)

Board of Mine Safety Examination

Central Mine Safety Committee
(5 standing subcommittees)

Export and Import Transaction
Council (15 standing
committees)

Export Inspection Council
(8 standing committees)

Export Insurance Council

Design Council

Trade Conference
(4 standing committees)

Commodity Exchange Council

Industrial Location and Water
Council (3 standing
committees)

Large-Scale Retail Council
(8 standing committees)

Credit Sale Council
(2 standing committees)

Consumer Product Safety and
Household Goods Labelling
Council (2 standing
committees)

Chemical Product Council
(6 standing committees)

Electronics Machinery Industry
Council (2 standing
committees)

Data Processing Promotion Council

Weights and Measures Administration Council (8 standing committees)

Aircraft-Machinery Industry Council (3 standing committees)

Vehicle Races Council (3 standing committees)

High Pressure Gas and Explosives Safety Council (2 standing committees)

Textile Industry Council (3 standing committees)

Traditional Craft Industry Council

Advisory Committee for Energy (7 standing subcommittees)

Mining Industry Council (2 standing committees)

Petroleum and Inflammable Natural Gas Resources Development Council (5 standing committees)

Petroleum Council

Coal Mining Council (5 standing committees)

Coal Mining Area Development Council (5 standing committees)

Electricity Utility Industry Council (2 standing committees)

Electric Chief Engineer Qualification Examination Committee

Industrial Property Council (2 standing committees)

Patent Attorney Examination and Disciplinary Committee (2 standing subcommittees)

Small and Medium Enterprise Policy Making Council (6 standing subcommittees)

Small and Medium Enterprise Stabilization Council

Central Small and Medium Enterprise Mediation Council

Small and Medium Enterprise Modernization Council (16 standing committees)

Japanese Industrial Standards Committee (30 standing subcommittees)

APPENDIX II
CONSTITUTION OF
ADVISORY COUNCILS—1979

	AIRCRAFT-MACHINERY COUNCIL	INDUSTRIAL STRUCTURE COUNCIL
Trade Association	29	28
Manufacturer	9	20
Trading Company	–	2
Quasi Government Institution	13 (3)*	3 (3)*
Commercial Bank	1	1
University	7	11
Newspaper	4	2
Labor Union	3	4
Consumers' Union	–	3**
Other	3	8***
TOTAL	69	82

NOTES:
  *Means the number of government financial institutions
  **Includes the Housewives' Federation
  ***Includes Governors' Conference and Mayors' Conference

APPENDIX III

A MEMBERSHIP LIST OF

INDUSTRIAL STRUCTURE COUNCIL (June 1, 1979)

NAME	COUNCIL CAPACITY	PRIMARY EMPLOYMENT AFFILIATION IS OR WAS WITH:
CHAIRMAN		
T. Doko	Chairman, Federation of Economic Organizations (Keidanren)	Chairman, Tokyo Shibaura Electric Co., Ltd. (Toshiba)
MEMBERS		
1. Trade Associations (28)		
S. Shindo	Chairman, Japan Electrical Manufacturers' Association	President, Mitsubishi Electric Corporation
K. Iwata	Chairman, Japan Electronic Industry Development Association	President, Tokyo Shibaura Electric Co., Ltd. (Toshiba)
H. Hyuga	Chairman, Kansai Federation of Economic Organizations	President, Sumitomo Metal Industries, Ltd.
B. Sasaki	Executive Director, Japan Chamber of Commerce & Industry	
T. Okuhara	Executive Director, Federation of Economic Organizations	
S. Ichijo	Chairman, Japan Mining Industry Association	

235

NAME	COUNCIL CAPACITY	PRIMARY EMPLOYMENT AFFILIATION IS OR WAS WITH:
MEMBERS		
1. Trade Associations (28) (Cont'd)		
Y. Inayama	Chairman, Japan Iron & Steel Federation	Chairman, Nippon Steel Corporation
T. Akashi	Vice-Chairman, Federation of Bankers' Association of Japan	
Y. Ogawa	Chairman, Light Metal Rolling Industry Association	
K. Osumi	Director, Japan Machine Tool Builders' Association	
K. Otani	Chairman, Japan Spinners' Association	
T. Okumura	Executive Director, Japan Iron & Steel Federation	
K. Kawamura	Chairman, Japanese Electric Wire and Cable Makers' Association	
K. Kuwae	Chairman, Japan Information Processing Center Association	
T. Kosuge	Chairman, Japan Department Stores Association	President, Isetan Co., Ltd.
Y. Koyama	Chairman, Japan Information Processing Development Center	
Y. Shimazaki	Vice-Chairman, Japan Gas Association	
Y. Shimada	President, Machinery and Electronic Inspection and Examination Association	

Y. Shimoyama	President, Japan Chemical Fibers Association
T. Takayanagi	Vice-Chairman, Securities Dealers Association of Japan
T. Tomioka	Chairman, Japan Ferro-Alloy Industry Association
E. Toyoda	Chairman, Japan Automobile Manufacturers' Associations, Inc.
K. Toyonaga	Vice-Chairman, Japan Paper Association
K. Nakamura	Director, Life Insurance Association of Japan
I. Nakayama	Chairman, Light Metal Association
S. Hiraishi	Executive Director, Product Safety Association
S. Iijima	Executive Director, Industry Location Center of Japan

2. *Manufacturers* (20)

T. Tanaka	President, Nippon Electric Co., Ltd.
S. Hiraiwa	President, Tokyo Electric Power Co., Ltd.
E. Saito	President, Nippon Steel Corporation
T. Hirai	Counsellor, Nippon Steel Corporation
N. Kumagai	President, Sumitomo Metal Industries, Ltd.
H. Iwamura	President, Kawasaki Steel Corporation
S. Akazawa	Vice-President, Fujitsu Limited
R. Kawai	President, Komatsu Ltd.
K. Inamori	President, Kyoto Ceramic Co., Ltd.
	President, Toyota Motor Co., Ltd.
	President, Jujo Paper Co., Ltd.
	Former Vice-Minister, MITI
	Former Vice-Minister, MITI
	Former General Manager, MITI
	Former Manager, MITI

237

NAME	COUNCIL CAPACITY	PRIMARY EMPLOYMENT AFFILIATION IS OR WAS WITH:
MEMBERS		
2. *Manufacturers* (20) (*Cont'd*)		
Y. Imai	President, Nippon Petrochemical Industries, Ltd.	Former Vice-Minister, MITI
R. Uenishi	President, Shimazu Seisakusho, Ltd.	
K. Kitagawa	Counsellor, Sumitomo Electric Industries, Ltd.	
S. Kobayashi	President, Japan Steel Works, Ltd.	
H. Suzuki	President, Showa Denko K. K.	
K. Takahashi	President, Kobe Steel, Ltd.	
Y. Takeda	President, Daido Steel Co., Ltd.	Former Managing Director, Nippon Steel Corporation
Y. Yasuda	President, Toshin Steel Co., Ltd.	
I. Yamashita	President, Mitsui Engineering & Shipbuilding Co., Ltd.	
T. Harashima	President, Nihon Cement Co., Ltd.	
K. Fujita	President, Fujita Corporation	
3. *Trading Companies* (2)		
Y. Ikeda	President, Mitsui & Co., Ltd.	
B. Tanabe	President, Mitsubishi Corporation	
4. *Quasi-government Institutions* (3)		
T. Tajima	Managing Director, Bank of Japan	

| E. Kageyama | President, Shoko Chukin Bank |
| K. Ueno | Chairman, Venture Enterprise Center |

5. Commercial Bank (1)

| Y. Ikeura | President, Industrial Bank of Japan |

6. Universities (11)

H. Arisawa	Professor, University of Tokyo
H. Inoue	Professor, University of Tokyo
T. Uchida	Professor, University of Tokyo
Z. Kitagawa	Professor, Kyoto University
T. Sakai	Professor, Kyoto University
T. Matsuda	Professor, Tokyo Technical University
K. Moriguchi	Professor, Electric and Communication University
K. Tsujimura	Professor, Keio University
M. Ueno	Professor, Waseda University
H. Ueno	Professor, Seikei University
M. Shinohara	Professor, Seikei University

7. Newspaper Publishing Companies (2)

| H. Uchida | Editor, Japan Economic Journal |
| H. Takashiro | President, Daily Industrial Journal |

8. Labor Unions (4)

| M. Tomizuka | Chairman, General Council of Trade Unions of Japan |

239

NAME	COUNCIL CAPACITY	PRIMARY EMPLOYMENT AFFILIATION IS OR WAS WITH:
MEMBERS		
8. Labor Unions (4) (Cont'd)		
R. Tanaka	Vice-Chairman, Japanese Confederation of Labor	
Y. Miyata	Chairman, Japanese Federation of Iron & Steel Workers' Unions	
T. Usami	Chairman, Japan Federation of Textile Workers' Unions	
9. Consumers' Unions (3)		
H. Shimizu	Chairman, The Housewives' Federation	
S. Tanaka	Chairman, Federation of Regional Women's Union	
A. Mitsumaki	Chairman, Consumer Science Association	
10. Others (8)		
M. Nakajima	President, Japan Electronic Computer Co., Ltd. (JECC)	
N. Iwasa	Chairman, Institute of Asian Economic Affairs	Former President, Fuji Bank, Ltd.
R. Okuda	Chairman, National Governors' Conference	Governor, Kyoto Prefecture
H. Hirayama	Chairman, National Mayors' Conference	Mayor, Odawara City
K. Tsuchiya	Chairman, Research Institute of General Policy	

T. Hattori	President, Research Institute of Structure Planning
M. Nakajima	President, Mitsubishi Research Institute, Ltd.
S. Sato	Former Chairman, Board of Audit

Compiled by Osamu Suruga, December 1982

APPENDIX IV

A MEMBERSHIP LIST OF AIRCRAFT-MACHINERY INDUSTRY COUNCIL (June 1, 1979)

NAME	COUNCIL CAPACITY	PRIMARY EMPLOYMENT AFFILIATION IS OR WAS WITH:
CHAIRMAN		
R. Taouchi	Chairman, Japan Machinery Federation	President, Ishikawajima Harima Heavy Industries Co., Ltd.
MEMBERS		
1. Trade Associations		
S. Shindo	Chairman, Japan Electrical Manufacturers' Association	President, Mitsubishi Electric Corporation
T. Yamashita	Chairman, Electronic Industries Association of Japan	President, Matsushita Electric Industrial Co., Ltd.
D. Kobayashi	Chairman, Japan Electronic Industry Development Association	President, Fujitsu Limited
S. Yokogawa	Chairman, Japan Electric Measuring Instruments Manufacturers' Association	President, Yokogawa Electric Works, Ltd.
G. Moriya	Chairman, The Japan Society of Industrial Machinery Manufacturers	President, Mitsubishi Heavy Industries, Ltd.
T. Tomita	Chairman, Japan Machine Tool Builders' Association	President, Toyoda Machine Works, Ltd.

243

NAME	COUNCIL CAPACITY	PRIMARY EMPLOYMENT AFFILIATION IS OR WAS WITH:
MEMBERS *1. Trade Associations (Cont'd)*		
T. Nakamura	Director, Japan Automobile Manufacturers' Associations, Inc.	President, Hino Motors, Ltd.
K. Fujioka	Chairman, Japan Auto Parts Industries Association	President, NHK Spring Co., Ltd.
R. Hanesaka	Managing Director, Japan Iron and Steel Federation	Former General Manager, Bureau of MITI
R. Uenishi	Chairman, Japan Analytical Instruments Federation	President, Shimazu Seisakusho, Ltd.
J. Kashima	Chairman, Japan Measuring Instruments Federation	President, Oval Gear Engineering Co., Ltd.
T. Shirakawa	Chairman, Japan Oil-Pressure Machinery Manufacturers' Association	President, Kayaba Industry Co., Ltd.
M. Daitoku	Chairman, Japan Casting Industry Association	
T. Takamatsu	Chairman, Japan Bearing Industrial Association	
A. Tamaki	Chairman, Engineering Development Association	President, Chiyoda Chemical Engineering & Construction Co., Ltd.
T. Yamaoka	Chairman, The Japan Society of Agricultural Machinery Manufacturers	President, Yammer Diesel Co., Ltd.
K. Yomoto	Chairman, The Society of Japan Aerospace Companies Inc.	President, Kawasaki Heavy Industries, Ltd.

M. Miyake	Chairman, Communication Industries Association of Japan	Former General Manager, Bureau of NTTPC
F. Iwata	President, VLSI Technical Research Association	President, Tokyo Shibaura Electric Co., Ltd.
S. Iwata	Chairman, Japan Printed Circuit Industry Association	
M. Oshima	Chairman, The Medical Information System Development Center	Professor, Medical Department, University of Tokyo
K. Kuwae	Chairman, Japan Information Processing Center Association	President, Japan Business Consultant Ltd.
T. Nomiyama	Chairman, Information-Technology Promotion Agency, Japan (IPA)	Former Manager, Section of MITI
T. Hattori	Chairman, Japan Software Industry Association	
T. Senga	Managing Director, Federation of Economic Organizations	
K. Aida	Chairman, Japan Beating Pressure Machinery Manufacturers' Association	
M. Kawai	Chairman, International Development Center	Former Manager, Bureau of Administrative Management Agency
S. Kobayashi	Chairman, General Casting Center	President, Japan Steel Works, Ltd.
2. Manufacturers		
T. Tanaka	President, Nippon Electric Co., Ltd.	
H. Yoshiyama	President, Hitachi, Ltd.	
S. Akazawa	Vice-President, Fujitsu, Ltd.	Former General Manager, Bureau of MITI

NAME	COUNCIL CAPACITY	PRIMARY EMPLOYMENT AFFILIATION IS OR WAS WITH:
MEMBERS		
2. *Manufacturers* (Cont'd)		
E. Ohara	President, Fuji Heavy Industries, Ltd.	Former Managing Director, Industrial Bank of Japan
K. Kataoka	President, Alps Electric Co., Ltd.	
R. Kawai	President, Komatsu Ltd.	
N. Shimizu	Vice-President, All Nippon Airways Co., Ltd.	
I. Tanaka	President, Toa Domestic Airlines Co., Ltd.	
O. Nagano	Counsellor, Ishikawajima Harima Heavy Industries, Co., Ltd.	
3. *Quasi-government Institutions*		
F. Koguchi	Managing Director, Nippon Telegraph & Telephone Public Corporation	
M. Ozeki	Managing Director, Japan National Railways	
S. Asada	President, Japan Air Lines Co., Ltd.	Former Vice-Minister, Ministry of Transport
K. Abiru	President, Nihon Aeroplane Manufacturing Co.	Former General Manager, Bureau o' MITI
J. Kondo	Vice-President, National Environmental Pollution Research Institute	
S. Sahashi	President, Industrial Economy Research Institute	Former Vice-Minister, MITI

Y. Tateyasu	President, Research Development Corporation of Japan	Former Manager, Bureau of Science & Technology Agency
M. Kogure	Chairman, Farm Mechanization Research Institute	Former General Manager, Bureau of Ministry of Agriculture & Forestry
S. Tateno	Manager, The Research Institute of Electronics and Communication	
M. Tomuro	Manager, Small Business Promotion Corporation	
K. Azuma	Manager, Japan Development Bank	
M. Takeuchi	President, Export-Import Bank of Japan	Former Vice-Minister, Ministry of Finance
T. Oda	Manager, Smaller Business Finance Corporation	
4. Commercial Bank		
T. Tajima	Managing Director, Industrial Bank of Japan	
5. Universities		
H. Arisawa	Professor, University of Tokyo	
A. Watari	Professor, University of Tokyo	
H. Kimura	Professor, Nihon University	
Z. Sawai	Professor, Nihon University	
M. Shinohara	Professor, Seikei University	
K. Hatta	Professor, Tokai University	
N. Fusamura	Professor, Waseda University	
6. Newspaper Publishing Companies		
K. Noyama	Editor, *Japan Economic Journal*	

NAME	COUNCIL CAPACITY	PRIMARY EMPLOYMENT AFFILIATION IS OR WAS WITH:
MEMBERS		
6. Newspaper Publishing Companies (Cont'd)		
T. Fujiyoshi	Editor in chief, *Daily Industrial News*	
S. Kawamoto	Editor in chief, *Nihon Industrial News*	
H. Shinohara	Editor, Asahi Shinbun, Co., Ltd.	
7. Labor Unions		
K. Oikawa	Vice-Chairman, General Council of Trade Unions of Japan	
S. Doi	Vice-Chairman, Japanese Confederation of Labor	
T. Kashiyama	Chairman, Federation of Independent Unions	
8. Others		
N. Makino	Executive Director, Mitsubishi Research Institute, Inc.	
H. Inaba	Chairman, Industry Research Institute	
K. Tsuchiya	Chairman, Research Institute of General Policy	

Compiled by Osamu Suruga, December 1982

KEIDANREN
JAPAN FEDERATION OF
ECONOMIC ORGANIZATIONS—1982

Chairman
Yoshihiro Inayama
> Director, Honorary Chairman Nippon Steel Corporation

Vice-Chairmen
Katsuji Kawamata
> Chairman, Nissan Motor Co., Ltd.

Norishige Hasegawa
> Chairman, Sumitomo Chemical Co., Ltd.

Isamu Saheki
> Chairman, Kinki Nippon Railway Co., Ltd.

Gaishi Hiraiwa
> President, The Tokyo Electric Power Co., Inc.

Masami Ishida
> Executive Advisor, Idemitsu Kosan Co., Ltd.

Isamu Yamashita
> Chairman, Mitsui Engineering & Shipbuilding Co., Ltd.

Hirokichi Yoshiyama
> Chairman, Hitachi Ltd.

Toshio Nakamura
Chairman, The Mitsubishi Bank, Ltd.

Eishiro Saito
Chairman, Nippon Steel Corporation

Nihachiro Hanamura
Director General, Keidanren

Chairman of the Board of Councillors
Yoshizane Iwasa
Advisor, The Fuji Bank, Ltd.

Honorary Chairman
Toshiwo Doko
Counsellor, Toshiba Corporation

Committee Chairmen
Committee on General Economic Policy
Katsuji Kawamata—Chairman, Nissan Motor Co., Ltd.

Committee on Economic Research
Binsuke Sugiura—Chairman, The Long-Term Credit Bank of Japan, Ltd.

Committee on Industrial Policy
Ryoichi Kawai—Chairman, Komatsu, Ltd.

Committee on Natural Resources
Shinpei Omoto—Senior Advisor, Mitsui Mining & Smelting Co., Ltd.

Committee on Environment and Safety
Eiro Iwamura—Chairman, Kawasaki Steel Corporation

Ad Hoc Committee on Reform of Administrative Structure
Masami Ishida—Executive Advisor, Idemitsu Kosan Co.

Committee on Prices
Munetada Murata—Chairman, The Nomura Securities Co.

Committee on Energy
Tomiichiro Shirasawa—Counsellor, The Japan Atomic Power Company

Committee on Distribution
Seiko Tozaki—President, C. Itoh & Co., Ltd.

Committee on Land Development and Utilization
Shojiro Nishikawa—Director and Advisor, The Dai-Ichi Kangyo Bank, Ltd.

Committee on Public Affairs
Nihachiro Hanamura—Vice Chairman Keidanren

Committee on Statistics
Hisashi Kurokawa—Chairman, Mitsubishi Petrochemical Co., Ltd.

Executive Committee on Coal
Yoshihiro Inayama—Director, Honorary Chairman, Nippon Steel Corporation

Committee on Transportation
Shojiro Kikuchi—Chairman, Nippon Yusen K.K.

Committee on Agricultural Policy
Bunzo Watanabe—Honorary Chairman Ajinomoto Co., Inc.

Committee on Data Processing
Taiyu Kobayashi—Chairman Fujitsu Limited

Committee on International Finance
Yasushi Watanabe—President, The Bank of Tokyo, Ltd.

Committee on Economic Legislation
Haruo Suzuki—Chairman, Showa Denko K.K.

Committee on Oceanic Resources
Kazuo Maeda—President, Mitsui Engineering & Shipbuilding Co., Ltd.

Committee on Foreign Trade
Tatsuzo Mizukami—President, Japan Foreign Trade Council, Inc.

Committee on Overseas Projects
Takeo Atsumi—Chairman and Chief Executive Officer, Kajima Corporation

Committee on Relations with Small and Medium Business
Masaya Hanai—Senior Advisor, Toyota Motor Corporation

Committee on Taxation
Kazuo Iwata—Toshiba Corporation

Committee on Life Science
Eiji Suzuki—Chairman, Mitsubishi Chemical Industries Ltd.

Committee on International Investment and Technology Exchange
Akio Morita—Chairman and Chief Executive Officer, Sony Corporation

BIAC (Business and Industry Advisory Committee to OECD) Japan
Yoshizo Ikeda—Senior Advisor, Mitsui & Co., Ltd.

Committee on Fiscal and Monetary Policies
Takuji Matsuzawa—Chairman, The Fuji Bank, Ltd.

Committee on Capital Market
Eiji Toyoda—Chairman, Toyota Motor Corporation

Committee on Industrial Technology
Sadakazu Shindo—Chairman, Mitsubishi Electric Corporation

Committee on Foreign Relations
Kisaburo Ikeura—President, The Industrial Bank of Japan, Ltd.

Committee on Economic Cooperation
Taiichiro Matsuo—Chairman, Marubeni Corporation

Atlantic Institute Committee
Seiki Tozaki—President, C. Itoh & Co., Ltd.

Special Committee on Europe
Toshio Nakamura—Chairman, The Mitsubishi Bank, Ltd.

Committee on Cooperation with Indonesia
Eiichi Hashimoto—Senior Advisor, Mitsui and Co., Ltd.

Japan-Venezuela Economic Cooperation Conference
Renzo Taguchi—Counsellor, Ishikawajima-Harima, Heavy Industries Co., Ltd.

Committee on Mexico-Japan Steel Cooperation
Yoshihiro Inayama—Director, Honorary Chairman, Nippon Steel Corporation

Japan-Canada Economic Committee
Hisao Makita—Chairman, Nippon Kokan K.K.

Japan-Brazil Economic Committee
Yutaka Takeda—President, Nippon Steel Corporation

Committee on Cooperation with Africa
Masao Kanamori—Chairman, Mitsubishi Heavy Industries, Ltd.

Committee on SOMISA
Nihachiro Hanamura—Vice-Chairman, Keidanren

Committee on Japan-Thailand Cooperation
Bunichiro Tanabe—Chairman, Mitsubishi Corporation

Japan-Mexico Business Cooperation Committee
Takashi Ishihara—President, Nissan Motor Co., Ltd.

Japan-Algeria Business Cooperation Committee
Binsuke Sugiura—Chairman, The Long-Term Credit Bank of Japan, Ltd.

Defense Production Committee
Gakuji Moriya—Counsellor, Mitsubishi Heavy Industries, Ltd.

Space Activities Promotion Council
Koji Kobayashi—Chairman, Nippon Electric Co., Ltd.

APPENDIX VIa
ORGANIZATION CHART OF MITI—1983

MINISTRY OF INTERNATIONAL TRADE AND INDUSTRY

MINISTER

VICE-MINISTERS

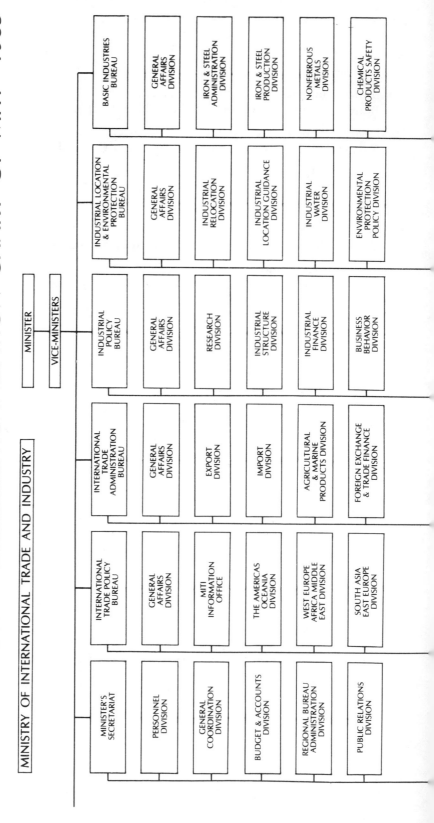

MINISTER'S SECRETARIAT
- PERSONNEL DIVISION
- GENERAL COORDINATION DIVISION
- BUDGET & ACCOUNTS DIVISION
- REGIONAL BUREAU ADMINISTRATION DIVISION
- PUBLIC RELATIONS DIVISION

INTERNATIONAL TRADE POLICY BUREAU
- GENERAL AFFAIRS DIVISION
- MITI INFORMATION OFFICE
- THE AMERICAS OCEANIA DIVISION
- WEST EUROPE AFRICA MIDDLE EAST DIVISION
- SOUTH ASIA EAST EUROPE DIVISION

INTERNATIONAL TRADE ADMINISTRATION BUREAU
- GENERAL AFFAIRS DIVISION
- EXPORT DIVISION
- IMPORT DIVISION
- AGRICULTURAL & MARINE PRODUCTS DIVISION
- FOREIGN EXCHANGE & TRADE FINANCE DIVISION

INDUSTRIAL POLICY BUREAU
- GENERAL AFFAIRS DIVISION
- RESEARCH DIVISION
- INDUSTRIAL STRUCTURE DIVISION
- INDUSTRIAL FINANCE DIVISION
- BUSINESS BEHAVIOR DIVISION

INDUSTRIAL LOCATION & ENVIRONMENTAL PROTECTION BUREAU
- GENERAL AFFAIRS DIVISION
- INDUSTRIAL RELOCATION DIVISION
- INDUSTRIAL LOCATION GUIDANCE DIVISION
- INDUSTRIAL WATER DIVISION
- ENVIRONMENTAL PROTECTION POLICY DIVISION

BASIC INDUSTRIES BUREAU
- GENERAL AFFAIRS DIVISION
- IRON & STEEL ADMINISTRATION DIVISION
- IRON & STEEL PRODUCTION DIVISION
- NONFERROUS METALS DIVISION
- CHEMICAL PRODUCTS SAFETY DIVISION

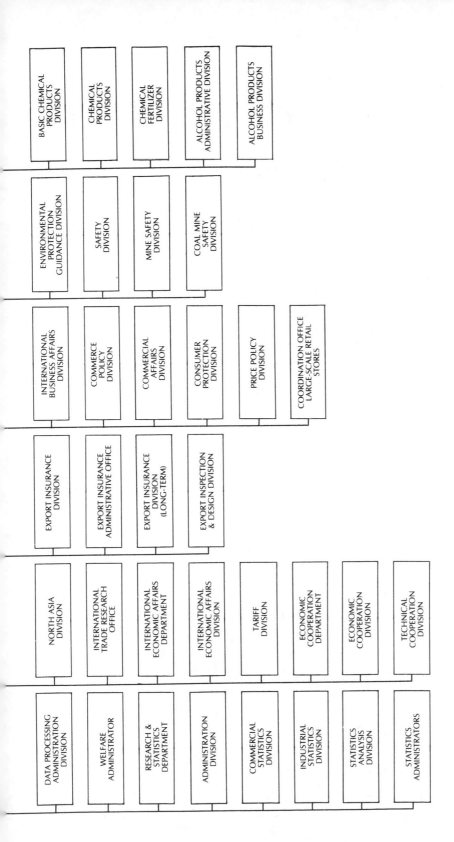

BASIC CHEMICAL PRODUCTS DIVISION

CHEMICAL PRODUCTS DIVISION

CHEMICAL FERTILIZER DIVISION

ALCOHOL PRODUCTS ADMINISTRATIVE DIVISION

ALCOHOL PRODUCTS BUSINESS DIVISION

ENVIRONMENTAL PROTECTION GUIDANCE DIVISION

SAFETY DIVISION

MINE SAFETY DIVISION

COAL MINE SAFETY DIVISION

INTERNATIONAL BUSINESS AFFAIRS DIVISION

COMMERCE POLICY DIVISION

COMMERCIAL AFFAIRS DIVISION

CONSUMER PROTECTION DIVISION

PRICE POLICY DIVISION

COORDINATION OFFICE LARGE-SCALE RETAIL STORES

EXPORT INSURANCE DIVISION

EXPORT INSURANCE ADMINISTRATIVE OFFICE

EXPORT INSURANCE DIVISION (LONG-TERM)

EXPORT INSPECTION & DESIGN DIVISION

NORTH ASIA DIVISION

INTERNATIONAL TRADE RESEARCH OFFICE

INTERNATIONAL ECONOMIC AFFAIRS DEPARTMENT

INTERNATIONAL ECONOMIC AFFAIRS DIVISION

TARIFF DIVISION

ECONOMIC COOPERATION DEPARTMENT

ECONOMIC COOPERATION DIVISION

TECHNICAL COOPERATION DIVISION

DATA PROCESSING ADMINISTRATION DIVISION

WELFARE ADMINISTRATOR

RESEARCH & STATISTICS DEPARTMENT

ADMINISTRATION DIVISION

COMMERCIAL STATISTICS DIVISION

INDUSTRIAL STATISTICS DIVISION

STATISTICS ANALYSIS DIVISION

STATISTICS ADMINISTRATORS

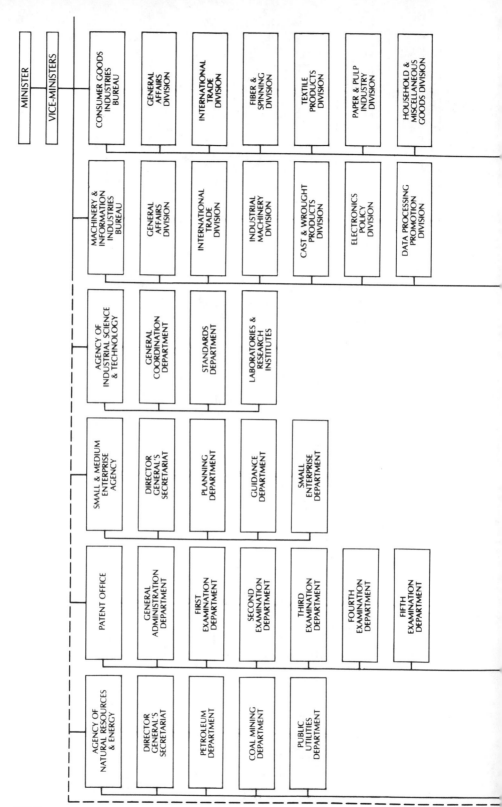

MINISTER

VICE-MINISTERS

CONSUMER GOODS INDUSTRIES BUREAU
- GENERAL AFFAIRS DIVISION
- INTERNATIONAL TRADE DIVISION
- FIBER & SPINNING DIVISION
- TEXTILE PRODUCTS DIVISION
- PAPER & PULP INDUSTRY DIVISION
- HOUSEHOLD & MISCELLANEOUS GOODS DIVISION

MACHINERY & INFORMATION INDUSTRIES BUREAU
- GENERAL AFFAIRS DIVISION
- INTERNATIONAL TRADE DIVISION
- INDUSTRIAL MACHINERY DIVISION
- CAST & WROUGHT PRODUCTS DIVISION
- ELECTRONICS POLICY DIVISION
- DATA PROCESSING PROMOTION DIVISION

AGENCY OF INDUSTRIAL SCIENCE & TECHNOLOGY
- GENERAL COORDINATION DEPARTMENT
- STANDARDS DEPARTMENT
- LABORATORIES & RESEARCH INSTITUTES

SMALL & MEDIUM ENTERPRISE AGENCY
- DIRECTOR GENERAL'S SECRETARIAT
- PLANNING DEPARTMENT
- GUIDANCE DEPARTMENT
- SMALL ENTERPRISE DEPARTMENT

PATENT OFFICE
- GENERAL ADMINISTRATION DEPARTMENT
- FIRST EXAMINATION DEPARTMENT
- SECOND EXAMINATION DEPARTMENT
- THIRD EXAMINATION DEPARTMENT
- FOURTH EXAMINATION DEPARTMENT
- FIFTH EXAMINATION DEPARTMENT

AGENCY OF NATURAL RESOURCES & ENERGY
- DIRECTOR GENERAL'S SECRETARIAT
- PETROLEUM DEPARTMENT
- COAL MINING DEPARTMENT
- PUBLIC UTILITIES DEPARTMENT

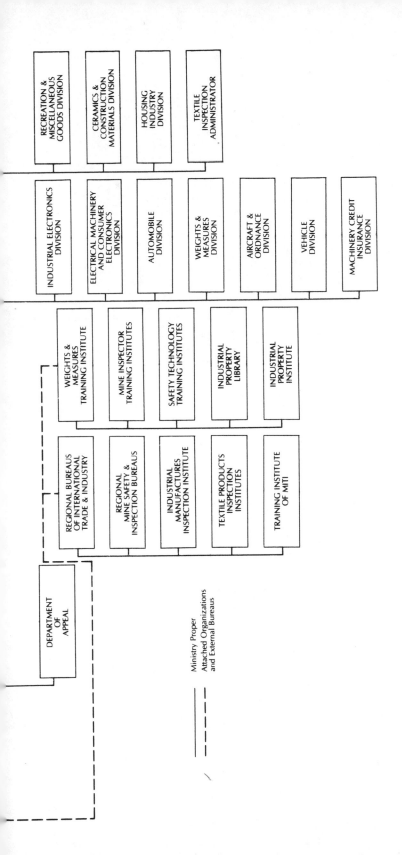

DEPARTMENT OF APPEAL

RECREATION & MISCELLANEOUS GOODS DIVISION

CERAMICS & CONSTRUCTION MATERIALS DIVISION

HOUSING INDUSTRY DIVISION

TEXTILE INSPECTION ADMINISTRATOR

INDUSTRIAL ELECTRONICS DIVISION

ELECTRICAL MACHINERY AND CONSUMER ELECTRONICS DIVISION

AUTOMOBILE DIVISION

WEIGHTS & MEASURES DIVISION

AIRCRAFT & ORDNANCE DIVISION

VEHICLE DIVISION

MACHINERY CREDIT INSURANCE DIVISION

WEIGHTS & MEASURES TRAINING INSTITUTE

MINE INSPECTOR TRAINING INSTITUTES

SAFETY TECHNOLOGY TRAINING INSTITUTES

INDUSTRIAL PROPERTY LIBRARY

INDUSTRIAL PROPERTY INSTITUTE

REGIONAL BUREAUS OF INTERNATIONAL TRADE & INDUSTRY

REGIONAL MINE SAFETY & INSPECTION BUREAUS

INDUSTRIAL MANUFACTURES INSPECTION INSTITUTE

TEXTILE PRODUCTS INSPECTION INSTITUTES

TRAINING INSTITUTE OF MITI

Ministry Proper

Attached Organizations and External Bureaus

257

APPENDIX VIb

DEPARTMENT OF COMMERCE

CHART 3   SECRETARY OF COMMERCE

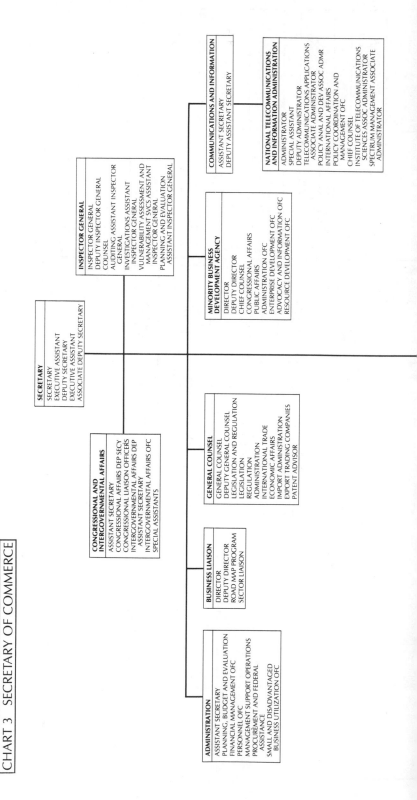

SECRETARY
SECRETARY
EXECUTIVE ASSISTANT
DEPUTY SECRETARY
EXECUTIVE ASSISTANT
ASSOCIATE DEPUTY SECRETARY

CONGRESSIONAL AND INTERGOVERNMENTAL AFFAIRS
ASSISTANT SECRETARY
CONGRESSIONAL AFFAIRS DEP SECY
CONGRESSIONAL LIAISON OFFICERS
INTERGOVERNMENTAL AFFAIRS DEP ASSISTANT SECRETARY
INTERGOVERNMENTAL AFFAIRS OFC
SPECIAL ASSISTANTS

INSPECTOR GENERAL
INSPECTOR GENERAL
DEPUTY INSPECTOR GENERAL
COUNSEL
AUDITING ASSISTANT INSPECTOR GENERAL
INVESTIGATIONS ASSISTANT INSPECTOR GENERAL
VULNERABILITY ASSESSMENT AND MANAGEMENT SVCS ASSISTANT INSPECTOR GENERAL
PLANNING AND EVALUATION ASSISTANT INSPECTOR GENERAL

COMMUNICATIONS AND INFORMATION
ASSISTANT SECRETARY
DEPUTY ASSISTANT SECRETARY

NATIONAL TELECOMMUNICATIONS AND INFORMATION ADMINISTRATION
ADMINISTRATOR
SPECIAL ASSISTANT
DEPUTY ADMINISTRATOR
TELECOMMUNICATIONS APPLICATIONS ASSOCIATE ADMINISTRATOR
POLICY ANAL AND DEV ASSOC ADMR
INTERNATIONAL AFFAIRS
POLICY COORDINATION AND MANAGEMENT OFC
CHIEF COUNSEL
INSTITUTE OF TELECOMMUNICATIONS SCIENCES ASSOC ADMINISTRATOR
SPECTRUM MANAGEMENT ASSOCIATE ADMINISTRATOR

MINORITY BUSINESS DEVELOPMENT AGENCY
DIRECTOR
DEPUTY DIRECTOR
CHIEF COUNSEL
CONGRESSIONAL AFFAIRS
PUBLIC AFFAIRS
ADMINISTRATION OFC
ENTERPRISE DEVELOPMENT OFC
ADVOCACY AND INFORMATION OFC
RESOURCE DEVELOPMENT OFC

GENERAL COUNSEL
GENERAL COUNSEL
DEPUTY GENERAL COUNSEL
LEGISLATION AND REGULATION
LEGISLATION
REGULATION
ADMINISTRATION
INTERNATIONAL TRADE
ECONOMIC AFFAIRS
IMPORT ADMINISTRATION
EXPORT TRADING COMPANIES
PATENT ADVISOR

BUSINESS LIAISON
DIRECTOR
DEPUTY DIRECTOR
ROAD MAP PROGRAM
SECTOR LIAISON

ADMINISTRATION
ASSISTANT SECRETARY
PLANNING, BUDGET AND EVALUATION
FINANCIAL MANAGEMENT OFC
PERSONNEL OFC
MANAGEMENT SUPPORT OPERATIONS
PROCUREMENT AND FEDERAL ASSISTANCE
SMALL AND DISADVANTAGED BUSINESS UTILIZATION OFC

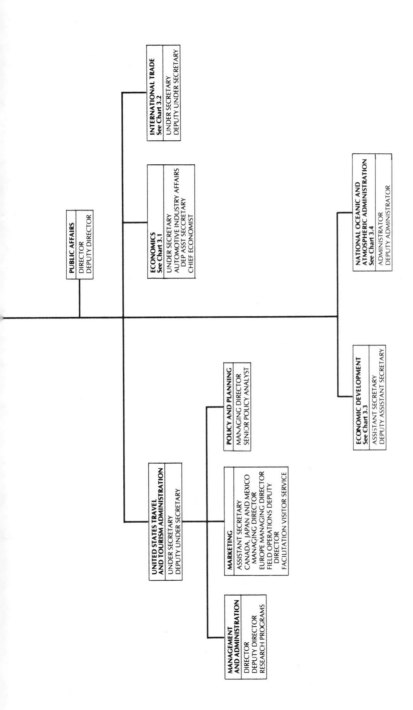

PUBLIC AFFAIRS
DIRECTOR
DEPUTY DIRECTOR

INTERNATIONAL TRADE
See Chart 3.2
UNDER SECRETARY
DEPUTY UNDER SECRETARY

ECONOMICS
See Chart 3.1
UNDER SECRETARY
AUTOMOTIVE INDUSTRY AFFAIRS
DEP ASST SECRETARY
CHIEF ECONOMIST

NATIONAL OCEANIC AND
ATMOSPHERIC ADMINISTRATION
See Chart 3.4
ADMINISTRATOR
DEPUTY ADMINISTRATOR

UNITED STATES TRAVEL
AND TOURISM ADMINISTRATION
UNDER SECRETARY
DEPUTY UNDER SECRETARY

POLICY AND PLANNING
MANAGING DIRECTOR
SENIOR POLICY ANALYST

ECONOMIC DEVELOPMENT
See Chart 3.3
ASSISTANT SECRETARY
DEPUTY ASSISTANT SECRETARY

MARKETING
ASSISTANT SECRETARY
CANADA, JAPAN AND MEXICO
MANAGING DIRECTOR
EUROPE MANAGING DIRECTOR
FIELD OPERATIONS DEPUTY
DIRECTOR
FACILITATION VISITOR SERVICE

MANAGEMENT
AND ADMINISTRATION
DIRECTOR
DEPUTY DIRECTOR
RESEARCH PROGRAMS

260

CHART 3.1 UNDER SECRETARY FOR ECONOMIC AFFAIRS

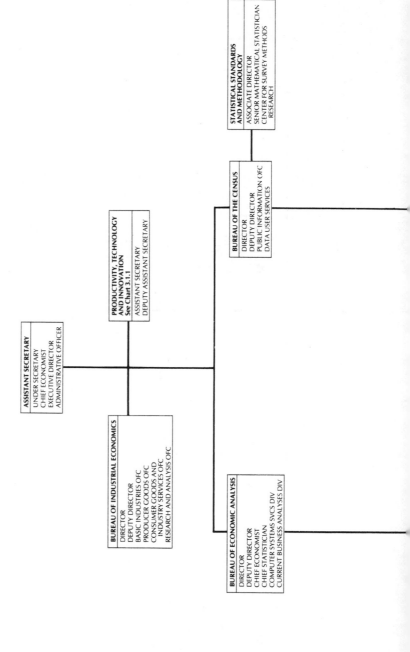

ASSISTANT SECRETARY
UNDER SECRETARY
CHIEF ECONOMIST
EXECUTIVE DIRECTOR
ADMINISTRATIVE OFFICER

PRODUCTIVITY, TECHNOLOGY AND INNOVATION
See Chart 3.1.1
ASSISTANT SECRETARY
DEPUTY ASSISTANT SECRETARY

STATISTICAL STANDARDS AND METHODOLOGY
ASSOCIATE DIRECTOR
SENIOR MATHEMATICAL STATISTICIAN
CENTER FOR SURVEY METHODS RESEARCH

BUREAU OF INDUSTRIAL ECONOMICS
DIRECTOR
DEPUTY DIRECTOR
BASIC INDUSTRIES OFC
PRODUCER GOODS OFC
CONSUMER GOODS AND INDUSTRY SERVICES OFC
RESEARCH AND ANALYSIS OFC

BUREAU OF THE CENSUS
DIRECTOR
DEPUTY DIRECTOR
PUBLIC INFORMATION OFC
DATA USER SERVICES

BUREAU OF ECONOMIC ANALYSIS
DIRECTOR
DEPUTY DIRECTOR
CHIEF ECONOMIST
CHIEF STATISTICIAN
COMPUTER SYSTEMS SVCS DIV
CURRENT BUSINESS ANALYSES DIV

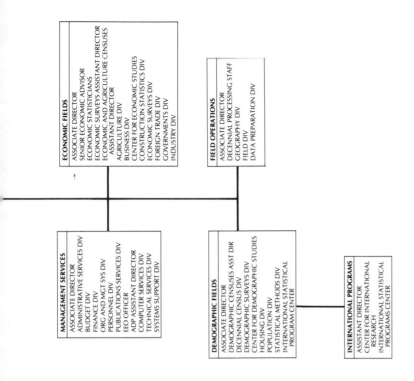

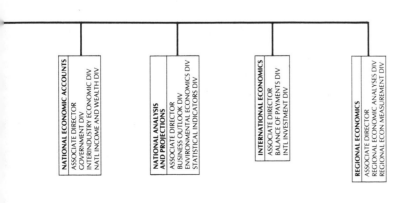

CHART 3.1.1 ASSISTANT SECRETARY FOR PRODUCTIVITY TECHNOLOGY AND INNOVATION

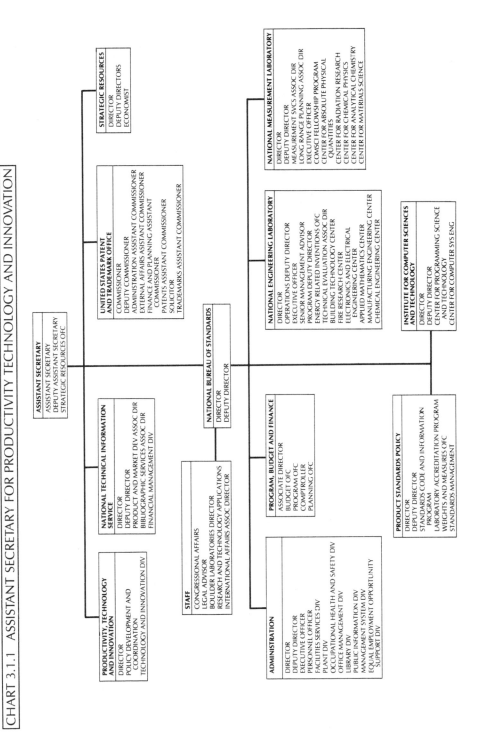

ASSISTANT SECRETARY
ASSISTANT SECRETARY
DEPUTY ASSISTANT SECRETARY
STRATEGIC RESOURCES OFC

STRATEGIC RESOURCES
DIRECTOR
DEPUTY DIRECTORS
ECONOMIST

NATIONAL MEASUREMENT LABORATORY
DIRECTOR
DEPUTY DIRECTOR
MEASUREMENT SVCS ASSOC DIR
LONG RANGE PLANNING ASSOC DIR
EXECUTIVE OFFICER
COMSCI FELLOWSHIP PROGRAM
CENTER FOR ABSOLUTE PHYSICAL
   QUANTITIES
CENTER FOR RADIATION RESEARCH
CENTER FOR CHEMICAL PHYSICS
CENTER FOR ANALYTICAL CHEMISTRY
CENTER FOR MATERIALS SCIENCE

UNITED STATES PATENT AND TRADEMARK OFFICE
COMMISSIONER
DEPUTY COMMISSIONER
ADMINISTRATION ASSISTANT COMMISSIONER
EXTERNAL AFFAIRS ASISTANT COMMISSIONER
FINANCE AND PLANNING ASSISTANT
   COMMISSIONER
PATENTS ASSISTANT COMMISSIONER
SOLICITOR
TRADEMARKS ASSISTANT COMMISSIONER

NATIONAL ENGINEERING LABORATORY
DIRECTOR
OPERATIONS DEPUTY DIRECTOR
EXECUTIVE OFFICER
SENIOR MANAGEMENT ADVISOR
PROGRAM DEPUTY DIRECTOR
ENERGY RELATED INVENTIONS OFC
TECHNICAL EVALUATION ASSOC DIR
BUILDING TECHNOLOGY CENTER
FIRE RESEARCH CENTER
ELECTRONICS AND ELECTRICAL
   ENGINEERING CENTER
APPLIED MATHEMATICS CENTER
MANUFACTURING ENGINEERING CENTER
CHEMICAL ENGINEERING CENTER

PRODUCTIVITY, TECHNOLOGY AND INNOVATION
DIRECTOR
POLICY DEVELOPMENT AND
   COORDINATION
TECHNOLOGY AND INNOVATION DIV

NATIONAL TECHNICAL INFORMATION SERVICE
DIRECTOR
DEPUTY DIRECTOR
PRODUCT AND MARKET DEV ASSOC DIR
BIBLIOGRAPHIC SERVICES ASSOC DIR
FINANCIAL MANAGEMENT DIV

INSTITUTE FOR COMPUTER SCIENCES AND TECHNOLOGY
DIRECTOR
DEPUTY DIRECTOR
CENTER FOR PROGRAMMING SCIENCE
   AND TECHNOLOGY
CENTER FOR COMPUTER SYS ENG

NATIONAL BUREAU OF STANDARDS
DIRECTOR
DEPUTY DIRECTOR

STAFF
CONGRESSIONAL AFFAIRS
LEGAL ADVISOR
BOULDER LABORATORIES DIRECTOR
RESEARCH AND TECHNOLOGY APPLICATIONS
INTERNATIONAL AFFAIRS ASSOC DIRECTOR

PROGRAM, BUDGET AND FINANCE
ASSOCIATE DIRECTOR
BUDGET OFC
PROGRAM OFC
COMPTROLLER
PLANNING OFC

PRODUCT STANDARDS POLICY
DIRECTOR
DEPUTY DIRECTOR
STANDARDS CODE AND INFORMATION
   PROGRAM
LABORATORY ACCREDITATION PROGRAM
WEIGHTS AND MEASURES OFC
STANDARDS MANAGEMENT

ADMINISTRATION
DIRECTOR
DEPUTY DIRECTOR
EXECUTIVE OFFICER
PERSONNEL OFFICER
FACILITIES SERVICES DIV
PLANT DIV
OCCUPATIONAL HEALTH AND SAFETY DIV
OFFICE MANAGEMENT DIV
LIBRARY DIV
PUBLIC INFORMATION DIV
MANAGEMENT SYSTEM DIV
EQUAL EMPLOYMENT OPPORTUNITY
   SUPPORT DIV

CHART 3.2 UNDER SECRETARY FOR INTERNATIONAL TRADE

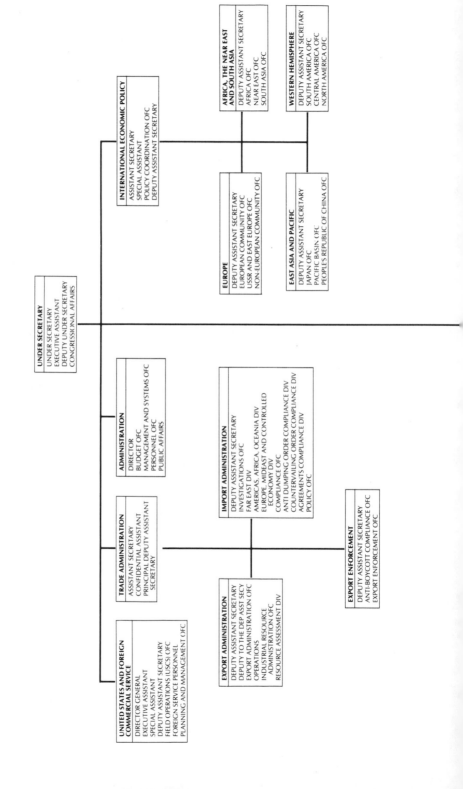

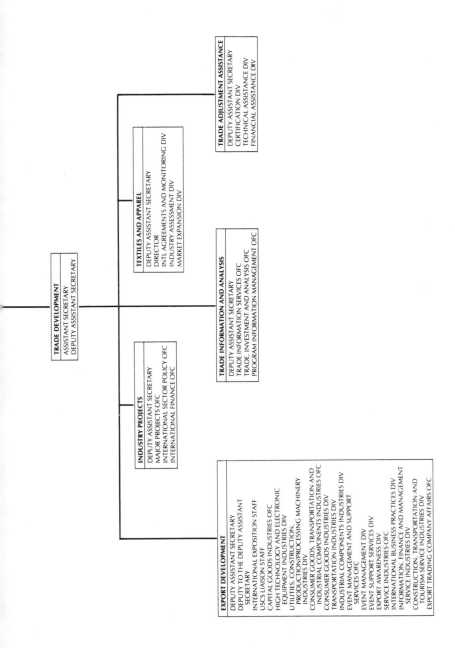

TRADE DEVELOPMENT
ASSISTANT SECRETARY
DEPUTY ASSISTANT SECRETARY

INDUSTRY PROJECTS
DEPUTY ASSISTANT SECRETARY
MAJOR PROJECTS OFC
INTERNATIONAL SECTOR POLICY OFC
INTERNATIONAL FINANCE OFC

TEXTILES AND APPAREL
DEPUTY ASSISTANT SECRETARY
DIRECTOR
INT'L AGREEMENTS AND MONITORING DIV
INDUSTRY ASSESSMENT DIV
MARKET EXPANSION DIV

TRADE ADJUSTMENT ASSISTANCE
DEPUTY ASSISTANT SECRETARY
CERTIFICATION DIV
TECHNICAL ASSISTANCE DIV
FINANCIAL ASSISTANCE DIV

TRADE INFORMATION AND ANALYSIS
DEPUTY ASSISTANT SECRETARY
TRADE INFORMATION SERVICES OFC
TRADE, INVESTMENT AND ANALYSIS OFC
PROGRAM INFORMATION MANAGEMENT OFC

EXPORT DEVELOPMENT
DEPUTY ASSISTANT SECRETARY
DEPUTY TO THE DEPUTY ASSISTANT
   SECRETARY
INTERNATIONAL EXPOSITION STAFF
USCS LIAISON STAFF
CAPITAL GOODS INDUSTRIES OFC
HIGH TECHNOLOGY AND ELECTRONIC
   EQUIPMENT INDUSTRIES DIV
UTILITIES, CONSTRUCTION,
   PRODUCTION/PROCESSING MACHINERY
   INDUSTRIES DIV
CONSUMER GOODS, TRANSPORTATION AND
   INDUSTRIAL COMPONENTS INDUSTRIES OFC
CONSUMER GOODS INDUSTRIES DIV
TRANSPORTATION INDUSTRIES DIV
INDUSTRIAL COMPONENTS INDUSTRIES DIV
EVENT MANAGEMENT AND SUPPORT
   SERVICES OFC
EVENT MANAGEMENT DIV
EVENT SUPPORT SERVICES DIV
EXPORT AWARENESS DIV
SERVICE INDUSTRIES OFC
INTERNATIONAL BUSINESS PRACTICES DIV
INFORMATION, FINANCE AND MANAGEMENT
   SERVICE INDUSTRIES DIV
CONSTRUCTION, TRANSPORTATION AND
   TOURISM SERVICE INDUSTRIES DIV
EXPORT TRADING COMPANY AFFAIRS OFC

CHART 3.3   ASSISTANT SECRETARY FOR ECONOMIC DEVELOPMENT

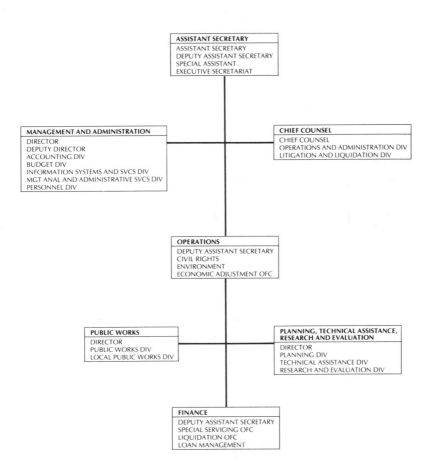

ASSISTANT SECRETARY
ASSISTANT SECRETARY
DEPUTY ASSISTANT SECRETARY
SPECIAL ASSISTANT
EXECUTIVE SECRETARIAT

MANAGEMENT AND ADMINISTRATION
DIRECTOR
DEPUTY DIRECTOR
ACCOUNTING DIV
BUDGET DIV
INFORMATION SYSTEMS AND SVCS DIV
MGT ANAL AND ADMINISTRATIVE SVCS DIV
PERSONNEL DIV

CHIEF COUNSEL
CHIEF COUNSEL
OPERATIONS AND ADMINISTRATION DIV
LITIGATION AND LIQUIDATION DIV

OPERATIONS
DEPUTY ASSISTANT SECRETARY
CIVIL RIGHTS
ENVIRONMENT
ECONOMIC ADJUSTMENT OFC

PUBLIC WORKS
DIRECTOR
PUBLIC WORKS DIV
LOCAL PUBLIC WORKS DIV

PLANNING, TECHNICAL ASSISTANCE, RESEARCH AND EVALUATION
DIRECTOR
PLANNING DIV
TECHNICAL ASSISTANCE DIV
RESEARCH AND EVALUATION DIV

FINANCE
DEPUTY ASSISTANT SECRETARY
SPECIAL SERVICING OFC
LIQUIDATION OFC
LOAN MANAGEMENT

CHART 3.4 NATIONAL OCEANIC AND ATMOSPHERIC ADMINISTRATION

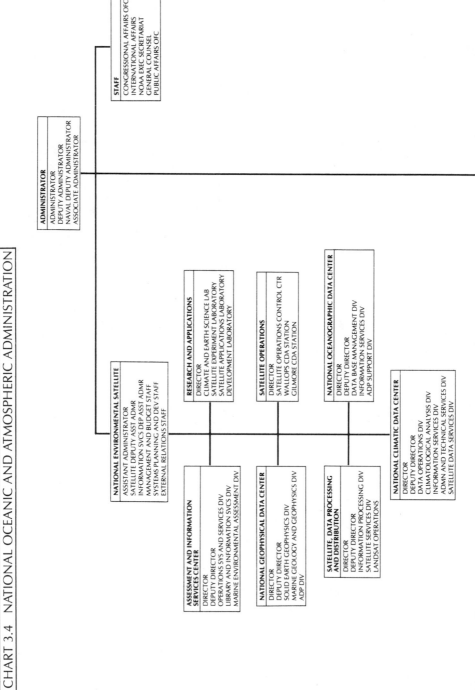

ADMINISTRATOR
ADMINISTRATOR
DEPUTY ADMINISTRATOR
NAVAL DEPUTY ADMINISTRATOR
ASSOCIATE ADMINISTRATOR

STAFF
CONGRESSIONAL AFFAIRS OFC
INTERNATIONAL AFFAIRS
NOAA EXEC SECRETARIAT
GENERAL COUNSEL
PUBLIC AFFAIRS OFC

NATIONAL ENVIRONMENTAL SATELLITE
ASSISTANT ADMINISTRATOR
SATELLITE DEPUTY ASST ADMR
INFORMATION SVCS DEP ASST ADMR
MANAGEMENT AND BUDGET STAFF
SYSTEMS PLANNING AND DEV STAFF
EXTERNAL RELATIONS STAFF

RESEARCH AND APPLICATIONS
DIRECTOR
CLIMATE AND EARTH SCIENCE LAB
SATELLITE EXPERIMENT LABORATORY
SATELLITE APPLICATIONS LABORATORY
DEVELOPMENT LABORATORY

SATELLITE OPERATIONS
DIRECTOR
SATELLITE OPERATIONS CONTROL CTR
WALLOPS CDA STATION
GILMORE CDA STATION

NATIONAL OCEANOGRAPHIC DATA CENTER
DIRECTOR
DEPUTY DIRECTOR
DATA BASE MANAGEMENT DIV
INFORMATION SERVICES DIV
ADP SUPPORT DIV

**ASSESSMENT AND INFORMATION
SERVICES CENTER**
DIRECTOR
DEPUTY DIRECTOR
OPERATIONS SYS AND SERVICES DIV
LIBRARY AND INFORMATION SVCS DIV
MARINE ENVIRONMENTAL ASSESSMENT DIV

NATIONAL GEOPHYSICAL DATA CENTER
DIRECTOR
DEPUTY DIRECTOR
SOLID EARTH GEOPHYSICS DIV
MARINE GEOLOGY AND GEOPHYSICS DIV
ADP DIV

**SATELLITE, DATA PROCESSING
AND DISTRIBUTION**
DIRECTOR
DEPUTY DIRECTOR
INFORMATION PROCESSING DIV
SATELLITE SERVICES DIV
LANDSAT OPERATIONS

NATIONAL CLIMATIC DATA CENTER
DIRECTOR
DEPUTY DIRECTOR
DATA OPERATIONS DIV
CLIMATOLOGICAL ANALYSIS DIV
INFORMATION SERVICES DIV
ADMN AND TECHNICAL SERVICES DIV
SATELLITE DATA SERVICES DIV

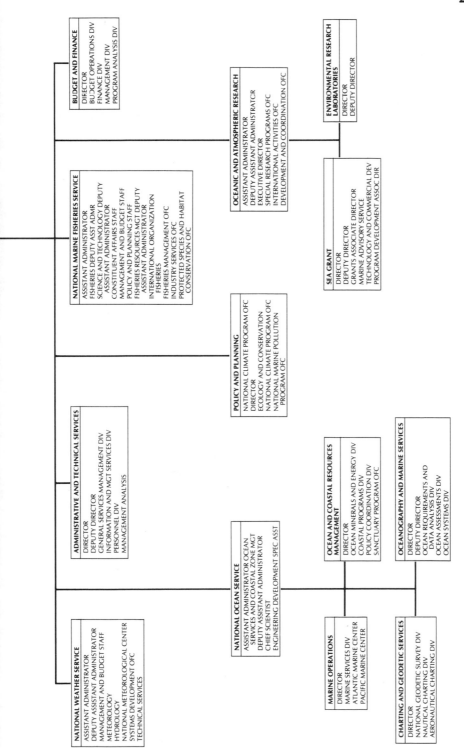

NATIONAL WEATHER SERVICE
ASSISTANT ADMINISTRATOR
DEPUTY ASSISTANT ADMINISTRATOR
MANAGEMENT AND BUDGET STAFF
METEOROLOGY
HYDROLOGY
NATIONAL METEOROLOGICAL CENTER
SYSTEMS DEVELOPMENT OFC
TECHNICAL SERVICES

ADMINISTRATIVE AND TECHNICAL SERVICES
DIRECTOR
DEPUTY DIRECTOR
GENERAL SERVICES MANAGEMENT DIV
INFORMATION AND MGT SERVICES DIV
PERSONNEL DIV
MANAGEMENT ANALYSIS

NATIONAL MARINE FISHERIES SERVICE
ASSISTANT ADMINISTRATOR
FISHERIES DEPUTY ASST ADMR
SCIENCE AND TECHNOLOGY DEPUTY
    ASSISTANT ADMINISTRATOR
CONSTITUENT AFFAIRS STAFF
MANAGEMENT AND BUDGET STAFF
POLICY AND PLANNING STAFF
FISHERIES RESOURCES MGT DEPUTY
    ASSISTANT ADMINISTRATOR
INTERNATIONAL ORGANIZATION
    FISHERIES
FISHERIES MANAGEMENT OFC
INDUSTRY SERVICES OFC
PROTECTED SPECIES AND HABITAT
    CONSERVATION OFC

BUDGET AND FINANCE
DIRECTOR
BUDGET OPERATIONS DIV
FINANCE DIV
MANAGEMENT DIV
PROGRAM ANALYSIS DIV

NATIONAL OCEAN SERVICE
ASSISTANT ADMINISTRATOR OCEAN
    SERVICES AND COASTAL ZONE MGT
DEPUTY ASSISTANT ADMINISTRATOR
CHIEF SCIENTIST
ENGINEERING DEVELOPMENT SPEC ASST

POLICY AND PLANNING
NATIONAL CLIMATE PROGRAM OFC
DIRECTOR
ECOLOGY AND CONSERVATION
NATIONAL CLIMATE PROGRAM OFC
NATIONAL MARINE POLLUTION
    PROGRAM OFC

OCEANIC AND ATMOSPHERIC RESEARCH
ASSISTANT ADMINISTRATOR
DEPUTY ASSISTANT ADMINISTRATCR
EXECUTIVE DIRECTOR
SPECIAL RESEARCH PROGRAMS OFC
INTERNATIONAL ACTIVITIES OFC
DEVELOPMENT AND COORDINATION OFC

**OCEAN AND COASTAL RESOURCES
MANAGEMENT**
DIRECTOR
OCEAN MINERALS AND ENERGY DIV
COASTAL PROGRAMS DIV
POLICY COORDINATION DIV
SANCTUARY PROGRAM OFC

OCEANOGRAPHY AND MARINE SERVICES
DIRECTOR
DEPUTY DIRECTOR
OCEAN REQUIREMENTS AND
    DATA ANALYSIS DIV
OCEAN ASSESSMENTS DIV
OCEAN SYSTEMS DIV

SEA GRANT
DIRECTOR
DEPUTY DIRECTOR
GRANTS ASSOCIATE DIRECTOR
MARINE ADVISORY SERVICE
TECHNOLOGY AND COMMERCIAL DEV
PROGRAM DEVELOPMENT ASSOC DIR

**ENVIRONMENTAL RESEARCH
LABORATORIES**
DIRECTOR
DEPUTY DIRECTOR

MARINE OPERATIONS
DIRECTOR
MARINE SERVICES DIV
ATLANTIC MARINE CENTER
PACIFIC MARINE CENTER

CHARTING AND GEODETIC SERVICES
DIRECTOR
NATIONAL GEODETIC SURVEY DIV
NAUTICAL CHARTING DIV
AERONAUTICAL CHARTING DIV

CHART 3.4.1 ENVIRONMENTAL RESEARCH LABORATORIES

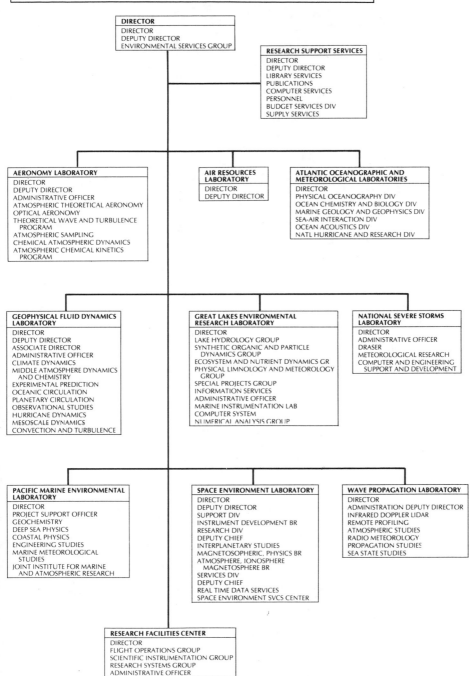

DIRECTOR
DIRECTOR
DEPUTY DIRECTOR
ENVIRONMENTAL SERVICES GROUP

RESEARCH SUPPORT SERVICES
DIRECTOR
DEPUTY DIRECTOR
LIBRARY SERVICES
PUBLICATIONS
COMPUTER SERVICES
PERSONNEL
BUDGET SERVICES DIV
SUPPLY SERVICES

AERONOMY LABORATORY
DIRECTOR
DEPUTY DIRECTOR
ADMINISTRATIVE OFFICER
ATMOSPHERIC THEORETICAL AERONOMY
OPTICAL AERONOMY
THEORETICAL WAVE AND TURBULENCE
  PROGRAM
ATMOSPHERIC SAMPLING
CHEMICAL ATMOSPHERIC DYNAMICS
ATMOSPHERIC CHEMICAL KINETICS
  PROGRAM

AIR RESOURCES LABORATORY
DIRECTOR
DEPUTY DIRECTOR

ATLANTIC OCEANOGRAPHIC AND METEOROLOGICAL LABORATORIES
DIRECTOR
PHYSICAL OCEANOGRAPHY DIV
OCEAN CHEMISTRY AND BIOLOGY DIV
MARINE GEOLOGY AND GEOPHYSICS DIV
SEA-AIR INTERACTION DIV
OCEAN ACOUSTICS DIV
NATL HURRICANE AND RESEARCH DIV

GEOPHYSICAL FLUID DYNAMICS LABORATORY
DIRECTOR
DEPUTY DIRECTOR
ASSOCIATE DIRECTOR
ADMINISTRATIVE OFFICER
CLIMATE DYNAMICS
MIDDLE ATMOSPHERE DYNAMICS
  AND CHEMISTRY
EXPERIMENTAL PREDICTION
OCEANIC CIRCULATION
PLANETARY CIRCULATION
OBSERVATIONAL STUDIES
HURRICANE DYNAMICS
MESOSCALE DYNAMICS
CONVECTION AND TURBULENCE

GREAT LAKES ENVIRONMENTAL RESEARCH LABORATORY
DIRECTOR
LAKE HYDROLOGY GROUP
SYNTHETIC ORGANIC AND PARTICLE
  DYNAMICS GROUP
ECOSYSTEM AND NUTRIENT DYNAMICS GR
PHYSICAL LIMNOLOGY AND METEOROLOGY
  GROUP
SPECIAL PROJECTS GROUP
INFORMATION SERVICES
ADMINISTRATIVE OFFICER
MARINE INSTRUMENTATION LAB
COMPUTER SYSTEM
NUMERICAL ANALYSIS GROUP

NATIONAL SEVERE STORMS LABORATORY
DIRECTOR
ADMINISTRATIVE OFFICER
DRASER
METEOROLOGICAL RESEARCH
COMPUTER AND ENGINEERING
  SUPPORT AND DEVELOPMENT

PACIFIC MARINE ENVIRONMENTAL LABORATORY
DIRECTOR
PROJECT SUPPORT OFFICER
GEOCHEMISTRY
DEEP SEA PHYSICS
COASTAL PHYSICS
ENGINEERING STUDIES
MARINE METEOROLOGICAL
  STUDIES
JOINT INSTITUTE FOR MARINE
  AND ATMOSPHERIC RESEARCH

SPACE ENVIRONMENT LABORATORY
DIRECTOR
DEPUTY DIRECTOR
SUPPORT DIV
INSTRUMENT DEVELOPMENT BR
RESEARCH DIV
DEPUTY CHIEF
INTERPLANETARY STUDIES
MAGNETOSPHERIC, PHYSICS BR
ATMOSPHERE, IONOSPHERE
  MAGNETOSPHERE BR
SERVICES DIV
DEPUTY CHIEF
REAL TIME DATA SERVICES
SPACE ENVIRONMENT SVCS CENTER

WAVE PROPAGATION LABORATORY
DIRECTOR
ADMINISTRATION DEPUTY DIRECTOR
INFRARED DOPPLER LIDAR
REMOTE PROFILING
ATMOSPHERIC STUDIES
RADIO METEOROLOGY
PROPAGATION STUDIES
SEA STATE STUDIES

RESEARCH FACILITIES CENTER
DIRECTOR
FLIGHT OPERATIONS GROUP
SCIENTIFIC INSTRUMENTATION GROUP
RESEARCH SYSTEMS GROUP
ADMINISTRATIVE OFFICER

Meetings are gatherings of members at which the Association's business is transacted and represent the opportunity to legitimately further the Association's goals. Because a trade association is, by definition, a combination of competitors, SAMA meetings must be conducted to avoid even the appearance that members are taking common action which might unreasonably restrain trade.

SAMA meetings are carefully structured and monitored. An agenda is prepared and circulated in advance, and is carefully followed at the meeting. A SAMA staff member attends all SAMA meetings and is responsible for preparing the minutes of each meeting. SAMA counsel attends all Association membership meetings, Board meetings, and other Association meetings at which sensitive issues are discussed and counsel reviews the minutes of these meetings. There are no informal meetings of the Association or any of its Committees; discussion of Association matters must never occur outside of formal meetings.

It is difficult to delineate in a set of guidelines the permissible limits of discussion at a SAMA meeting because so much is dependent upon the context in which any particular subject is to be raised. However, to avoid the most sensitive areas, there should never be a discussion of the following at a SAMA meeting:

1. Price or any elements of price or pricing policies, including costs.
2. Discounts, terms and conditions of sale, warranty terms, profits,

market shares, sales territories, and rejection or termination of customers.
3. Identified individual company statistics, inventories, or merchandising methods.
4. Particular competitors.
5. Anything dealing with trade abuses or excluding or controlling competition.

By following the guidelines herein set forth, the members can meet to transact lawful Association business for the betterment of our industries.

Source: 1981–1982 Membership Directory/Organization Manual, Scientific Apparatus Makers Association, p. 9.

COMPUTING THE COST OF
CAPITAL FOR U.S. AND
JAPANESE COMPANIES
by Jay B. Barney

Introduction

According to modern financial theory, the close relationship between banks and firms in Japan that leads to more efficient information flow, better control, and lower bankruptcy costs, together with the beneficial risk-sharing properties of profit sharing bonuses, should both be reflected in the weighted average cost of capital for Japanese firms. This weighted average cost of capital, or WACC, consists of two components, a firm's cost of debt (i.e., its cost of obtaining funds through long-term loans, short-term loans, corporate bonds, etc.) and its cost of equity (i.e., its cost of obtaining funds through selling stock), each weighted by the percent of total assets a firm holds in the form of debts or equity. The underlying hypotheses put forward in Chapter 4 is easily translated into weighted average cost of capital terms. If potential investors have excellent information concerning the true value of a firm in which they might invest, they face less uncertainty about the future value of their investment, and thus lower risk. They will, in turn, not need to require as large a risk premium for making their funds available to these firms as less well-informed potential investors. The lower the risk premium charged to a firm, the lower the weighted average cost of capital for that firm.

At various points in Chapter 4, the WACC was reported for several U.S. and Japanese electronics companies. The purpose of this appendix is to outline how these figures were computed. While the principles underlying the computation of the WACC in firms in the United States and Japanese are identical, because of the complicating factor of compensating balances, we will focus on the Japanese case here. However, except for controlling for compensating balances in computing the cost of debt, the process of estimating the WACC for U.S. and Japanese electronics firms is substantially the same.

Before-Tax Cost of Debt

Temporarily setting aside the compensating balance problem, computing the overall before tax cost of debt for a firm is quite straightforward. If a firm's total debt is $1,000,000, and it pays $85,000 in interest payments on that debt, then its before-tax cost of debt is 8.5 percent. However, this calculation is significantly complicated if compensating balances are included. If a firm's total debt is $1,000,000 and it pays $85,000 in interest payments, but $400,000 of its total indebtedness is in the form of a compensating balance, receiving interest at 5.0 percent, the actual before-tax cost of that debt is 13.7 percent, substantially higher than the 8.5 percent cost of debt one obtains if compensating balances are not taken into consideration.[1]

If compensating balances are small as a percentage of a firm's total indebtedness, then the failure to include them into calculations of the cost of debt is not likely to affect the results greatly. This is the situation among the U.S. companies we studied. However, if compensating balances are large, they can have a substantial impact. This is the situation in Japan. Thus, a primary issue for us became estimating the size of the compensating balance for the Japanese firms in our study. Unfortunately, there are no statistically rigorous ways to estimate this compensating balance figure in Japan. In our calculations, we relied on our interviews with Japanese bankers and banking officials and U.S. bankers in Japan. These interviews suggested two rules of thumb. The first was that, on average, 90 percent of a firm's cash and deposits should be considered as a compensating balance. The second was that, on average, 40 percent of a firm's total indebtedness will be held as a compensating balance.[2] Application of these two rules of thumb normally generates approximately the same result, i.e., for most firms, about 40 percent of a firm's total indebtedness equals about 90 percent of that firm's cash and deposits.[3] Armed with this estimate of a firm's compensating balances, we then computed the cost of debt for the Japanese firms we studied as in the previous example.

After-Tax Cost of Debt

One of the advantages of debt over equity financing in the United States and Japan is that interest payments on debt in both countries are tax deductible. Thus, while the before-tax cost of debt is of some interest, the after-tax cost of debt represents the actual cost of borrowing money for a firm. Modern financial theory has shown that the effect of interest payment deductions on the cost of debt can be computed by multiplying the before-tax cost of debt times one minus the marginal tax rate for the firm. This was done to obtain the figures reported in Chapter 4.

Cost of Equity

The cost of debt, as an interest payment, is intuitively understandable to most people. After all, we buy houses by borrowing money, and the interest we pay on these loans is the cost of using that money. However, because these interest payments are tax deductible, the actual cost of borrowing the money is less than the interest rate we are paying. This is directly analogous to the before- and after-tax costs of debt. However, while the cost of debt may be intuitively clear to most people, the costs to a firm issuing stock are not so obvious. To many people, it might appear that there are no costs to issuing stock. Firms offer stock to potential investors, and those investors either do or do not buy it. If they buy it, then the firm has raised capital. Except for the costs of selling the stock, printing up stock certificates, and the inevitable lawyer fees, where is the cost to the firm?

The costs of issuing equity can be found in the return that firms must earn for their equity holders in order to attract and use these investor's funds. Suppose you are approached to invest $10,000 in a firm. In return, you will receive stock in the firm. Usually, you will only be willing to do this if two conditions exist. First, the return you would need to receive from investing this $10,000 in the firm must be greater than the return you would receive from investing the same money in, say, risk-free government bonds. If your return is *less* than this risk-free rate of return, then it would not make any sense to accept any risks at all by investing in the firm. It would be better to put your money into government securities and sleep soundly at night, for your return will be just as large and absolutely certain. Thus, for the firm to attract your money, it must generate a return on your investment larger than the return you would receive on risk-free government securities. Second, in order for you to be willing to invest this $10,000 in the firm, the actual return from your investment would depend on the individual riskiness of the investment. If the investment is very risky, the return you would need to receive from your investment in order for you to be willing to invest must be greater than what you would obtain from a less risky investment. If the investment is on the low-risk side, the return you would need to receive from your investment in order for you to be willing to invest will be less than in the high-risk case, but still higher than the return you could obtain from making a no-risk investment. Thus, for this firm to attract your money, it must generate a return consistent with the individual riskiness of the investment. The riskier the investment, the higher the required return.

These concepts have been formalized in what is known as the Capital Asset Pricing Model, or CAPM. This financial model can be used to estimate the rate of return firms must provide for stockholders in order for these stockholders to be willing to invest in the firm. The minimally acceptable rate of return is the cost of equity capital for a firm and is calculated by adding a "risk premium" to a risk-free rate of return. The risk premium is computed in two steps. First, the overall riskiness of investing in the stock market as opposed to investing in no-risk government securities is estimated by calculating the return one could expect from investing in a fully diversified portfolio of stock and holding this portfolio for an extended period of time. The difference between this average "market" rate of return and the risk-free rate of return is the return attributable to accepting the risk of investing in stocks instead of risk-free securities. Second, once this "average" return is calculated, the individual riskiness of a particular firm's stock is evaluated by comparing the extent to which the returns to that stock move together with overall market trends. If the returns to a firm's stocks vary independently of overall market trends, then future returns to that stock are likely to be difficult to predict and anticipate, and this investment should be considered relatively more risky. If the returns to a firm's stock, on the other hand, are quite predictable as a function of overall market trends, then this investment is less risky. The overall market return for investing in the stock market must be adjusted by the individual riskiness of an investment. Investments with higher risk must generate more return if they are to attract investors. Investments with lower risk need not generate such high returns.

A Numerical Example

A simple numerical example will help explain how we calculated the cost of equity. Computing the cost of equity for firms in Japan in 1980, we took the risk-free rate of return to be equal to the interest paid on short term deposits in major city banks. These deposits are fully insured by the Japanese government, much like FDIC insured deposits in the United States. Because they are fully insured, these deposits are subject to essentially no risk. Theoretically, people investing their money in this way could only lose it if the government of Japan ceased to exist or went totally bankrupt. In 1980, the interest paid on these risk-free investments was 4.09 percent, thus, the risk-free rate of return equalled 4.09 percent. To calculate the market rate of return for buying a fully diversified portfolio of stocks on the Tokyo stock market, holding them for a substantial period of time, and then selling it, we did the following. First, we calculated the return an investor would have received from buying one share of every stock in the Tokyo stock exchange in 1962, holding it for ten years, and then selling it all in 1971. We then repeated this calculation for ten ten-year periods, each period beginning from 1962 to 1971. We then averaged all these market returns to generate one average market rate of return for the last nineteen years. This return was 15.8 percent.[4] Finally, to estimate the individual riskiness of each firm as an equity investment, we compared the variance in the returns of that individual stock to the variance in the returns in the overall market. If these two returns moved closely together over time, then this investment was on the low-risk side. If these two returns moved independently of one another, then it was a high-risk investment. The particular measure of "covariation" between individual stock and overall market returns we used is contructed so that high-risk investments have a figure greater than 1.0, and low-risk investments have a figure less than 1.0.[5] In 1980, for example, this figure was .6947 for Hitachi, indicating that investments in Hitachi were very low-risk in character. For Toshiba, this figure in 1980 was 1.296, indicating that the individual risk of investing in Toshiba was such that this firm had to generate a return greater than the return that could be had from investing in a fully diversified portfolio of stocks in order to attract investors. To compute the cost of equity, we took the risk-free rate of return (4.09 percent) and added to it the difference between the market rate of return (15.8 percent) and the risk-free rate of return multiplied by the measure of the individual riskiness of the return to a stock (.6947 for Hitachi and 1.296 for Toshiba). The cost of equity in 1980 for Hitachi was 12.22 percent, while the cost of equity for Toshiba in 1980 was 19.26 percent.[6]

The Weighted Average Cost of Capital

The total cost of capital is a weighted average of the after-tax cost of debt and the cost of equity. Because interest payments are tax deductible, debt costs less to use than equity, so firms in general will attempt to increase the amount of debt they hold, as compared to equity, until those lending them money are unwilling to accept any more risk by lending them still more. All other things being equal, firms with more debt than equity will have a lower WACC than firms with more equity then debt.

To weigh the cost of debt and equity in the final calculation, the percentage of total assets held as debt and equity were calculated. The costs of debt and equity were then multiplied by the percentage of debt and percentage of equity, respectively, and these products were then added together. This sum is the final weighted average cost of capital for the firm.

Notes

1. The actual calculation is of the form:
   Before tax cost of debt = Interest Paid of Debt
   (Total debt − compensating balance) + (Compensating
                    balance × interest rate paid on compensating balance)
   In the example:

   $$\text{Before tax cost of debt} = \frac{\$85,000}{(1,000,000 - 400,000)} + (.05 \times 400,000) = 13.71\%$$

2. The first rule of thumb was explained to us by several MITI and MOF officials, while the second rule of thumb was applied by several different Japanese bankers.

3. For a small number of firms with very low percentages of debt, the first rule of thumb generates unrealistically large estimates of compensating balances. For those firms, we adapted only the second rule.

4. The calculation was done this way to avoid any unusual economic conditions for a short period of years, as well as to avoid last period problems.

5. This is, of course, BETA. The numbers reported are unlevered BETA's, and therefore, the unlevered cost of equity.

6. The actual calculation is of the form:

Cost of Equity = Risk Free Rate + (Market Rule of Return − Risk Free Rate of Return) Individual Riskiness of the Investment

For Hitachi: $4.09 + (15.8 − 4.09) .6947 = 12.22$

For Toshiba: $4.09 + (15.8 − 4.09) 1.296 = 19.26$

APPENDIX IX
JAPANESE GOVERNMENT SOURCES OF FUNDING FOR NEW TECHNOLOGIES

Most MITI-related projects are not financed through JDB, but through one or another of the several alternative sources which are available. Let me briefly summarize these, drawing from a working paper written by Nicholas E. Benes, a member of our research team at UCLA.

The Important Technologies Research and Development Subsidy Program

This program is intended to support private R & D efforts in industry, ordinarily by paying for one-half of the research expenses incurred. Any association of firms may apply, and many of the "research associations" apply for these funds. Applicants must state the nature of their project and set forth detailed financial, technical, and organizational plans. The minimum grant is for $50,000, which means the smallest total project cost must be $100,000, and most applicants envision multiyear projects. The firms keep title to any patents that result, but any profits attributable to the joint research must be shared with MITI for a period of five or six years after the conclusion of the research. The exact sharing formula is set by MITI, which prefers to keep its share low enough to encourage firms to apply. In recent years, 80 percent to 90 percent of the applications have been funded, which implies that no one applies unless extensive discussions have been held with the appropriate discussion councils and MITI staff and that the trade associations involved support the proposal.

The Technology Improvement
Subsidy Program

While the important technologies program supports mostly the major firms, the TIS is aimed at small and medium enterprises which want to undertake R & D projects. Depending on the type of research, either one-half or three-fourths of total costs will be covered by MITI, with a minimum MITI grant of $15,000 and a maximum of $60,000. Although companies own their patents, MITI is empowered to force companies in this program to license their patents to others, presumably to guard against the chance that a small company may develop an important new technology that it is unable to bring to market but is irrationally unwilling to license to anyone else. In recent years, the important technologies program has provided funding of approximately $12 million per year, while TIS has provided about $4 million per year.

The National Technologies
Promotion Financing Program

In 1980, this program provided loan funds of $200 million through the JDB. Proposals are scrutinized by AIST and Industrial Policy Bureau staff within MITI, and require support from the relevant industry associations. The project must hold out the promise of a significant advance in technology and a high level of risk. If all parties concur, an application and recommendation for funding is forwarded by MITI to the Japan Development Bank. For most projects, the program will provide 50 percent to 70 percent of total research expenses with loan funds. The interest rates are only slightly below nominal bank rates, but payments ordinarily do not begin until after a grace period of two or three years and may be stretched out over as many as ten years, which is far beyond what a bank could withstand for such risky projects.

Financing for the Utilization
of New Technologies, Extended
by the Small and Medium
Enterprises Lending Fund

The purposes of this program are identical with the NTPF just described: to reduce the financial risks associated with important R & D by extending long-term loans. In this case, however, the program is limited to small and medium enterprises and is intended to enable such companies to move their new inventions into manufacturing and distribution. Total funds disbursed in 1980 was $20 million. Maximum loans are for $1 million, with a grace period of two years or less and a payback period of ten years or less.

The Mining and Manufacturing Technologies Research Associations Program

This is the program that supported both the VLSI Research Association and the Fifth Generation Project and which, in 1980, was supporting thirty-one research associations. This program is intended to support those projects so large in size and scope that they would not otherwise be undertaken. The total budget figures were unavailable to our research team, but the VLSI Research Association alone received $35 million of subsidies from this program in 1979. Funds are grants rather than loans and require very strong support from MOF as well as from the MITI staff to be granted. If the project succeeds in developing commercial products, then the grant must be repaid. Patents are held by the research associations, which in turn are owned by their corporate members. The association is under no obligation to license or otherwise make its technology available to nonmembers. If a government laboratory participates in the research, then patents are jointly owned by the research association and the government.

Debt Guarantee Operations by the R & D-Based Companies Promotion Center (VEC)

VEC was established in 1975 by the Machinery and Information Industries Bureau of MITI and received as its loan funds the receipts from the government-owned bicycle-racing betting monopoly. VEC is intended to aid R & D intensive small and medium companies by providing unsecured debt guarantees of up to 80 percent of a loan. This is important to small and medium companies, which often lack the mortgageable assets that banks require as collateral. The company pays an annual fee of 2 percent of the guaranteed amount, and if the funded project is a success, then the company must also pay a bonus to VEC of 5 percent to 50 percent of the guaranteed amount, the percentage to be set on a case-by-case basis by VEC. The maximum guarantee is $400,000 per project for up to eight years, although successful applicants are also eligible for very low-interest (4 percent in 1983) loans also from VEC. VEC is quite small, guaranteeing from ten to forty loans each year with a total value of $1 million to $5 million. The total guarantees outstanding at any one time may not go much beyond $12 million. It is probably a good thing that VEC is small, because it appears to be under constant pressure from politicians to bail out companies in their home districts.

The Small and Medium Enterprises Investment Promotion Companies

IPC's are stock companies held by a combination of private and public investors. Three such IPC's exist and have invested a total of $190 million in small and medium business, with some concentration on information-processing services and softwear development firms which are already successful but in need of growth capital. In order to avoid undue political meddling, each IPC has both nonvoting stock, which is the only kind that national government bodies may own, and voting stock, which is the only kind that regional governments and private industry may own. Eighty percent of IPC stock is held by private industry, and 75 percent of the private industry holding is by banks, with the remainder held mostly by securities firms. IPC's prefer to invest in medium-sized companies that are nearly big enough to be publicly listed on the stock exchanges.

The New Technologies Development Association

The NTDA was established by the prime minister's office as a quasi-independent body in 1961. Since that time, it has supported 181 projects in amounts from $200,000 up to $7 million, with most projects at about $2 million. In each case, NTDA brings together two parties: an original researcher who holds a patent or other technology that might have important applications in a new technological application or industry; and a contract researcher, who thinks that he or she can develop that patent into a successful major new application. NTDA serves as a clearinghouse introducing these two kinds of parties to one another and then inviting them to apply for funding. Funding is ordinarily 70 percent to 90 percent of the total project costs. Within five years after the completion of the project, the researcher must pay back the entire sum to NTDA (interest-free) if the project has been successful. In addition, the contract researcher must pay a royalty (usually 1 percent to 3 percent) on sales of the resulting products to NTDA, which in turn gives half of those royalties to the original researcher. All patents stemming from the contract research are owned jointly by the contract researcher, the original researcher, and NTDA, and NTDA normally has the right to license other firms to use the technology, although the contract researcher may be able to bargain for exclusive rights for up to three years. If the research is judged to have been a failure, then the NTDA funds do not have to be repaid, but the researcher must return to NTDA all equipment bought with the funding.

One may view this collection of funding routes as either a creative bazaar of responses to differing needs or as a patchwork of bureaucratically invented ad hoc measures. It is notable that this assemblage of financing resembles in many respects the variety of financing available through the U.S. government to its agricultural industries, the industry in which the United States is clearly the world leader. More importantly, however, it is obvious that these public funds could easily be dissipated into marginal uses if they were subjected to political pressures from narrowly self-interested special-interest groups. An observer cannot help but feel that the more highly developed capital markets of the United States and Western Europe and Canada today carry out most of the activities undertaken by these public bodies in Japan, and might thus conclude that public financing of this scope is unnecessary in those Western nations. However, it also becomes evident that in every economy there are many forms of economic development that cannot be undertaken by private markets, either because they involve nearly public goods that no private investor could capture, or because they represent a level of risk so great that no private consortium could withstand it. In such cases, if the project also represents a positive externality of great potential value to the society as a whole, it must be undertaken through public financing if it is to occur at all. None of this is possible, however, unless public financing can operate within a highly disciplined political framework in which all interested parties can be involved, so that narrow self-interest is deterred, social memory assured, and serial equity protected.

APPENDIX X
THE HISTORICAL ROLE OF THE ZAIBATSU AND THE PRESENT ROLE OF THE SOGO SOSHA IN FINANCING JAPANESE INDUSTRY

Any discussion of the financial system in Japan would be incomplete without some mention of the historical antecedents of today's industrial groups, the zaibatsu of pre-World War II Japan. Extensive treatments of this subject have been written by Yoshihara and by Young, and the reader interested in the topic should read theirs and other accounts of the zaibatsu and of their inheritors, the sogo sosha, or major trading companies.[1] Here we will touch only on a few major points of interest.

The major industrial groups that we have described are rather loose couplings of ten to thirty companies each. Banks stand at the center of these groups, which are held together by common stockholdings and through a natural affinity to trade with one another. To a limited extent, the companies may send directors to one another's boards, but ordinarily 80 or 90 percent of a company's directors are drawn from the ranks of its own top executives.

The Zaibatsu

The predecessors of these loose alliances of the 1980s (the Keiretsu) were the much more tightly knit zaibatsu. As Rodney Clark describes them: "Each zaibatsu had at its center a holding company, controlled by the founder family. This would own a large proportion of each of the dozen or so core companies, including the bank, the trading company, the trust company, and the insurance company. Each of the core companies would own a further percentage of the equity of many of the others, so that the zaibatsu as a group controlled 40 to

287

100 percent of the capital of each of the major members. Each core company might have one or two associates, affiliates or subsidiaries, so that the whole zaibatsu appeared as a vast agglomeration of related companies extending over a range of different industries.[2] By 1941, according to Clark, the zaibatsu controlled 32 percent of the national investment in heavy industry and nearly 50 percent of banking. The zaibatsu however, had developed intimate ties with the military during World War II, and in 1946 the occupation forces dismantled them, breaking Mitsui & Co., then the largest, into 170 separate companies and Mitsubishi, today the largest trading firm, into 139 entities.[3]

Today, the situation is greatly altered. Public opinion in Japan has run against the major industrial groups, with most of the attention focused on the six major groups, of which three are descended from zaibatsu (Mitsui, Mitsubishi, and Sumitomo), and three are relatively new groups led by banks (Fuyo-Fuji, Dai-Ichi Kangyo, and Sanwa). In June of 1983, the Anti-Monopoly Council of the Japanese Fair Trade Commission released a new report on these groups. The average shareholding of any group member in other group members is now down to 1.78 percent of each company's outstanding stock, with a company on average holding shares in half of all of the other companies in the group. Among members of boards of directors, 9 percent are from other companies in the group. The strongest link remains financing, with companies on average receiving 18.8 percent of their total debt financing from within the group (down from 21.3 percent in 1979), according to a report in the Japan Economic Journal.

As Alexander Young points out: "The big six conglomerate groups, as of March 31, 1974, consisted of 187 financial, industrial, and trading giants of Japan . . . The number of group firms varied, ranging from the Sumitomo group's 16 to the Dai-Ichi Kangyo Bank group's 57 . . . According to the Japan Fair Trade Commission, the Mitsubishi group firms owned 31 percent of the total number of stock issued by group firms . . . The mutual stock holdings of the Sumitomo group calculated on the same basis amounted to about 28 percent."[4]

The Sogo Sosha—Japan's Major Trading Companies

The large company groups are sometimes confused with the major trading companies, or sogo sosha. Yoshihara Kunio provides a concise definition of this genre, which today includes nine companies in Japan: "For a trading company to be a sogo sosha, it had to deal with many products (not concentrating in one product group, such as textiles or steel), engage in both export and import, have offices in various parts of the world, and wield considerable power in the spheres of marketing and finance."[5] Because Japan has few raw materials, it has always needed specialist companies that could scour the world for copper, cotton, and oil. More recently, although the largest companies can maintain their own worldwide sales networks, the trading companies have served as sales agents for the medium-sized and smaller companies. The trading companies have thus become important, with more than 4,000 trading companies in business today. However, the sogo sosha arc in a different class, with the nine companies as a group accounting for slightly more than one-half of Japan's total foreign trade in recent years.

The sogo sosha are of interest here particularly as financial intermediaries. On the one hand, the sogo sosha as a group borrow 97 percent of their total capital, with only 3 percent equity, a figure that seems incredible. On the other hand, their profits on equity have been in the range of 15 to 16 percent during the recent past. The trading companies typically provide credit to both buyers and sellers of goods, and because they invest not in plant and equipment but for short periods of time in goods for trade, their risk of ending up with 5,000 dead sheep is minimal. More importantly, the companies specialize in information, in knowing where to find cotton and where to sell machine tools, and as a result of knowing what is demanded, they are in a good position to safely lend money for thirty days or so to finance the buyer or seller.

The trading companies have filled a need not only because Japanese manufacturers must import raw materials, but also because so many manufacturers in Japan are too small to maintain their own foreign sales organizations. In 1970, for example, there were more than 500,000 small and medium-sized manufacturing companies in Japan, accounting for 68 percent of all manufacturing workers. In the United States in 1967, by comparison, small and medium sized enterprises accounted for only 40 percent of manufacturing jobs.[6] According to a 1979 MITI study, textile companies in Japan have an average of 36 subcontractors each, general machinery companies 105 subcontractors each, and transport machinery companies 136 subcontractors each.[7]

Small business remains an important sector in Japan, accounting for 95 percent of all businesses and 66 percent of all jobs. More importantly, small business remains the source of future growth. For example, among 120 electronics companies that had grown beyond "small or medium-size" (at least $4 million of capital) in 1979, 54 had been small or medium in 1955.[8] These small businesses depend on the trading companies for a good deal of their credit, although they borrow also from local banks, credit associations, and other financial institutions created for small business. But a bank would find it too risky to lend large sums for one year to a fledgling company, and it would be too costly for both parties for the bank to arrange financing only for the time that it takes to ship one machine tool from Nagoya to Sandusky. The trading companies, however, already possess the information necessary to knowing how safe such a loan is and can therefore provide such financing.

In recent years, both the large industrial groups and the sogo sosha have been under public attack. As Yoshihara Kunio describes the period, it sounds a lot like the United States during that same era: "The one-and-a-half-year period from early 1973 was an ordeal for sogo sosha. They were reviled as 'traitors,' 'wicked traders,' 'parasites,' 'Shylocks of Tokyo,' and 'Dracula sucking the blood of the public.' They were attacked by consumer groups that leveled emotional charges. Senior citizens staged sit-ins in front of their headquarters. They also faced criticism from the right. One right-wing newspaper warned them that it might become necessary to take 'direct action' against them 'for the sake of social justice.' The cause? They were accused of speculating in land and commodities, such as soybeans and wood, and became the whipping-boy for inflationary pressure.[9]

It may seem on the surface that the sogo sosha and, more directly, the major industrial groups of Japan are organized as H-Form entities, which we have described as being unsuccessful over the long run. However, recall that within the true H-Form or U.S. conglomerate, each company is owned 100 percent by a central corporation, whereas in the Japanese case, investors outside of the group typically own 60 or 70 percent of each company in the group. If necessary, then, a company in the group can raise its own additional capital through new stock or loans, so that a bright star is not encumbered with the stodgy reputation of a larger corporation. In addition, each member company in a Japanese group is subject to scrutiny by several outside banks, each of which has the rights of an equity owner to probe deeply in the company's affairs. On the other hand, each company has to deal with only ten or fifteen providers of capital, rather than ten thousand or one million as is true of large U.S. companies with many shareholders.

One consequence is that the Japanese company is able to communicate to its providers of capital the need for long-term investment in research and development, training of employees, and modernizing facilities. Those investments may be necessary to build a future for the company, but they will inevitably tend to depress current profits. If the owners are few in number and expert in ability, they can appraise these plans firsthand and decide whether patience is in order or not. If there are ten thousand owners, however, they cannot possibly grasp such subtleties, and will rely instead on only the most gross measures of corporate performance, such as quarterly earnings reports and newspaper accounts of good news or bad.

NOTES

Chapter 1

1. The Business Week Team, *The Reindustrialization of America* (New York: McGraw-Hill, 1982), p. 10.
2. Mancur Olson, *The Rise and Decline of Nations* (New Haven: Yale University Press, 1982).
3. The Business–Higher Education Forum, "America's Competitive Challenge: The Report in Brief" (Washington, DC, April 1983), p. 2.
4. International Management and Development Institute, "The Renewal of America in the 1980's," report on Phase I of the Fowler-McCracken Commission on Improving Government-Business Cooperation in the Conduct of U.S. International Economic Policy (Washington, DC, Spring 1982).
5. Special Task Force on Long-Term Economic Policy, Democratic Caucus/U.S. House of Representatives, "Rebuilding the Road to Opportunity," September 1982.

Chapter 2

1. Richard P. Rumelt, "Diversification Strategy and Profitability," *Strategic Management Journal* III (1982), p. 359; also Richard P. Rumelt, *Strategy, Structure,*

and Economic Performance (Boston: Division of Research, Harvard Business School, 1974); also David J. Teece, "Towards a Theory of the Multiproduct Firm," working paper, Graduate School of Business, Stanford University, July 1980; Richard E. Caves, "Industrial Organization, Corporate Strategy and Structure," *Journal of Economic Literature*, March 1980.

2. Oliver E. Williamson, *Markets and Hierarchies* (New York: Free Press, 1975).

3. As stated by Williamson, the M-form hypothesis is this: "The organization and operation of the large enterprise along the lines of the M-form favors goal pursuit and least-cost behavior more nearly associated with the neoclassical profit maximization hypothesis than does the U-form organizational alternative" (ibid., p. 150).

4. For a discussion of these and other types, see ibid., pp. 151–154.

5. Robert B. Reich, *The Next American Frontier* (New York: Times Books, 1983), Chapter VIII.

6. For example, see Eugene F. Fama, "Agency Problems and the Theory of the Firm," *Journal of Political Economy*, April 1982; see also Michael C. Jensen and William H. Meckling, "Theory of the Firm: Managerial Behavior, Agency Costs, and Ownership Structure," *Journal of Financial Economics*, October 1976, pp. 305–360.

7. See Alfred D. Chandler, Jr., *Strategy and Structure: Chapters in the History of the Industrial Enterprise* (Cambridge, MA: MIT Press, 1962), *The Visible Hand: The Managerial Revolution in American Business* (Cambridge, MA: Harvard University Press, Belknap Press, 1977).

8. William G. Ouchi, "Markets, Bureaucracies, and Clans," *Administrative Science Quarterly*, March 1980, pp. 129–141.

9. Alvin W. Gouldner, "The Norm of Reciprocity: A Preliminary Statement," *American Sociological Review*, April 1960, pp. 161–178. See also J. Stacey Adams, "Inequity in Social Exchange," *Advances in Experimental Social Psychology* 1 (1965); and B. F. Meeker, "Decisions and Exchange," *American Sociological Review*, June 1971.

10. For a complete description of this natural selection approach as it applies to organizations, see William McKelvey, *Organizational Systematics* (Berkeley: University of California Press, 1983).

11. For a discussion, see Peter M. Blau and W. R. Scott, *Formal Organizations* (San Francisco: Chandler Publishing Co., 1962). The most incisive discussion of the contracting problem in employment is in Herbert A. Simon, *Models of Man* (New York: John Wiley and Sons, 1958).

12. For a more thorough discussion of this problem, see Armen A. Alchian and Harold Demsetz, "Production, Information Costs and Economic Organization," *American Economic Review*, December 1972, pp. 666–695.

13. Andrew H. Van de Ven, "Three R's of Administrative Behavior: Rational, Random, and Reasonable—and the Greatest of These Is Reason," working paper presented at the Albany Conference on Organizational Theory and Public Policy, April 1–2, 1982.

14. Charles E. Lindbloom, *Politics and Markets—The World's Political–Economic Systems* (New York: Basic Books, 1977).

Chapter 3

1. Pascale Buch, "Three Weeks at MITI," *Journal of Japanese Trade and Industry*, January/February 1983, pp. 62–64.
2. T. J. Pempel, *Policy and Politics in Japan—Creative Conservatism* (Philadelphia: Temple University Press, 1982), pp. 270–271.
3. Ibid., pp. 269–270.
4. Ibid., p. 146.
5. Chalmers Johnson, *MITI and the Japanese Miracle—The Growth of Industrial Policy, 1925–1975* (Stanford, CA: Stanford University Press, 1982), pp. 20–21.
6. Ezra F. Vogel, "Guided Free Enterprise in Japan," *Harvard Business Review*, May–June 1978, pp. 161–170.
7. ". . . the new minister of commerce and industry, working with and on the inspiration of his chief of the Documents Section, Yoshino Shinji, undertook an initiative that is acknowledged to be the beginning of modern Japanese industrial policy. On May 23, 1927, Minister Nakahashi set up within MCI a Commerce and Industry Deliberation Council (Shoko Shingikai). Its charter was to examine broadly what was ailing the Japanese economy and what the government ought to do about it. As a joint public-private forum, it is the direct antecedent of the 1950's-era Industrial Rationalization Council and its successor, the Industrial Structure Council—MITI's number one official channel to the business community. . . . The Council achieved unprecedented results. It convinced MCI to strengthen its compilation of industrial statistics, authorized some 30 million yen in loans to medium and smaller enterprises (a figure ten times larger than any previous loans), proposed for the first time the amalgamation of the Yawata steel works with private steel firms (an idea that came to pass in 1934), and underscored the need for improved trade intelligence and subsidies for export industries." Johnson, *MITI and the Japanese Miracle*, p. 102.
8. Keidanren—1982, Tokyo; Keidanren.
9. Interview notes, Keidanren staff, August 13 and 19, 1982.
10. "Profile of Keizai Doyukai," draft mimeo (Tokyo: Keizai Doyukai, no date given).
11. As Pempel points out, however, this atomized union structure of Japan has also produced political impotence for organized labor: "Nearly 40 percent of the 12,500 unions in Japan lack any affiliation with a national federation. Sohyo, the largest of these bodies, represents only 38 percent of the unionized work force" (*Policy and Politics*, p. 96). Pempel also points to one very important consequence of this labor structure: in Japan, the enterprise union had no access to the national government and instead concentrated its efforts on winning employment security, better wages, and better working conditions from the management of its own company. Companies, having the long-term view of their employees permitted by well-informed bankers and shareholders, had a similar desire. By contrast, the U.S. was characterized by national unions which could effectively influence the Congress, while business had no na-

tional associations with which to counterbalance the political power of labor, and the short-run view of American managers was often sharply at odds with the goals of workers. As a result, labor in the U.S. won its case in the U.S. Congress with no effective opposition from industry.

12. Chamber of Commerce of the United States, "A Glimpse of the U.S. Chamber 1981–82," Washington, DC.

13. Some examples: Industrial Policy Committee, Foreign Trade Committee, Taxation System Committee, Distribution System Study Committee, Sub-Contracting Affairs Committee, Tourism Committee, Foreign Exchange Committee. The Chamber also runs seven divisions, each specialized to discuss the problems of a specific industry group such as the retail division, the manufacturing division, the mining division, and so on. In order to ensure member participation, the Tokyo Chamber has as its chief decision-making body a General Meeting of Councillors. Of the 150 Councillors, 76 are elected at-large by members, 52 represent the seven divisions and are chosen by them, and 22 are selected by the president of the chamber.

14. A 1949 law established the National Federation of Small and Medium Enterprises, with offices in each of the forty-seven prefectures of Japan (similar to the fifty states of the U.S.). Each prefectural federation consists of several local associations, and the prefectural federation receives funds from both the national government and the prefectural governments. Some of the activities of these prefectural federations include providing fire insurance, forming co-operatives for warehousing and manufacturing by many small businesses in common, collective bargaining for better terms from large corporate customers, and organizing credit cooperatives. Several additional laws passed since 1949 have assisted small businesses. One provides for special tax deductions for small businesses; another allows small business proprietors to charge as a business loss their annual contributions to a credit cooperative for the purpose of potential bankruptcy-avoidance loans (which may be up to ten times the accumulated deposits and are government-financed); and another requires large chain stores to apply for permission to open any unit of more than 500 square meters, and if that new unit should seriously endanger small retailers in the area, the application may be denied or altered. Clearly, small business is a potent political constituency in Japan.

15. "Promotion of Small and Medium Enterprise in Japan," *Now in Japan*, no. 31 (Tokyo: Japan External Trade Organization [JETRO], no date given).

16. Ibid., p. 23.

17. Ibid., p. 4.

18. Pempel, *Policy and Politics*, p. 20.

19. "Summary of Electronic Industries Association of Japan" (Tokyo: EIAJ, no date given).

20. Interview notes, EIAJ staff, August 11, 1982.

21. Interview notes, Keidanren staff, August 19, 1982.

22. Interview notes, Electric Wire and Cable Makers Association, August 17, 1982.

23. Interview notes, JEMIMA staff, August 18, 1982.

24. Interview notes, former MITI official, January 7, 1983.

25. Koichi Kishimoto, "Diet Structure, Organization, and Procedure," in *The*

Japanese Diet and the U.S. Congress, ed. Francis R. Valeo and Charles E. Morrison (Boulder, CO: Westview Press, 1983), pp. 51–52.

26. Nicholas Benes, "Recent Trends in Industry Rationalization in Japan: The Designated Depressed Industries Law," working paper, School of Law, UCLA, 1983.

27. Eugene J. Kaplan, *Japan: The Government–Business Relationship* (Washington, DC: U.S. Government Printing Office, U.S. Department of Commerce, Bureau of International Commerce, 1972), pp. 106–136.

28. Ibid.

29. Ibid., p. 122.

30. Ibid.

Chapter 4

1. David Packard, "High Technology, High Stakes: An Agenda for the Eighties," speech at the conference on "High Technology Industries: Public Policies for the 1980's," sponsored by the Government Research Corporation, Washington, DC, February 1–2, 1983.

2. Harold Demsetz, "The Structure of Corporate Ownership and Economic Efficiency," mimeo, Department of Economics, UCLA, no date given.

3. "U.S. and Japanese Semiconductor Industries: A Financial Comparison," prepared by Chase Financial Policy, copyright Semiconductor Industry Association, 1980, p. 12.

4. Ibid., pp. 8.7–8.8.

5. All figures are based on 1979. Figures for Japanese cost of equity and all U.S. figures are from the Chase Financial Policy report.

6. "The Financing of Japanese Industry," *Bank of England Quarterly Bulletin* 21 (December 1981), pp. 513–515.

7. Interview notes, Mitsubishi Bank, Tokyo, September 10, 1982.

8. A. A. Berle and G. C. Means, *The Modern Corporation and Private Property* (New York: Commerce Clearing House, 1932).

9. Rodney Clark, *The Japanese Company* (New Haven: Yale University Press, 1979), p. 75.

10. Julian Gresser, "High Technology and Japanese Industrial Policy: A Strategy for U.S. Policymakers," Subcommittee on Trade of the Committee on Ways and Means, U.S. House of Representatives, Washington, DC: U.S. Government Printing Office, October 1, 1980.

11. T. F. M. Adams and Iwao Hoshii, *A Financial History of the New Japan* (Tokyo: Kodansha, 1972), pp. 92–93.

12. Ibid., p. 105.

13. Comptroller General of the United States, "Industry Policy: Japan's Flexible Approach" (Washington, DC: U.S. General Accounting Office, no date given), ID 82-32, p. 4.

14. John Jay Knox, *A History of Banking in the United States* (New York: Bradford Rhodes and Company, 1900).

15. Susan Estabrook Kennedy, *The Banking Crisis of 1933* (Lexington, KY: The University Press of Kentucky, 1973), p. 229.

16. Ibid., pp. 79–80.

17. Ibid., p. 212.

18. U.S. Congress, Senate, Subcommittee of the Committee on Banking and Currency, *Hearings on S. Res. 84 and S. Res. 239,* 72d Cong., 2d sess., January 11, 12, 1933; see especially part 6, pp. 1762–1826.

19. See Margaret H. Douglas-Hamilton, Esq., "ALI-ABA Resource Materials: Banking and Commercial Lending Law—1980," Some Problems Associated with Creditor Control of Debtor Companies (Boston, MA: Bingham, Dana and Gould), pp. 330–357.

20. Ibid., p. 351.

21. Ibid., p. 353.

22. *Portsmouth Cotton Oil Refining Corp.* v. *Fourth National Bank of Montgomery,* 280 f. 879 (M.D. Ala., 1922), aff'd, 284 f. 718.

23. Chicago Mill and Lumber Co. v. Boatmen's Bank, 234 f. 41 (8th Cir. 1916).

24. Interview notes, Mitsubishi Bank, August 31, 1982.

Chapter 5

1. "The Colossus That Works," *Time,* July 11, 1983, p. 45. During this period Japan assessed tariffs of 15 percent from 1955 to 1972 on U.S.-made mainframes, a rate that declined to 13.5 percent during 1972–1978, to 10.5 percent from 1978 to 1980, and to 4.9 percent in 1982 under the GATT Geneva Accord, compared to a U.S. tariff of 5.5 percent on Japanese-made mainframes, thus giving an advantage to the Japanese firms. Nonetheless, the development of the Japanese industry in such a technology-intensive field in so short a time is impressive.

2. Guido Krickx, "A Brief Overview of the History of the Japanese Computer Industry," unpublished monograph, Graduate School of Management, UCLA, November 3, 1982, p. 102.

3. Edward Feigenbaum and Pamela McCorduck, *The Fifth Generation* (Reading, MA: Addison-Wesley, 1983), p. 12.

4. Krickx, "History of the Japanese Computer Industry," p. 5.

5. Kaplan, *Japan,* p. 82.

6. *Fuji Bank Bulletin,* September 1960, p. 25.

7. *Fuji Bank Bulletin,* March 1966, p. 51.

8. Kaplan, *Japan,* p. 83.

9. Johnson, *MITI and the Japanese Miracle,* pp. 246–247.

10. Krickx, "History of the Japanese Computer Industry," p. 75.

11. Ibid., p. 76.
12. Ibid., p. 77.
13. Kaplan, *Japan*, p. 86.
14. Comptroller General of the United States, "United States–Japan Trade: Issues and Problems" (Washington, DC: U.S. General Accounting Office, September 21, 1979), ID 79-53, p. 11.
15. I. C. Magaziner and T. M. Hout, "Japanese Industrial Policy," Policy Papers in International Affairs no. 15, (Institute of International Studies, University of California at Berkeley, 1980), p. 105.
16. Kaplan, *Japan*, p. 88.
17. Ibid., p. 87.
18. Interview notes, Shohei Kurihara, Vice Minister for International Affairs, MITI, August 11, 1982, p. 26.
19. Kaplan, *Japan*, p. 87.
20. Interview notes, JECC staff, August 30, 1982, pp. 152–154.
21. Kaplan, *Japan*, p. 88.
22. Interview notes, LASDEC staff, August 19, 1982, p. 112.
23. J. E. Tilton, "International Diffusion of Technology: The Case of Semiconductors" (Washington, DC: Brookings Institution, 1972); for a summary, see Krickx, "History of the Japanese Computer Industry," p. 74.
24. Translation of this law by Nicholas Benes, UCLA Law School and Graduate School of Management, 1982.
25. Gresser, "High Technology and Japanese Industrial Policy," p. 10. After 1964, AIST entered a new era with the creation in 1966 of the National Research and Development Program. This program was intended to create, fund, and assist only very large-scale research projects in industry. As of 1983, the new agency had completed eleven such projects and had eight more in process. These included a project to develop desulfurization processes to remove the noxious gases from power plants and other heavy users of heavy oil, a project to develop economical means to make fresh water from salt water, a project to develop an electric car for urban, limited-range use, and a project to develop a robotic garment sewing factory of the future. As might be expected of high-risk projects, not all have been fully successful, but all may be considered to be exactly the sort of project that no one company can afford to undertake but that represent a social endowment and should be undertaken by the nation.

  In the computer industry, AIST under the new organization undertook the super-computer project, PIPS, and the High Speed Computing Project. The super-computer project (1966–1971, $44 million of public funds) joined together the AIST Electro-Technical Laboratory with Hitachi, Fujitsu, NEC, Toshiba, Oki, Mitsubishi, and the University of Tokyo. The objective was to match IBM's 360, and the method, recalling the shortage of skilled scientists, was for each company to specialize in the research area at which it was best. In order to then disseminate the results to all parties in a thorough and orderly fashion, AIST established in 1969 a new arm, the Japan Industrial Technology Association (JITA), as a nonprofit organization chartered to diffuse all technology obtained through AIST by license to companies in Japan and abroad.

Computers are essentially semiconductors plus software. The need for software development was just as critical, and thus in 1967 the Japan Information Processing Development Center (JIPDEC) was created. JIPDEC, unlike JEIDA, is funded by MITI and by the Ministry of Posts and Telecommunications. It carries out research on software, does contract research for government agencies, and carries out many training seminars. JIPDEC serves as software consultant to government agencies, publishes reports, and conducts conferences. Thus JIPDEC assists the industry by engaging in information-gathering on a scale that no company could afford and by serving as a discussion place in which business and government can informally and early on develop future policy through a sustained and well-informed dialogue.

Several other joint activities had occurred during the 1960s. From 1962 to 1965, Oki-Univac, NEC, and Fujitsu had collaborated on FONTAC, a project to develop a large computer. From 1968 to 1973 Fujitsu, Hitachi, and NEC had collaborated on DIPS, a project to connect "large-scale on-line (time-sharing) computer systems to electronic exchange and transmission systems." In 1969, at the request of the six remaining computer makers, MITI arranged a "rationalization cartel" which directed the companies to consolidate seven types of punched card and paper tape equipment, adding line printers and magnetic drums in 1970, so that higher productivity could be achieved through volumes and lower costs.

In each case, it should be noted that the initiatives came from the private sector, from profit-seeking firms, each attempting to gain some special advantage or assistance. The objectives were no different from the objectives of every U.S. company that approaches our government seeking price protection, depletion allowances, land leases, or tax benefits and outright subsidies. Instead of dealing with each company one-on-one or asking each company to attempt to build political support for its position, however, the Japanese government encouraged the development of new trade associations. These were followed by new governmental bodies that could carry out an informed dialogue with the business community. See Magaziner and Hout, "Japanese Industrial Policy," p. 103, and Gresser, "High Technology and Japanese Industrial Policy," p. 10.

The response of the Japanese companies to the third-generation IBM computer was swift. In 1969 a MITI committee produced a report on the consensus among manufacturers, the wider business community, the Diet, and the bureaucracy on next steps. The report called for software development, personnel training, and time-sharing. The time-sharing proposal was implemented by 1972. Training was upgraded by merging the Information Technology Institute into JIPDEC, the software organization. The institute began programs to train systems analysts and programmers around the nation, coordinated with seven regional university-based computer training centers sponsored by the Ministry of Education. Software development was addressed through the creation in 1970 of the Information Technology Promotion Agency, funded half by government funds and half by the six computer makers. The majority of the agency's funds were to be used to develop software applicable to the entire industry; the remaining funds were earmarked as deposits at private banks, to be used to guarantee loans from those banks to small, start-up software development companies. The program was qualified for Japan Development Bank funds, thus providing for tremendous leverage. With only $1.1 million of initial capitalization, the agency made available over $30 million of loans to small software companies in 1971, its first full year of operation. By 1972 there were forty software houses in existence, the majority having begun after 1970. Ultimately, the agency's objective was to funnel $720 million into the software industry, consisting of private and government funds.

26. Kaplan, *Japan*, p. 95.
27. Krickx, "History of the Japanese Computer Industry," p. 75.
28. Ibid., pp. 22, 25.
29. Gresser, "High Technology and Japanese Industrial Policy," p. 13.
30. Kaplan, *Japan*, p. 100.
31. Ibid., p. 82.
32. Market share estimates are from an interview with the Toshiba staff, December 18, 1981.
33. Gresser, "High Technology and Japanese Industrial Policy," p. 112.
34. Krickx, "History of the Japanese Computer Industry," p. 25. Fujitsu invested in Amdahl, a U.S. firm making IBM-compatible computers, while Hitachi, which was financially much stronger than Fujitsu but less technically advanced at the time, was building a licensed RCA design that was itself IBM-compatible. NEC was working under licenses from Honeywell, which had absorbed the computer business of GE, under whose licenses Toshiba was working. Oki and Mitsubishi did not have as good a technical fit since Oki was a licensee of Remington-Univac in a joint venture, whereas Mitsubishi's Melcom computer was a Japanese version of a Xerox computer.
35. Gresser, "High Technology and Japanese Industrial Policy," pp. 12–13.
36. Krickx, "History of the Japanese Computer Industry," p. 31.
37. *Forbes*, May 15, 1977, p. 60; and Krickx, "History of the Japanese Computer Industry," p. 31.
38. Krickx, "History of the Japanese Computer Industry," p. 32.
39. Interview notes, JEIDA staff, August 20, 1982.
40. Interview notes, Staff of Electronics Policy Division, MITI, August 26, 1982.
41. Interview notes, Fujitsu staff, September 7, 1982.
42. Interview notes, Dr. Yasuo Tarui, January 10, 1983.
43. This and other details of the VLSI Joint Laboratory are drawn from "Minutes of the Second Special Study Group on High Technology Management," which was held June 21, 1982, at the Economics Club (Keizai Kurabu) on the theme "Operation of the VLSI Research Association." The principal speaker was Mr. Masato Nebashi. Translation of these minutes was by Nicholas Benes in December 1982.
44. Ibid., pp. 5–6.
45. Ibid., p. 11.
46. Institute for New Generation Computer Technology (ICOT), "Outline of Research and Development Plans for Fifth Generation Computer Systems" (Tokyo: Japan Information Processing Development Center, May 1982), pp. 1–2.
47. The decision was not to create a research association under the 1961 law,

perhaps for two reasons. First, the chief financial advantage of the research association is the accelerated depreciation on equipment purchased by the member companies, but in this case virtually all of the funding at the outset comes from the government, thus leaving no expenses for companies to deduct for tax purposes. Second, the research association requires that the member companies take equity positions. In this case there are more than the usual number of companies, and their precise involvement is difficult to forecast at present; so the equity shares could probably not be set in a manner that all would find acceptable.

Chapter 6

1. Guido Krickx, "A Note on the Photovoltaic Industry," Graduate School of Management, UCLA, March 1983, p. 1.
2. Ibid.
3. Ibid.
4. Science Applications, Inc., "Characterization and Assessment of Potential European and Japanese Competition in Photovoltaics" (McLean, VA: Solar Energy Research Institute, October 1979), SERI/TR-8251, p. 4–3.
5. See Krickx, "Photovoltaic Industry," and Appendixes 3 and 4.
6. Ibid., p. 8.
7. Ibid., p. 9, from SERI reports and from Committee on Appropriations, House of Representatives.
8. "Principal Conclusions of the American Physical Society Study Group on Solar Photovoltaic Energy Conversion" (New York: The American Physical Society, January 1979), pp. 2, 173.
9. Richard Bolling and John Bowles, *America's Competitive Edge—How to Get Our Country Moving Again* (New York: McGraw-Hill, 1982), p. 126.
10. James Botkin, Dan Dimancescu, and Ray Stata, *Global Stakes: The Future of High Technology in America* (Cambridge, MA: Ballinger, 1982), p. 76.
11. Bolling and Bowles, *America's Competitive Edge*, pp. 125–130.
12. Botkin, Dimancescu, and Stata, *Global Stakes*, p. 77.
13. Ibid., p. 25.
14. Ibid., p. 212; also Donald W. Burlage, "The Very High Speed Integrated Circuits Program," Office of the Under Secretary of Defense for Research and Engineering (no date given).
15. Bolling and Bowles, *America's Competitive Edge*, p. 126.
16. Burlage, "The Very High Speed Integrated Circuits Program," p. 196.
17. Dr. Edith Martin, "The Next Decade and Beyond in Defense Technology," Office of the Under Secretary of Defense for Research and Engineering, speech delivered at GOMAC-82.

18. Ibid.
19. Botkin, Dimancescu, and Stata, *Global Stakes*, p. 75.
20. Interview notes, Leonard Weisberg, February 25, 1983.
21. Defense Science Board, "Report of the Task Force on Very High Speed Integrated Circuits (VHSIC) Program" (Washington, DC: Office of the Under Secretary of Defense, Research and Engineering, February 17, 1982), p. 5.
22. Interview notes, VHSIC staff, January 18, 1983.
23. Interview notes, VHSIC staff, January 20, 1983.
24. Interview notes, Harley Cloud, February 1, 1983.
25. Jim Martin, "Very High Speed Integrated Circuits into the Second Generation," *Military Electronics/Countermeasures*, December 1981, p. 72.

Chapter 7

1. Michael Useem, "The Social Organization of the American Business Elite and Participation of Corporation Directors in the Governance of American Institutions," *American Sociological Review* 44 (August 1978), pp. 553–572.
2. Michael D. Cohen and James G. March, *Leadership and Ambiguity: The American College President*, a general report prepared for the Carnegie Commission on Higher Education (New York: McGraw-Hill, 1974), pp. 81–91.
3. Ibid., p. 91.
4. Kan Ori, "The Diet in the Japanese Political System," in *The Japanese Diet*, ed. Valeo and Morrison, p. 14.
5. Koichi Kishimoto, "Diet Structure, Organization, and Procedures," in *The Japanese Diet*, ed. Valeo and Morrison, pp. 51–52.
6. Ralph D. Nurnberger, "The Making of a Law," in *The Japanese Diet*, ed. Valeo and Morrison, p. 144.
7. Ibid., p. 145.
8. Ori, "The Diet," p. 13.
9. Hiroshi Yamamoto, "Political Parties and the Diet," in *The Japanese Diet*, ed. Valeo and Morrison, pp. 25–29.
10. Ori, "The Diet," p. 13.
11. Robert L. Peabody, "The U.S. Congress: Structure, Party Organization, and Leadership," in *The Japanese Diet*, ed. Valeo and Morrison, p. 136.
12. Izumi Shoichi, "Diet Members," in *The Japanese Diet*, ed. Valeo and Morrison, p. 75.
13. Kishimoto, in *The Japanese Diet*, p. 54.
14. Susan Webb Hammond, "The Member of the U.S. Congress," ed. Valeo and Morrison, pp. 163–165.
15. Charles E. Morrison, "The U.S. Congress in Foreign Relations, Trade and Defense," in *The Japanese Diet*, ed. Valeo and Morrison, p. 183.

16. Roger B. Porter, "Organizing Economic Advice to the President: A Modest Proposal," *The American Economic Review* 72, no. 2 (May 1982), p. 357; also Anne Colamosca, "The Trade Association Hustle," *New Republic,* November 3, 1979, pp. 16–19; also SAMA 1980 Annual Report (Washington, DC: Scientific Apparatus Makers Association, 1980).
17. Lewis Anthony Dexter, *How Organizations Are Represented in Washington* (New York: Bobbs-Merrill, 1969), p. 21.
18. Chamber of Commerce of the United States, 1982 Annual Report.
19. Interview notes, Alexander Trowbridge, February 24, 1983.
20. Interview notes, Jack Albertine, March 1, 1983.
21. Kim McQuaid, "The Roundtable: Getting Results in Washington," *Harvard Business Review,* May/June 1981, pp. 114–123.
22. Ibid., p. 117. The Business Council meets only twice yearly to hear and react to talks by high government officials.
23. The 1981 bill discriminated against schools of business administration, which train those engineers to be managers. Members of Congress please take note!
24. "NEMA 1982," Washington, DC, NEMA, p. 6.
25. 1980 Annual Report—SAMA, Washington, DC, p. 9.
26. Alfred D. Chandler, Jr., "The Adversaries," *Harvard Business Review,* November–December 1979, pp. 88–102.
27. Ibid., p. 90.
28. Ibid., p. 89.
29. Pempel, *Policy and Politics,* p. 48.
30. Chandler, "The Adversaries," pp. 88–89.

Chapter 8

1. Bolling and Bowles, *America's Competitive Edge,* p. 153.
2. "The International Microelectronic Challenge," The Semiconductor Industry Association, May 1981, p. 10.
3. Robert Wolcott Johnson, "The Passage of the Investment Act of 1978: A Case Study of Business Influencing Public Policy," unpublished doctoral dissertation, Graduate School of Business Administration, Harvard University, 1980, p. 41. Available through University Microfilms International, Ann Arbor, Michigan.
4. Ibid.
5. Ibid., pp. 45–46.
6. Ibid., p. 49.
7. Ibid., p. 50.
8. Ibid., pp. 57–58.
9. Ibid., p. 70.
10. Ibid., p. 74.
11. Ibid., p. 77.
12. Ibid., p. 81.
13. Ibid., p. 83.
14. Ibid., p. 86.

15. Ibid., p. 98.
16. Ibid., p. 126.
17. Ibid., p. 152.
18. Ibid., p. 167.
19. Ibid., p. 195.
20. "Stupendous Steiger," *The Wall Street Journal*, April 26, 1978.
21. Johnson, "The Passage of the Investment Act of 1978," pp. 216–217.
22. Ibid., p. 228.
23. Ibid., p. 249.
24. Ibid., p. 279.
25. Ibid., p. 278.
26. Chris Reidy, "AEA Is Making Inroads on Capitol Hill," *The Peninsula Times Tribune*, August 17, 1982.
27. Interview notes, Ken Hagerty, January 27, 1982.
28. Interview notes, Ed Ferrey, January 27, 1982.
29. Ibid.
30. *American Electronics Association Update*, March 1983.
31. John C. Aplin and W. Harvey Hegarty, "Political Influence: Strategies Employed by Organizations to Impact Legislation in Business and Economic Matters," *Academy of Management Journal* 23, no. 3 (1980), pp. 438–450.
32. Lester M. Salamon and John J. Siegfried, "Economic Power and Political Influence: The Impact of Industry Structure on Public Policy," *The American Political Science Review*, September 1977, pp. 1026–1043.
33. David E. Price, "Policy Making in Congressional Committees: The Impact of 'Environmental' Factors," *The American Political Science Review*, June 1978, pp. 548–574.
34. Ibid., p. 552.
35. Ibid., p. 555.
36. Ibid., p. 556.
37. Ibid., p. 560.
38. Salamon and Siegfried, "Economic Power and Political Influence," p. 1030.
39. Joel Kotkin and Don Gevirtz, "Why Entrepreneurs Trust No Politician," *The Washington Post*, January 16, 1983.
40. Interview notes, White House Staff, March 1, 1983.

Chapter 9

1. John Brandl and Ronnie Brooks, "Public-Private Cooperation for Urban Revitalization: The Minneapolis and St. Paul Experience," in *Public-Private Partnership in American Cities: Seven Case Studies*, ed. R. Scott Foster and Renee A. Berger (Lexington, MA: Lexington Books, 1982), p. 164.
2. These historical facts are drawn from a book by Don W. Larson, *Land of the Giants* (Minneapolis: Dorn Books, 1979).
3. Ibid., pp. 90–91.
4. Ibid., p. 21.
5. Ibid., pp. 140–142.

6. Ibid., p. 161.
7. Dick Schaaf, "The 5% Solution," *Republic Scene,* February 1982, p. 47.
8. Joseph Galaskiewicz, Wolfgang Bielefield, and Patti Mullaney, "Corporate Nonprofit Linkages in Minneapolis-St. Paul: Preliminary Findings from Three Surveys," Department of Sociology, University of Minnesota, November 1982, p. 55. I am indebted to Congressman Bruce F. Vento of the 4th District, Minnesota, for providing me with this and other information.
9. Ibid., pp. 60–64.
10. "Minneapolis Businesses Make Habit of Donations," Associated Press story in the *Fergus Falls Daily Journal,* July 28, 1977.
11. John Brandl and Ronnie Brooks, "Public-Private Cooperation for Urban Revitalization," p. 165.
12. Judson Bemis and John A. Cairns, "In Minnesota Business Is Part of the Solution," *Harvard Business Review,* July–August 1981, pp. 85–93.

Chapter 10

1. Paul R. Lawrence and Jay W. Lorsch, *Organization and Environment: Managing Differentiation and Integration* (Boston: Division of Research, Graduate School of Business Administration, Harvard University, 1967).
2. Interview notes, Senator Inouye, March 2, 1983.
3. Emile Durkheim, *The Division of Labor in Society,* trans. George Simpson (New York: The Free Press, 1933), original published in French in 1893.
4. Ibid., p. 5.

Appendix X

1. Yoshihara Kunio, *Sogo Sosha—The Vanguard of the Japanese Economy* (Tokyo: Oxford University Press, 1982), and Alexander K. Young, *The Sogo Sosha—Japan's Multi-National Trading Companies* (Tokyo: Charles E. Tuttle Company, 1979).
2. Rodney Clark, *The Japanese Company* (New Haven: Yale University Press, 1979), p. 42–43.
3. Young, *The Sogo Sosha,* p. 35.
4. Ibid., pp. 37, 42.
5. Yoshihara, *Sogo Sosha,* p. 10.
6. Ibid., p. 213.
7. "Chusho Kigyo Hakusho, Showa 54 Men," (White paper on Small Medium Enterprise, 1979), Small-Medium Enterprise Agency, MITI, 1980, translation of tables by Sayoko Benes, April 1983, p. 158.
8. Ibid., p. 336.
9. Yoshihara, *Sogo Sosha,* pp. 263–264.

INDEX